Robert Macklin was born in Queensland and educated at Brisbane Grammar School, the University of Queensland and the Australian National University. He began his journalistic career at the *Courier-Mail* and subsequently wrote for *The Age* and *The Bulletin*, and was associate editor of the *Canberra Times* until 2003.

His 2016 biography *Hamilton Hume* revived national interest in Australia's greatest explorer, and the acclaimed *Dark Paradise* exposed the horror of colonial sadism in the penal colony of Norfolk Island. His history of Australia's Special Forces, *Warrior Elite*, is required reading in the fields of military security and intelligence. His bestselling biography of Rob Maylor, *SAS Sniper*, revealed in graphic detail the battles against Islamist fanatics.

Robert has won numerous literary prizes including, with Peter Thompson, the 2009 Blake Dawson Prize for Business Literature for their classic, *The Big Fella: The Rise and Rise of BHP Billiton*.

Robert is the author of 29 books including the biography of Kevin Rudd, four novels and a number of works of history. He is a graduate of the Australian Film Television and Radio School and has written and directed documentary films in 33 countries in Asia and the South Pacific. Robert now lives in Canberra and Tuross Head, and divides his time between his books and screenplays.

Castaway

The extraordinary survival story of
Narcisse Pelletier, a young French cabin boy
shipwrecked on Cape York in 1858

Robert Macklin

hachette
AUSTRALIA

First published in Australia and New Zealand in 2019
by Hachette Australia
(an imprint of Hachette Australia Pty Limited)
Level 17, 207 Kent Street, Sydney NSW 2000
www.hachette.com.au

This edition published in 2021

10 9 8 7 6 5 4 3 2 1

 A catalogue record for this
book is available from the
NATIONAL LIBRARY OF AUSTRALIA   National Library of Australia

ISBN: 978 0 7336 4506 8 (paperback)

Full cover by Luke Causby, Blue Cork
Cover photographs courtesy of iStock and Queensland State Archives
Text design by Bookhouse, Sydney
Typeset in Bembo MT Pro by Bookhouse, Sydney
Printed and bound in Australia by McPherson's Printing Group

*This is for Donald Thomson, and for the Aboriginal people
who gave refuge to a stranger, In Memoriam*

CONTENTS

Author's Note   xi

PART ONE

1   Narcisse   3

PART TWO

2   Australia   27

PART THREE

3   Narcisse/Amglo   47
4   Queensland   54
5   Narcisse/Amglo   70

PART FOUR

6   Queensland   81
7   Amglo   92
8   Queensland   99
9   Amglo   106
10   Queensland   117
11   Amglo   123

PART FIVE

12   Queensland   135
13   Amglo   139
14   Cape York   148
15   Amglo   154
16   Cape York   160

17 Amglo   164
18 Cape York   171

PART SIX

19 Amglo   181
20 Queensland   186
21 Amglo   193
22 Cape York   202
23 Amglo   207

PART SEVEN

24 Cape York   223
25 Amglo   228
26 Cape York   240
27 Amglo   245

PART EIGHT

28 Somerset   253
29 Amglo/Narcisse   256

PART NINE

30 Saint-Gilles-Sur-Vie   269
31 Queensland   280
32 Narcisse/Amglo   287

Epilogue   295

Acknowledgements   301
Abridged Bibliography   303
Notes   306
Index   311

'The imagination is the power to
disimprison the soul of fact'

Samuel Taylor Coleridge (attrib.)

AUTHOR'S NOTE

I first heard the raw outline of the castaway story from a family friend, the late Jimi Bostock, whom I had known long ago when making documentary films. He was now on the staff of the Aboriginal leader Noel Pearson, and he arranged to have lunch with me during a holiday in Cairns.

As a Queenslander, and an historian, I was both amazed that I had never heard of it before and delighted to discover it at a time when Australia is at last willing to listen to the real story of the colonial treatment of the Aboriginal people. For I knew almost at once that given the time frame of Narcisse Pelletier's seventeen years with the Aboriginal people of Far North Queensland – 1858 to 1875 – it would be a perfect counterpoint to the Frontier War that raged in Queensland throughout that period. And ironically some of its most vicious perpetrators were the officers and men of the Native Mounted Police Force.

It would complete my planned Australian History Quartet, which began with *Dark Paradise,* the shocking savagery of the convict story played out on Norfolk Island; followed by *Hamilton Hume*, the narrative of the first eighty years of our colonial history as seen through the life of our greatest explorer; and then

Dragon and Kangaroo, telling of our remarkable shared relations with China for the last 200 years.

However, the *Castaway* story had complications not shared by the others. One was language. Narcisse was a fourteen-year-old French cabin boy when abandoned to his fate on the Far North Queensland beach. He spoke not a word of English. His saviours were Aboriginal people who spoke no language but their own. Yet I would be writing in English for a mainly English-speaking readership.

Another was the research into what he actually did during those seventeen years. On his reluctant return to France, he gave interviews to a surgeon turned historian that resulted in a book. But from all the evidence of its contents, he told the author very little indeed about his adventures and experiences, and virtually nothing about the intimate daily lives of his Aboriginal hosts-cum-extended family.

For this I embraced the man to whom this work is dedicated, one of Australia's greatest Aboriginal anthropologists, the late Donald Thomson. His field notes of his deep and authoritative study of this obscure and unique maritime people on the coast of Far North Queensland were of overwhelming value. I immersed myself in them. Indeed, in areas such as male initiation, marital, diplomatic and burial practice, I have followed his words almost to the letter.

For this access I wholeheartedly thank Lindy Allen, the then Senior Curator, Anthropology (Northern Australia) of Museums Victoria. And although full acknowledgements will be made at the back of this volume, I must also here thank Rita Metzenrath, the Senior Collections Officer at the Australian Institute of Aboriginal and Torres Strait Islander Studies (AIATSIS) and its library staffers whose assistance was wholehearted and unstinting. Though I hasten to say that neither Lindy Allen nor Rita Metzenrath participated in what flowed from my research.

Donald Thomson spurned convention and published his findings beyond the academic arena. Yet there remains a concern from some academics about an approach that delves beyond the usual constricted telling of Aboriginal society and customs – even to the sexual and initiation practices of the people in the years before the British invasion. The result has been that white Australians have been denied the full-bodied reality that reveals and affirms just what our Aboriginal and Torres Strait Islander compatriots – then and now – mean to the great land that we all now occupy. And to our future together.

The time, I believe, is long overdue for us to draw that veil aside. So, for the first time, guided by Thomson's field notes, his published work and his astonishing collection of artefacts and photographs of the Sandbeach people in their native state, I have written the story of Aboriginal society in Far North Queensland as I believe it was lived before the white man destroyed it.

My rendering, I freely admit, is inexact. It could hardly be otherwise since in addition to my not actually witnessing the events, they are seen through the eyes and actions of a four-teen-year-old French cabin boy growing to maturity within his Aboriginal clan.

But as well as the Thomson oeuvre and extensive reading of other anthropologists and historians, I was blessed by the 2009 academic work of Stephanie Anderson. In her *Pelletier: The Forgotten Castaway of Cape York,* she translated the book by French 'sociologist' Constant Merland who conducted the interviews with Pelletier on his return to France. More importantly, in Anderson's work, Merland's observations were enhanced by the commentaries and linguistics of some of Thomson's Australian successors, notably Professor Athol Chase and from time to time a very distinguished coterie, including Herbert Hale, Norman Tindale, David Thompson, Bruce Rigsby and Nicolas Peterson.

Like them, I too visited the area and established some enduring friendships with the local Aboriginal people. And from all these combined resources I have attempted to re-create the social and emotional reality of Narcisse/Amglo's seventeen years with the Night Islanders.

The other element of the book, the Frontier War conducted against the Aboriginal people by the white settlers and their government – powerfully reinforced by the Native Mounted Police drawn from southern Aboriginal nations – provided no such constraints. Written records abound and some very fine historical documentation was able to be drawn upon.

The Native Police conducted hundreds of massacres of the Aboriginal people in the most densely populated mainland colony of Queensland. These 'troopers' and, specifically, their white officers are the villains of the piece. But they only reflected the larger mindset of the time: that the Aboriginal people were simply an impediment to 'development' to be swept aside as quickly and as completely as possible.

No doubt the usual suspects will respond with their 'black armband' retorts. Truth is, there are not enough black armbands in Christendom to acknowledge the terrible carnage wrought by the bullets, poison and despair that our First Australians suffered. And if these seem angry words, I plead guilty as charged.

Robert Macklin
Canberra, 2019

LANGUAGE

Sadly, the language of the Night Island (Uutaalnganu) people is no longer sufficiently well known for an authoritative, independent vocabulary to have been collected and attested; however, the brilliant linguist and anthropologist David Thompson has preserved much of the very similar Sandbeach language of the neighbouring Kuuku Y'au and the Umpila people. And since there is good reason to believe that Uutaalnganu shared their vocabulary, I have drawn principally upon David Thompson's collection in the brief conversations between Amglo/Narcisse and his fellow clansmen. Note that certain words appear to have multiple meanings, while more than one word can have the same meaning.

PART
One

I

Narcisse

He loved the sea.

He loved the clean, salt tang of it when he reached the open deck each morning and the breeze blew away the sweaty exhalations of the night below.

He loved the sight of it, the deep blues and greens, the frothing snow-white curls topping the choppy swells that swept from one horizon to the other.

He loved the sound of it as the three-masted barque *Saint-Paul* cut through the lumpy surface like the swish of a cutlass blade and the sails snapped and billowed above him.

And he loved the moody spirit of it that lived beneath the waves and on the good days stayed calm and peaceful.

On those days, as the dawn broke he made his way along the deck towards the quartermaster's cabin balancing the hot water, the coffee pot and the fresh rolls from the galley with the expertise of a tightrope walker. And on the bad ones when the spirit was roused and raging he put his back to the wind and the stinging pellets of rain and spume, sheltering his master's *petit dejeuner* as the deck bucked and shuddered beneath his bare feet.

But still he loved it.

3

It was the greater part of his life and it had been since ever his fourteen-year-old brain could remember. Good memories. And as soft winds drove the *Saint-Paul* from Hong Kong east of the Philippines and down through the South Pacific into a darkening Bismarck Sea, Narcisse Pelletier leaned on the railing, with one hand hooked around the rigging, and played with the memories.

The best of them was Grand-père Babin, his mother's father, with his curly salt beard, who took him sailing in the boat which he'd named after the boy himself, *Le Jeune Narcisse*. When he was just eight years old, his *grand-père* had fetched him from his home in their beloved village of Saint-Gilles to take a journey in the little boat, up and down the Bay of Biscay on the Côte de Lumière. They carried small cargoes from place to place and it had lasted several months. He wished it would never end and thereafter nothing would do but to return to the joy of it, *avec grand plaisir*.

His father's profession – if you could call it that – held no attraction for him. Indeed, he knew that for Martin Pelletier himself, the role of *bottier*, or shoemaker, was barely endurable for the scion of a family that had fallen so far – from privileged and titled *Pelletier de Saint-Gilles* after the glorious revolution of 1789. That was when the people rose against the *aristos* and the Divine Right of kings and replaced them with the Rights of Man and the Tricolour. But though the Pelletiers had lost their land, they kept their heads and Narcisse knew his Père Martin as an honest toiler; he had trained his hands to mould the leather for workers' boots and the polished hightops of the town's merchants. And they too respected him.

Martin Pelletier married Narcisse's mother, Alphonsine Babin, beautiful and younger by eleven years, in February 1843 and they moved into the first of the three houses in Saint-Gilles of the *département Vendée* that the family would occupy. Only three months later she was pregnant with Narcisse. She named him for

Saint Narcissus, the Catholic Bishop of Jerusalem in the century after the Lord Jesus walked the holy land.

When the voyage with Grand-père Babin was done, Narcisse returned to the communal school and his endless battle – his *conflit* – with his teacher, M. Palvadeau. So fierce did it become that when Narcisse was only ten the *educateur* had written to the mayor of the town complaining of the boy's '*insubordination et insolence*'. The punishment for such offences was expulsion, but the authorities left it to Père Martin to mete out the penance. That was bad enough – he insisted Narcisse remain at school for two more years.[1]

But at least there was the consolation that after lessons he could hurry to the nearby rectory of the young priest known to the faithful as Monsieur le Curé. It was the priest's task to teach him the Catechism, but mostly he told of the miracles of the saints, including Narcisse's namesake who, he learned, had turned water into oil so the Easter lamps could be lit in the holy city. And that was but one of the wonders they performed. Theirs was a world of the spirit where everything was possible; and the Church, with its rich and mysterious rituals and its deep devotion to the Holy Spirit, soon became the other abiding presence in Narcisse's world.

It was a good place, for all around him was the sea and the River Vie with its crowds of bobbing vessels, from ships of the line to fishing smacks moored in the sparkling estuary. Their home was right on the bank; and as Alphonsine produced two young brothers in the five years since his own birth, the littoral became the joyous playground – *l'aire de jeu* – for Narcisse, Élie Jean-Félix and little Alphonse. They watched and marvelled as the new lighthouse rose at the entrance to the port of Saint-Gilles. Their days were filled with the activities of the ships, marred only once when the wash of a passing fishing boat upset their little dinghy and Alphonse was lost, forever it seemed, in the deep current of the Vie.

Narcisse dived below in a frantic race to find him, and through the murk, the *boue,* of the river he glimpsed his feet. He drove himself forward and grabbed an ankle but was carried down by the current to the river bed. Once his feet touched the bottom he flexed his knees then drove upwards with all his strength. When he reached the surface he took a great gulp of air and found himself close in to the bank where Élie Jean-Félix, in a blubber of tears, reached out a hand and they wrestled Alphonse to shore.

Narcisse dragged himself on to the land where Élie was frantically slapping his brother's face, imploring him to breathe, *'Respire! Respire!'* It was no use. Alphonse was turning blue. Narcisse recovered himself and began to push on to his brother's back. But then Élie lost all control and took Alphonse's face in his hands and blew into his mouth, blew and blew and blew until Narcisse reached out to push him away. But then the little boy vomited the river water on Élie and took a very big breath of his own, opened his eyes and started talking.

It was a miracle. Saint Narcissus himself had been watching over them.

Narcisse endured his classroom for those two final years until Grand-père Babin finally persuaded Martin and Alphonsine to release him. Then the old sailor, whose son Jean would soon become harbour master and who knew the captains of half the ships of France's *flotte maritime,* was able to secure him an apprenticeship as a cabin boy – a *mousse* – on the ketch *Le Furet.* So at twelve years old Narcisse said his solemn goodbyes to his father and Monsieur le Curé; he glowed in the eyes of Élie, two years below him, and felt a catch in his throat when little Alphonse kissed both his cheeks. But when he came to his mother suddenly he was drenched in her tears and though he tried his manly best to resist, his emotions had a mind of their own and the tears escaped him.

Finally, with his few clothes in a leather portmanteau crafted by Père Martin, Narcisse stepped aboard the small coastal trader.

He was back upon the sea.

There was little time to enjoy it. His duties were never-ending. And after *Le Furet* came a bigger vessel, the *Eugénie*. The work was not much different but now there was room to breathe and it felt like a promotion. When he wasn't helping the cook in his hot and boisterous galley, he was either carrying buckets of food to the forecastle where the ordinary seamen ate; running messages around the ship; learning to handle the sails, lines and ropes in all weathers; or scrambling up the rigging into the yards when the sails had to be trimmed.

He would stand watch with other crewmen and, when he'd learned to box a compass and the going was calm and steady, he would even be permitted to take the helm and keep the ship on course. That was a special thrill. But nothing compared with setting the top gallant from the yard so far above the deck that the crewmen below seemed like midgets and the sea went on forever.

The climb up Jacob's ladder was always a race, even if he was the only competitor. While others held back, he loved the excitement that rose from belly to chest and seemed ready to burst by the time he reached the top. Even with great swells amidships he held on and laughed into the wind. It made up for the times when he had to clean out the quartermaster's cabin and work in the stinking bilges.

Narcisse was making his way in the seaman's world and there was a *camaraderie* among the crew who included him in their jests – *leurs sales tours* – and their endless tales of shipboard escapades. But then in his second year he transferred to the *Reine des Mers*, for a voyage to Trieste, and for the first time he felt the rough, angry hands of seafaring.

The memory bit deep – the knife attack from the ship's first
mate and the pain that came with it. He was thirteen now and
was beginning to develop his young muscles. He might have
been of only medium height, but the mirror reflected his pleasing
features. His eyes were large and brown. They were well set
below a high forehead which was crowned by dark, glossy hair.
His mouth was quick to smile and pout and he spoke the rapid
patois of the Vendée. His manner was unforced and lively and
he retained the bouncy spirit that had so enraged M. Palvadeau.

As the blood flowed from his wound, the mate's excuse was
a foolish one: that he 'fell asleep while on watch'. No one truly
believed it though they would not contradict the officer, even
when he said he stabbed Narcisse to 'wake him up'. The truth
was never spoken but they knew it was his refusal to bend to the
big man's lustful demands as more timid cabin boys had done in
the naval fleets from time immemorial. The stab wound would
heal, but the memory would remain. And when the ship reached
Marseilles on its return run in July 1857, Narcisse left it without
a backward glance.[2]

By now he knew his trade and within a month he had signed
on to the *Saint-Paul* under Captain Emmanuel Pinard. This was
a real promotion. The 620-ton three-masted barque would cross
the globe on a voyage all the way to Bombay with its cargo of
Bordeaux wine. This was the sea in all her beauty and the spirit
in all its moods.

When they reached the crowded bustle of the Indian port, they
were surrounded by hundreds of jabbering locals all competing
for the task of unloading half the precious cargo for the British
colonial administrators and their memsahibs. It took a bevy of
uniformed sepoys led by a red-faced British officer to bring order
to the rabble.

Captain Pinard was a stern master with his broad chest,
black hair and eyebrows above a pair of grey eyes, and a round,

clean-shaven chin. He had been born in Nantes in 1816 and had made his career in *la marine marchande,* rising to *capitaine* in 1850. He decreed that the younger crewmen, Narcisse included, remain on board throughout their stay. So he watched as the older men left the vessel and were instantly surrounded by the eager harlots in their flashing red and green silk saris concealing and revealing their slim, sensuous bodies; and with their pimps – *les souteneurs* – negotiating the price. He would carry those visions to his hammock for many nights as they crossed the Indian Ocean, then negotiated the dangerous Straits of Malacca and set course north to Hong Kong.

There they discharged the remainder of their Bordeaux bounty while the captain and his local agent negotiated the loading of a new cargo. None of the crewmen knew what it was, though most said it would be tea or the *chinoiserie* that was beginning to be popular in Paris. Narcisse paid it little mind for Captain Pinard had relaxed his ban on shore leave for the cadets and apprentices.

He started out in a small party of shipmates but soon found himself alone among the crowded streets and byways of Wanchai as tough brown coolies became human ponies between the shafts of rickshaws. They pulled men lounging back in their seats and looking so much like pink walruses that he stopped and laughed aloud. He ate in tiny sidewalk cafés and marvelled at the tastes when finally they found a spoon for him instead of the impossible chopsticks. And while he always followed orders and returned to the *Saint-Paul* in the evenings, during the days that followed he retraced his steps and almost felt at home among the Chinese. They could speak no French but they understood his Gallic gestures and the friendliness of his smile.

On his fourteenth birthday, he made his way down the now familiar streets and in his shoulder bag he carried a bottle of the wine the crewmen had *libéré* from the cargo hold. When he reached his favourite café, he produced it and invited the happy, gap-toothed owner and his pretty daughter, who waited on the rickety tables, to share a glass.

The owner grinned and grabbed the bottle which he opened with an ancient metal corkscrew. The daughter produced three small glasses but when her father growled at her she blushed and put hers aside. Narcisse protested and the old man relented but took care to see that hers was no more than a taste. His own was filled to the brim and, to Narcisse's amazement, was consumed in a single draught before he scurried back to his wok which fitted neatly into the hole above the glowing coals of his oven.

The meal seemed almost endless. Just as one steaming plate of delicious food was dispensed with, another appeared from *le patron*'s tiny kitchen. And as the afternoon turned to evening, the regular clientele arrived and were introduced to the *shuǐshǒu Fǎguó de*, which Narcisse took to mean French sailor.

'*Je m'appelle Narcisse,*' he said as each arrived and nodded uncomprehendingly but with grins that convinced Narcisse that he was welcome in their midst.

By now the bounty of Bordeaux had long been replaced by a rice wine of such alcoholic potency that he felt his eyeballs bulging from his head as it passed his throat and coursed down his insides. His reaction caused such hilarity among the onlookers that he couldn't help but repeat the process and they all laughed the more.

Only when he finally rose to take a gracious leave did he realise – and then only dimly – that locomotion was quite beyond him. And the rumbling of his insides gave warning that all the hard work of *le patron* was in danger of returning unbidden.

Then it did.

Fortunately, he was able to stagger into the narrow alleyway-cum-drain at the side of the café before the explosion took place. When it was over he returned, deeply ashamed, to the small bamboo chair where he slumped and began a new struggle, this time to keep his eyes open as the darkness gathered round him.

The next he knew he was in a hard, narrow bed in almost complete blackness. As his eyes accustomed themselves, he realised he was in an upper room so small he could nearly touch the walls on either side. His throat was parched and as he turned on his side he became aware that he was totally undressed and on the floor beside him was a bowl of water. He buried his head in it and drank noisily before lying back again and listening for some clue to his whereabouts. It certainly wasn't the ship with the groans and snores and farts of the crewmen, though the room felt no more steady than the *Saint-Paul* at anchor. And with that realisation came a ripple of fear for the consequences from Captain Pinard.

The time. What could it be? The darkness was not quite complete and when he scanned his surroundings a shadow separated itself from the rest and loomed towards him. As it took shape he knew immediately it was the daughter and she had a finger pressed to her lips. Without a word she slipped in beside him and he was instantly, painfully aroused. She was wearing only a thin cotton chemise and the touch of her body set his heart beating against his chest. She gave small birdlike chirrups and nibbled his neck and ear, then moved above him and guided him into the depths of her warm, clenching *ouverture*. As she moved slowly upon him, she placed her soft hand over his mouth, muffling his groans as he exploded.

For a long moment they rested. And then, still without a word, she left the bed and retrieved his clothes and shoulder bag from a corner of the room. He struggled to dress as his head whirled and she guided him out of the room and down the flimsy stairs, through the kitchen and into the grey pre-dawn of Wanchai. She smiled as she kissed his cheek and pointed the way back to the ship.

* * *

By the time Narcisse arrived at the dock the sun was up and, as he approached the *Saint-Paul*'s berth, he was astonished to see a crowd of Chinese coolies lined up before the gangway. Just as he reached them, the bosun yelled an order and they began filing up the gangway. The walk from his overnight billet had cleared his head and he joined the Chinese, lowered his gaze, and shuffled up the walkway in their midst.

Once aboard he dropped his bag and hurriedly resumed the role of crewman, joining the knot of sailors watching the Chinese being directed below. In all the excitement, his absence, it seemed, had barely registered. They were the mysterious cargo coming aboard for the next leg of the journey. It would take them south to *Nouvelle-Hollande* where for the last eight years the greatest goldrush the world had known had been drawing hopeful miners from around the globe. But while Narcisse found the prospect an exciting one, the twenty-one officers and crew were not happy, and the cook and his galley hands were at the point of revolt. 'Three hundred and seventeen extra mouths to feed!' cried the cook. 'And they eat like savages!'

Narcisse made for his bunk, only to discover that sleeping arrangements were in chaos; his gear had been moved and the quartermaster's mate was waiting. He had been missed after all and as punishment he would do double watches throughout the journey south. Instead of four-hour shifts, his would be eight; and long before they reached the Australian coast he would be exhausted and aching in every muscle. That would be a lesson to him.

He took the penance on the chin. At least in those long nights at sea he would have a memory to sustain him, an experience in that café's upper room that capped all the others of his fourteen years.

By now the crew had joined with the cook in angry protest. The Chinese were eating their way through all the supplies. And the crew's rage increased with every passing meal until, after four days under sail, the captain responded. The first mate called the crew together and Pinard made his announcement from *le pont arrière*. The Chinese, he said, were consuming more than expected, so it was necessary to plot a new course to the destination. Instead of the usual route through the South China Sea, they would reduce their journey by veering east of the Philippines and running due south through the Louisiade Archipelago, discovered and named by the great French navigator, Louis-Antoine de Bougainville.

It was received in silence. But at least it stilled the more *activiste* among them. And for several days the ship made good progress until now, when Narcisse unhooked his arm from the rigging, left his favoured place by the ship's railing and made his way to the quarterdeck where he would spend the next few hours repairing torn sails. Then he would take his turn at the daily task of pumping out the water that seeped between the timber planking of the keel and the copper sheet that had recently been fitted to prevent marine worm.

Soon he noticed lightning flickering on the starboard horizon and the stars began to disappear behind a rolling bank of cloud. Then came a freshening wind from the same quarter and the rumble of approaching thunder. Narcisse watched as the swells rose. The spirit was waking from its slumber.

In the next few hours the swells became full-bodied waves and a curtain of rain swept in as Narcisse and his shipmates climbed the rigging and hauled in the sails. By now the lightning was all around and the thunder deafening. But it was not until the midnight hour that the storm unleashed its full fury on the *Saint-Paul*. It raised the waves to the height of the top gallants, lifted the ship to their dizzying peaks then flung the barquentine down their slopes, plunging it into the seawater that churned across the deck and swept the unwary off their feet, their screams lost in the roaring wind as they skidded on their backs into the safety rails.

For two days and nights, with varying degrees of intensity, the seas raged around the sailing ship and there were times, as the *Saint-Paul* groaned in its planking and screamed in its rigging, that Narcisse called upon his namesake for deliverance. On one occasion, as he threw his own weight to the helm beside that of the hulking sailing master, it seemed they were lost, that in the next moment the ship would finally capsize. And when, eventually, the *Saint-Paul* slowly righted herself and the water drained down the scuppers, he threw himself to his knees and thanked the Holy Spirit for their salvation.

At the height of the tempest he could sometimes detect the shouts and *cris de panique* from the Chinese below deck. And from time to time in ones and twos they put their heads above the hatches before retreating. When the worst was over, he visited them in the bowels of the ship. The stench was overwhelming, but they were all hard at work cleaning their shattered quarters with buckets and rags and anything else that came to hand. The next time he ventured below, order had been restored.

The one saving grace of the fearful episode was the food stores which were barely touched while the gale played itself out. But both passengers and crew made up for it in the next three days as the ship beat south through the first of the island chains on the approach to New Guinea's eastern tip.

No sooner had they reached the Louisiade group than they were blanketed by a seemingly endless fog. In some ways this was worse than the cyclone since the captain could take no sextant bearings, and the stars of the southern sky were hidden from view. The compass was their only guide and even that was no real indicator of their position in a barely charted sea dotted with a thousand atolls and islets.

Narcisse was on the second half of his watch, standing in the bow and peering through the heavy mist on all sides, when tragedy struck. They were travelling at just over ten knots when a shadowy mass to port suddenly emerged from the fog. He called a warning and Captain Pinard came on deck. But no sooner had he arrived than there came a terrifying thud from the depths followed by a shocking clatter and banging as the *Saint-Paul* came to a shuddering halt and anything not tied down crashed on to the decks. Then the mainmast canted forward and split at the base, bringing down the foremast and the sails.

There followed a moment of terrible silence when Narcisse wished himself anywhere but on a ship where the watch-keeper had failed so appallingly in his duty. It didn't matter that it would have happened to anyone else on watch at the time. It didn't matter that his senior watch-keeper at the helm was also to blame. He knew with *certitude absolue* that he, Narcisse Pelletier, would be damned by his captain and crew as the culprit, *le coupable*, the begetter of their distress.

And so it came to pass.

As the officers burst upon the deck with Pinard shouting orders, their gaze lighted upon him. When they learned the worst, their anger and contempt paralysed him and he was roughly pushed aside. The younger crewmen were no more sympathetic. They ignored him. It was almost as though he ceased to be. There were no orders to follow. Nothing to do. Then the terrified Chinese rushed on deck and the captain turned his rage upon them. The officers forced them back below. There was nothing to do but wait until a pallid sun rose behind the fog to reveal the true horror of their plight.

It could hardly have been worse. They were hard aground on the tip of a coral reef from which, as the fog cleared, Narcisse could see an island rising to a peak about a kilometre to the south. They were almost 3000 kilometres from any of the regular shipping lanes or anything that passed for civilisation. And with the waves crashing against its timbers, the *Saint-Paul* was threatening to break up completely. The captain ordered all hands to prepare to abandon ship.[3]

What to do with the Chinese? The barque carried only one longboat and two smaller dinghies. Fortunately, those not able to find a place in the boats – including Narcisse – were able to clamber over the exposed reef to its tiny islet; only about twenty by thirty metres, it was little more than a patch in the great ocean.

Some of the crewmen remained to salvage what food and water they could find in the shattered hold. It was a miserable haul – a few barrels of water-soaked flour, two or three quarters of salted meat and a handful of tinned food – but no fresh water. Clearly, if the 348 souls crowded onto the tiny atoll were to survive, quick action was required.

Captain Pinard filled the longboat with some of his officers and men, together with a few Chinese, and rowed for the hilly outcrop which quickly became known as the *Ilot du Refuge*, Refuge Isle.† There, at least, they should be able to find water. Narcisse, still *persona non grata*, remained with the Chinese until a second, third and fourth journey of all three boats ferried the remainder to the tiny island.

By the time he arrived, a visiting party of Melanesians had made contact with the shipwreck survivors and according to the Chinese they had given the white men some coconuts. There was also a tiny stream running down from the hill and everyone had slaked their thirst. But it was clear that it would soon dry up and there was no food to be found but for a few coconut trees. The survivors shared some of the salvaged food in an evening meal then bedded down on the beach with several fires that

---

† Later Heron Island, not to be confused with Heron Island east of Gladstone.

burned until they exhausted the fuel they had gathered from the surrounding scrubland. But as the sun rose, the 'hospitable' natives mounted a fierce attack and several of the crewmen and Chinese were killed, until finally the Frenchmen fought them off.

Narcisse and another cadet joined Pinard and were ordered to row with the senior crewmen to the much larger Rossel Island, about four kilometres to the east. Narcisse put his back into the task, as if by his exertions he might make up for his failure. But Pinard gave no sign that he noticed or cared.

When they reached Rossel Island, Narcisse was at the rear of the party when they were attacked with 'darts and stones'.[4] At least two were killed and another taken captive. Narcisse was struck behind the ear by a rock as he and the apprentice ran to the longboat where the other officers and men were making their escape. Once aboard, he crouched behind the sheltering timbers trying to staunch the blood from his wound as arrows swept overhead or fell short of the retreating vessel.

By the time they returned to the others, unbeknown to Narcisse, the captain had decided on a course of action. That night when most of the camp was sleeping, the signal to depart quietly spread among the crewmen who gathered what clothes and other belongings they had salvaged before gathering at the longboat tethered by anchor to the sandy beach. In the silent night, an unfamiliar noise woke Narcisse and in the moonlight he made out the shadowy figures of his so-called shipmates preparing to push off in the only boat that offered a chance to survive. Fear gripped him and it turned instantly to action as he raced for the departing vessel. He reached it in the shallows and flung himself over the side.

Pinard and the crew let him stay – to do otherwise would have wakened the Chinese with his cries – and with muffled oars they made for the open sea. The date was 2 October 1858.

* * *

Pinard would later claim to the authorities that he 'consulted' with the Chinese before abandoning them on the *Ilot du Refuge*. If so, he had given them no choice. He had ordered his men to load the seven-metre longboat with some of the boxes of tinned food rescued from the wreck and whatever fresh water could be carried in the available vessels, including – in some reports – the seamen's boots.[5]

The 300 Chinese, and at least one European, were left with very little food and water and only a few axes and firearms with which to defend themselves. Moreover, the guns were virtually useless. While they had powder and shot, the crewmen had not been able to rescue any of the percussion caps needed to fire the weapons. If attacked, a second man would have to use burning slivers of wood to touch off the firing mechanism in the way muskets were fired in the distant past.[6]

Nevertheless, they began organising to survive. They succeeded in making drinkable water by constructing a crude distillery made of big shells and a leather 'channel' salvaged from the *Saint-Paul*. They dug holes in the sand and lined them with canvas to conserve the water, but with such great numbers it was a losing battle. They had soon used up the meagre foodstuffs from the ship and foraged through the island for any game and plants that might still the pangs of hunger.

Two of their number died of starvation in those first weeks. But much worse was in store for the survivors. A month after their ordeal began, the Melanesians arrived in force from Rossel Island. By now the only European left was the ship's carpenter and when the club-wielding Papua New Guineans attacked, he waded into the melee with a cutlass in one hand and an axe in the other. But he was quickly overpowered and disarmed; and as the attackers surrounded the Chinese they sued for peace.

This brought an apparent change of mood among the Rossel Islanders who laid down their arms and their chieftain, known as Muwo, promised to supply the castaways with food and water. Moreover, he would arrange for them to be transported to the 'mainland'. But whether that referred to Rossel Island or distant New Guinea is unclear. In fact, he had no intention of permitting any of them to leave his domain alive.[7]

Muwo ruled his fellow islanders by fear. The son of a chief, his violent nature showed itself early when some dirt tossed by a playmate accidentally struck him on the face. Although the commoner apologised and made elaborate gifts in compensation, Muwo begged his father to kill the boy. Reluctantly, the chieftain agreed, even to Muwo's plea that he should eat some of the flesh.

This was the beginning of a craving for human flesh that came to obsess Muwo when he succeeded his father as chief. In fact, cannibalism was part of a religious ritual on Rossel Island. Their hero-god, Wonajo, dictated that when a chief died, a selected tribal member would be killed and eaten at the funeral feast. Payments would be made to the victim's family and they would be honoured for their sacrifice. However, Muwo's lusts were of a different order – they extended to the wealth of his neighbours and he acquired no fewer than ten wives, ten houses, five ceremonial canoes, five sailing canoes, fishnets, money and other valuables.

No one dared defeat him in a canoe race lest he claim the canoe for himself and if the owner protested he would be killed – and eaten – the same day. Historian Col Davidson says, 'Any excuse would do to satisfy his craving – being bitten by mosquitoes, his garden damaged by pigs, his hut by the weather. He would blame someone's sorcery and send his men to kill him. The victim would then be eaten.'[8]

It was at this time – the height of his power – that the *Saint-Paul* landed on Muwo's island doorstep. According to the single

Chinese survivor, the canoes arrived with supplies to keep them alive and to take them, three at a time, across the water to Rossel Island. Once out of sight of their compatriots, they were stripped, bashed and their pigtails pulled out by brute force before they were butchered, cooked and eaten. The island became a grisly human abattoir, its sandy soil drenched in their blood, their skulls scattered among the palms and bushes fringing the beach. And the dying fires carried the stench of roasted flesh.

Remarkably, the European ship's carpenter – believed to be Greek – was spared, together with four young Chinese who caught the fancy of Muwo's lesser chieftains. However, for all but one, their reprieve was only temporary.

* * *

In the open boat under a blazing tropic sun, Narcisse was living through his own special hell. The sea was endless, its spirit sleeping in the cold depths far beyond the reach of prayer. After four days, hunger and thirst had become constant aches with never a moment's rest. There was no place in the boat to find comfort or even to call his own. And never for a minute was he allowed to forget his part in the events that had brought his companions to their plight. If only he had cried a warning in time for the helmsman to spin the wheel and avoid the coral crag that had ripped open the belly of the *Saint-Paul*. If only he had stayed awake!

'*J'étais réveillé!*' I was awake!

'*Alors pourquoi?*' Then why?

'*Le brouillard . . . le brouillard . . .*' The fog . . . the fog . . .

'*Merde!*'

And so it went. He was last to receive the few morsels of tinned beef, last to be passed the rag soaked in their remaining boot of water; and when he tried with all his strength to squeeze the final drops from it, they sneered and turned away. He would never forget them: second mate, Alphonse d'Adhemar de Cransac from Rouen; sailing master Adolphe-Charles Per, from St-Malo; the cook, François Garcin; the bosun's mate, Pierre Lagnardette; seaman Jan-Michel Ovitali; and even his fellow *novice* Lauren Monteil.[9]

The captain had his dagger pistol and rounds of shot which he used to kill a seabird that landed on a rippled ocean just out of reach of the sailors' outstretched hands. But Narcisse received no more than a bone or two with the remains of its meagre flesh. Then the sailing master fired at a circling shark but the great fish merely swam away. And on the seventh day they began to drink sea water mixed with their own urine.

Narcisse fought to keep it down. He found a small space by the starboard bow and cooled his face with the spray from the whitecaps. His wound from the rock thrown at Rossel Island was becoming painful and he bathed it in salt water as they travelled. He tried to be invisible. He had heard the stories told with relish in the galleys and in the hammocks of castaways turned cannibal; and the first to go under the knife was always the cabin boy.

The only ray of hope was their progress under a rough sail with a nor'easter that was pushing them steadily westward. Then early one morning a dozen seagulls arrived from nowhere and the crewmen grabbed three before the others took fright. But what little he was spared was raw and rank. When the bosun's mate caught a decent sized fish, there was celebration all round. He scaled and gutted it before cutting the pieces grabbed by eager hands. And when Narcisse complained about the size of his portion, they offered him the guts.

On the tenth day they saw a smudge of land on the western horizon.

'*C'est la Nouvelle Hollande,*' said Pinard, and Narcisse prayed to his namesake that it was true. On the eleventh day they broached the coral barrier and knew in their hearts that deliverance was at hand. They steered for the land with its green foliage rising to

a range of tall mountains. And on the twelfth day they landed
on a long white beach. He would learn much later that they had
travelled some 1200 kilometres.

Pinard divided the crew into two parties, one to travel north,
the other south, in quest of water. Narcisse was assigned to the
first mate's party heading south and they set off at as brisk a
pace as they could manage. And soon enough they found a tiny
soak in scrubland back from the beach. The sailors drank first.
Then when they were done Narcisse buried his aching head in
the damp sand that remained.

They returned to the longboat and in the afternoon dark
clouds from the northwest glowered teasingly above them until
suddenly they gave up their liquid load in a mighty downpour.
It was over as quickly as it began. But at least it had brought a
temporary relief from their thirst and given them strength to
resume their search for food. They found many small crabs on the
rocks and after starting a fire on the beach they boiled them in
the iron bailing dish, but they provided very little nourishment.

By now the cut behind Narcisse's ear had become septic and
the pain was unceasing.

As the sun was setting they saw black men emerging from the
scrub further down the beach. They made threatening gestures
with their spears before disappearing back into the stunted trees.
Captain Pinard ordered a watch set and Narcisse was roughly
excused. But he barely slept for the throbbing of his wound
and the clouds of mosquitoes that feasted on the men until an
on-shore wind peppered them with flying sand.

Early next morning they boarded the longboat and travelled
south in search of a more safe and sheltered beach. When they
arrived at a potential site, the routine was resumed – two parties,
one north, one south – a vain quest for meat or fruit, a sad return
to the boat, a downpour followed by a fishing session that barely
filled their bellies, before they collapsed in sleep around a great

fire on the beach. The inhabitants stayed away but the smoke from their fires gave notice of their presence.

On the fourth day everything changed. That was the day his second life began. Narcisse could never quite remember all the details, but he knew he walked a long way with his group, his bare feet cut by coral as he came and went from the boat, trying to keep up with them, crossing a shallow waterway and pleased when he saw they had stopped up ahead and were bending to drink. But by the time he reached them, the waterhole was dry.

They ignored his protests. They told him he could stay until it filled again and they left him to continue their search. There through the mid-morning he stayed and watched, but the water didn't come. And when he tried to follow his group, the waterway they'd crossed had been filled by the turning tide. So he returned to the waterhole – still dry – to wait for their return. And in the afternoon sun he fell asleep.

When he woke, there was pain and dizziness in his head. There was no sign of the crewmen. He staggered to the waterway which had returned to its previous depth so he crossed it and headed in the direction of the boat. He walked until he fell to his knees. He rose again and walked unsteadily through the heavy sand. Now, he was sure, he had reached the place where the boat had come ashore. There were footprints in the sand, a furrow where the rope and anchor chain had held the boat fast to the beach.

It was gone.

Through swollen eyes he searched the sea, back and forth, all the way to the horizon. There was a small island straight ahead, but nothing else to catch the eye. He let himself fall to his rump and an unnatural darkness gathered around him. Only the throbbing of his head remained. Then that too faded to nothingness.

Time passed.

When he opened his eyes again, it was to the sound of soft voices and a vision of three round, dark faces bending over him.

Then there was water on his lips and trickling down his throat
. . . he coughed, and drank, and slept.

But not for long. Soon the muffled voices returned and he
came fully awake. Two naked men holding long spears in their
right hands were approaching. They spoke to him in words that
sounded like pebbles rolling down a stream and he stood and
responded, *'Bonjour messieurs, bonjour . . .'* knowing immediately
that it was meaningless to them. He sought some gesture, some
gift, but all he had was a worthless tin cup. It would have to
do. He picked it up from the sand and offered it to the bigger
man. He took it gently and both men examined it minutely
before the bigger man touched his chest. 'Maademan,' he said.

Narcisse understood. He tapped his own chest, *'Je suis Narcisse.'*
But it clearly meant nothing to the older man. He thrust his hand
into his pocket and withdrew his only other possession, a ragged
handkerchief. He offered it to Maademan. The man smiled and
exposed glistening white teeth minus a big one at the front as
he accepted the offering. Then he turned to the women who
had been hanging back and uttered a sentence or two. One of
them came forward with another gourd of water.

Maademan passed it to Narcisse and he drank. Suddenly a wave
of dizziness swept over him and he staggered back. The natives
reached him before he fell. Then, with their strong hands at his
shoulders, the two men on either side supported him as they
walked over the sand and into the bush. There was a moment
when he thought that he should feel fear, but they were warm to
his touch and he was reassured. When they spoke, the words were
unfamiliar but there was no hostility in them. They could have
been the voice of Monsieur le Curé telling his stories of the saints.

There was a fire in a clearing and they lowered him a small
distance from it. And he slept again.

PART
Two

2

Australia

The Great South Land that we now know as Australia has always been an enigma to the rest of the world. From the time it broke away from the vast Gondwana supercontinent almost 100 million years ago, it has followed its own unique and confounding path. Its marsupial fauna bound across a timeless landscape; the broad grey-green leaves of its remnant rainforests rustle their secret messages in the shadowy warmth of their ancient canopy; the most toxic serpents the world has known glide through their grassy camouflage like the silent spirits of Eden. And when *Homo sapiens* arrived from their journey out of Africa some 70,000 years ago, they discovered a land where no human foot had trod. The biggest island and smallest continent on the globe was theirs alone.

Many, perhaps most, reached it, we believe, through the tip of Cape York, having traversed the islands of the Arafura Sea and the perilous jungles and escarpments of New Guinea. And from that northern beachhead they spread and multiplied across the land. It was a world within a world, protected by an oceanic moat and containing a seemingly endless banquet of natural provender.

The great, awkward *Diprotodon*, a giant marsupial 'wombat' with the bulk of a hippopotamus; the *Zaglossus hacketti,* a sheep-sized echidna; massive flightless birds; *Thylacines* as big as lions;

kangaroos three metres tall – all fell to the clubs, spears and ambushes of the newcomers. Then as the regularity of the rains that sustained the cycle of abundant life disappeared from the hills and plains of the great island, so too did the trundling beasts.

The people adjusted to their new circumstance. They learned the principles of conservation. As the centuries turned to millennia, the Dreamtime stories on which they were founded became an all-embracing spirit world in which the land and the people were joined, each interacting with the other to produce an enduring harmony.

They cared for the land with fire; and the land gave up its bounty in the plants and animals that made their life possible and enjoyable. The longer they practised their spiritual sacraments, the more complex and sophisticated they became. Separate doctrines developed for the males and females and they found expression in stories and dances that each held dear. So too the relationships within the clan to regulate ties to the land and to pass along the songs and stories that bind and teach the wisdom of experience.

The land was so vast that as they spread across it the different groups in widely separated environments developed their own languages and the varieties of custom that their surroundings decreed. The further away, the greater the differences that arose between them. In time, the Great South Land became overlaid by a pattern of Aboriginal occupation like a massive spider's web where in some areas the filaments were densely crossed and others almost bare. In many ways, they were not unlike the population of Europe: their territories were clearly delineated and jealously guarded; their sense of communal ownership and pride was no less powerful than that of the Frenchman, the German or the Britisher.

Their songlines and trading interconnected the more than 250 language groupings. Within their regions, they became expert linguists. Most Aboriginal people would usually be fluent in at least two distinct languages. Moreover, they would have to know their social relationship to every other member of the clan, and to behave correctly in their presence.

But that was just the beginning. They must also be fully aware of the relationships between each clan member and all the others. In a typical group of perhaps fifty souls, the number of connections in play would test a modern computer, particularly when they mutated as members aged or altered their status by marriage, childbirth or initiation.

Their intimate relationship with the land and its bounty meant that ownership of the plants and animals that grew upon it was jealously guarded. Trespassing without permission was a call to arms; and appropriating the game of both land and sea was punishable by death. This meant that their nomadic lifestyles within the boundaries of their 'country', and their need for new genetic blood within the complexities of familial relationships, entangled them in constant conflict and diplomacy with their neighbours.

Indeed, the diplomatic niceties involved in the visitation of representatives to a neighbouring clan's territory were no less arduous and pettifogging than those practised by the envoys of Europe's medieval states. And as often as the Europeans, they failed in their mission. But unlike the slaughter that soaked other continents in blood, the Aboriginal affrays were largely ritual blood-lettings, followed in time by corroborees in which all mourned their fallen warriors.

However, while their overt conflicts were spasmodic and ritualistic, their reliance on the spirit world of spells and sorcery to wreak vengeance on their enemies was the greater part of their armoury; and it occupied a vitally important place in their perception of life and death. Indeed, the inner-life of the Aboriginal people – their busy intellect and their spiritual pageantry, leavened by a well-tuned sense of humour — was as complex and sophisticated as any on the globe.

Yet, in their daily routines, innovation in mechanical technology was unnecessary, where weaponry was adequate for the perceived threat, and their architecture fit for purpose and short-lived. Their mode of self-government seemed invisible yet produced a community that provided long and largely satisfying lives to its people as the seasons rolled on with the rhythm of millennia.

Other parts of the globe lived by different notions of time and place. Theirs was a restless world of innovation to meet the demands of a settled life and a rising population, where religious dispute and the quest for dominance too often resulted in a bloodied battlefield. But war brought progress as the techniques of metallurgy produced ploughs as well as swords; and the naval shipyards produced not only armadas of invasion but vessels of exploration. These were the fragile craft that crossed the great moat and finally made the link between the two worlds.

When they came together, each could hardly believe that they shared a common humanity. To the Aboriginal people, the white men — if indeed they were males beneath their fancy dress — were the ghosts of departed tribesmen. This was hardly surprising; to them the Great South Land *was* the world. All memory of their ancient journey across the globe had been lost. And white was the colour of death, the skin beneath the living pelt.

To the Europeans, the Aboriginal people were objects from another plane of existence whose *modus vivendi* was outrageously uncivilised. Yet remarkably, they comported themselves with a self-regard that would have been laughable were it not so genuinely unaffected. One of the first of the outlanders to find himself among them, the English Captain James Cook, was taken aback: 'They may appear to some to be the most wretched people upon Earth,' he wrote, 'but in reality they are far more happier than we Europeans; being wholly unacquainted not only with the superfluous but the necessary conveniences so much sought after in Europe, they are happy in not knowing the use of them . . . the Earth and sea of their own accord furnished them with all things necessary for life.'[1]

Cook had spent seven weeks repairing his ship, the HMS *Endeavour,* at the river mouth that now bears its name. It spills into the sea on the eastern side of Cape York. When he departed he first cleared the treacherous reefs then landed on a deserted island at the tip of the cape. There, on 22 August 1770, without reference to the Aboriginal people, he claimed possession of the entire eastern seaboard of their country for his king.[2]

Had the Aboriginal people learned of it at the time, it is tempting to imagine the knee-slapping laughter around the campfires that night. ('The whitefella did what!?') If so, it would have rung increasingly hollow in the years ahead, when the notion of 'black humour' acquired a new dimension . . .

★ ★ ★

Cook was one of several score of Europeans to have touched the edges of the continent they dubbed *Terra Australis Incognita.* The first recorded was the Netherlander, Willem Janszoon, who charted the shores of Cape York in 1606 in his fifty-ton *Duyfken.* The history is vague and contradictory, but the story as told by the Aboriginal people is that the Dutchmen landed on the western side of the cape and attempted to kidnap a young woman. The men of her clan reacted and the nine-man landing party fell to their spears and clubs. The *Duyfken* retreated to Java from whence it came.

Ten years later Janszoon's countryman Dirk Hartog was swept by a storm on to the western coast where he went ashore, but he merely left an inscribed pewter plate to record his brief landing. Another Dutchman, Abel Tasman, rode the Roaring Forties across the Indian Ocean and fetched up on the island he named

Van Diemen's Land for the governor of the East Indies, but which would eventually become Tasmania. He saw fires and heard voices, but the Aboriginal people made no contact.

Tasman was followed by some twenty-seven Dutch sea captains who charted patches of the island coastline they dubbed 'New Holland' but none left any descriptions of the inhabitants that encouraged either trade or settlement.

Cook's English compatriot, the buccaneer William Dampier, made landfall on the western coastline in 1688 and again eleven years later. He was scathing in his description of the inhabitants as 'the miserablest people in the world', tortured by flies, and quite without good sense. When he offered them an old pair of trousers and a tattered shirt as inducement to fill his ship's water barrels, they laughed in his face. Instead, they returned to their fishing 'by making [weirs] of stone across little coves or branches of the sea'.[3] Dampier's description of the land which supported them was equally discouraging. Indeed, his most significant contribution to Australian culture was his introduction of the word 'barbecue' to the English language.

In the eighteenth century, other European powers, notably the French, made forays into the southern hemisphere. By then their rivalry with the British was already an article of faith in both countries. From 1337 to 1453 they had engaged in the Hundred Years War, and from the 1660s for the next 150 years 'these two increasingly coherent and unified nations fought each other relentlessly. The stakes were high, no less than global dominance,' says historian Noelene Bloomfield.[4] The drama was to play out in the oceans of the world, including the South Pacific.

There is fragmentary evidence for the 1503 expedition by Binot Paulmier de Gonneville on behalf of the merchants of Honfleur in Northern France. A report of the voyage spoke of his men mixing with the 'natives' for six months. Their weapons were spears and bows and arrows. They grew vegetables and roots, 'their homes had a hole in the roof for a chimney, doors with wooden keys and bedding of woven reeds'.[5] The report was generally accepted as genuine and served to encourage further exploration of the Great South Land.

Other voyages touched on the west coast but it was not until Louis de Bougainville circumnavigated the world, beginning in 1766, that the French approached *la Nouvelle Hollande* from the east. Indeed, he would have landed on the east coast were it not for the Great Barrier Reef. Instead, he turned north and navigated through the island chains to the east of New Guinea, naming them the Louisiade Archipelago after his monarch Louis XV. (Or so he said; it was mere coincidence that they shared a Christian name.)

Louis de Bougainville later assisted in the extensive planning of another great venture into the region led by Jean-François de Galaup La Pérouse. It was a naval operation and La Perouse was chosen to lead it after he had distinguished himself in support of the American War of Independence against the British. He commanded a brace of vessels, the *Boussole* on which he sailed and the *Astrolabe* captained by his friend Fleuriot de Langle. On their approach from the South Pacific, they called by Samoa for fresh food and water, but after an initial friendly welcome, relations with the islanders collapsed and de Langle was dragged out of his longboat and clubbed to death.

A chastened La Perouse steered a course for 'New Holland'. France had accepted the British claim to the eastern seaboard and knew of their plans to use it as a convict colony. And since 1788 was a rare interregnum in their perennial warfare, La Perouse was hoping for a resupply from a thriving community. However, he reached Botany Bay just eight days after the arrival of Captain Arthur Phillip and his 759 convicts, their marine guards and civil officers of the First Fleet. Phillip himself had departed seeking a better site for a settlement and while his deputy, Captain John

Hunter, was sympathetic, there was little he could afford from his meagre stores to replenish the French *cellier*.

With Phillip's discovery of Port Jackson, the British relocated their crowded vessels while La Perouse remained in the bay where at least he was able to take on fresh water and repair his ships. His men fished and swam in Botany Bay's warm waters and wore a track to Sydney Cove in pursuit of the female convicts.

Relations with the Aboriginal people became troubled. Like their fellow British colonisers, the newcomers had no concept of the offence they had perpetrated on the Aboriginal owners of the area. They responded as a Frenchman would have done if some foreign force had occupied the streets of Paris. They attacked with their heaviest armoury – spears propelled by woomeras – and the new arrivals dug in behind a deep ditch and a walled stockade.

After six weeks, with the ships repaired and their water casks full, the French departed, only to be wrecked when swept by a storm-lashed sea into the coral reefs surrounding the island of Vanikoro between New Caledonia and the Solomon Islands. Their fate was unknown at the time and two years later the French National Assembly mounted an expedition to solve the mystery of their disappearance.

Led by Bruni d'Entrecasteaux, this expedition also consisted of two ships and they approached from the west and twice touched upon Tasmania where they mixed briefly with the Aboriginal people. They showered them with gifts and left behind a male and pregnant female goat in the hope that their progeny might provide protein for the hunter-gatherers.† D'Entrecasteaux also visited New Caledonia in 1793 where some sixty years later France would establish its own Pacific penal colony. However,

---

† Neither survived.

en route to Java and resupplies, he fell victim to scurvy and was buried at sea.

By 1800 Napoleon Bonaparte had risen from obscurity to become First Consul and he authorised a major expedition to explore the southern seas for their colonial potential. Led by Nicolas Baudin, it was not a happy voyage; many of the crewmen from both the *Geographe* and the *Naturaliste* died of scurvy and other diseases. Baudin also landed in Tasmania and resumed friendly contact with the Aboriginal people. But as so often happened, misunderstandings led to angry responses and the meeting ended badly.

In 1802 the French ships arrived at Port Jackson where they were greeted by the new governor, Philip Gidley King. However, on this occasion misunderstanding between the two colonial Europeans led to King's suspicion that the Frenchman was planning a settlement in the Port Phillip district. So he hurriedly sent a ship to King Island in Bass Strait to claim possession of it and keep watch on Baudin's activities in Western Port.

It is not known whether any Aboriginal people lived on the island at the time, but either way it was of no interest to either the British or the French. Baudin himself perished in Mauritius on the return journey. The one lasting achievement of his expedition was the artistic rendering of the Aboriginal people and the unique fauna by Charles-Alexandre Lesueur, one of several artists on board.

The French retained their interest in the region throughout the first half of the nineteenth century. Indeed, when New South Wales Governor Ralph Darling heard of a second visit to Western Port in 1825, he sent a naval flotilla of two vessels to found a settlement there. The British established the outline of a township with barracks, a timber mill and brickworks, a commandant's house and a hospital hut. But after three years defending it from the area's Aboriginal owners, they abandoned it.

By then the British had established their mastery of the seas and while French vessels engaged in whaling, sealing and other trade, the opportunity for colonising any substantial part of *Terra Australis* was lost forever. However, when news of the great gold discoveries of the 1850s reached Europe, the race was on for enterprising captains to transport the miners from around the world to the Victorian *El Dorado*.

* * *

Captain Pinard and his crewmen in the longboat continued their journey south. While the northern wet season had yet to begin, they were favoured by a series of rainstorms. They had collected coconuts that had washed ashore before departing the mainland, and had managed to kill several white-tailed rats, each weighing more than a kilogram, which they made into a stew. The waters were full of fish and over a coral reef they killed a turtle which provided a surprising amount of edible meat.

Nevertheless, they would undoubtedly have perished had they not been intercepted by the schooner *Prince of Denmark* on 15 October. Skippered by a Britisher, William MacKellar, she was en route to the Torres Strait where he had teams collecting *bêche-de-mer* to be gutted and dried on Elliott Island and eventually exported to Hong Kong. Only when that was completed did MacKellar sail Pinard and his crew to the French penal colony in New Caledonia.

There the captain and two of his officers boarded the French steamer *Styx* for the return trip to the *Ilot du Refuge*. They reached it on 5 January 1859, some seventy-seven days since he had left his stranded passengers. Sections of the *Saint-Paul* remained on the tiny coral atoll and 'it was immediately obvious how close the line had been between disaster and success – a few metres to one side and his ship would have missed the reef entirely'.[6]

They approached the *Ilot du Refuge* but it was apparently deserted; and when they landed the only evidence of the Chinese presence was a tattered tent, a small midden of shellfish shells and two shallow graves containing the bodies of Chinese men who had apparently died of starvation.

They reboarded the *Styx* and made for Rossel Island where they anchored at the mouth of a river and continued in one of the ship's smaller boats. They spotted two canoes carrying three natives each but they veered away and made for shore beyond the sight of the Frenchmen. As they rounded a point, they came upon a man in a cove, up to his waist in water, silently heading their way and waving frantically. According to an eyewitness, 'He was apparently too afraid to cry out and when the boat reached him, they found he was one of the shipwrecked Chinese. He threw himself into the arms of his rescuers crying, "All dead. All dead."'[7]

They took him back to the *Styx* where in broken French and English he told of the horrifying fate of his compatriots. He was one of the five – including the European ship's carpenter – who had been spared. When the Rossel Islanders sighted the *Styx,* he said, the other four had been taken up into the mountains. He had hidden himself in the rocks near the shore for two terrifying days and nights until the boat approached.

After some refreshment, he led them to a nearby village of about thirty islanders. The villagers first tried to entice the Chinese man to remain with them, then turned threatening when he refused. The French quietly retreated and found the area where Pinard and his men first came ashore after the shipwreck survivors had reached the *Ilot du Refuge*. This was the place where Muwo's cannibals had murdered so many of the passengers who had committed themselves to his care. The Chinese man pointed to the tree trunk where the necks of the Chinese were forced back for the cutting spear that ripped open their throats, before the body was disembowelled and the flesh apportioned among the Melanesians to be consumed at Muwo's evening feasts.

The Frenchmen were overwhelmed by the horror, Pinard most of all. But there was no time for self-recrimination as suddenly they found themselves under attack from a war party. They hastily retreated to the ship. But unwilling to leave while the four hostages remained on the island, they returned next morning to the village where they had been threatened.

When they were attacked by the village men who rushed at them with spears and clubs, the French party responded with a fusillade of rifle fire. They returned to the ship, but the following day made another foray with the same result, except that this time when they returned to the ship they fired a cannon at another hostile village then burned it to the ground. By then it was clear that nothing further could be done to save the hostages so, on 8 January, the French raised anchor and set sail for Sydney. They reached the British settlement on 26 January 1859, exactly seventy-one years from the founding of the Australian penal colony.

* * *

Those three score and eleven years since La Perouse met with the First Fleet in Botany Bay had wrought the most significant change in the Great South Land since the arrival of the Aboriginal people some 70,000 years earlier. The British explorers had crossed the Great Dividing Range to the fertile plains of New South Wales. They had forged a path to the Port Phillip district in the south, and in 1851, as the first big gold strike took place within its boundaries, it became the Colony of Victoria.

The northern districts, with a penal settlement at Moreton Bay, had just been granted separation to become the Colony of Queensland. And where once the colonies had drained the British treasury to feed and clothe the convicts, now they were producing gold by the ton and a woolclip to sustain the textile mills of England's Industrial Revolution. From every corner came the cry of 'pioneering', 'progress' and 'potential'. Australia was on the rise.

The one economic impediment was the Aboriginal people.

At first, their numbers had come as a surprise to the British arrivals. From William Dampier to the highly influential Joseph Banks, who had accompanied James Cook on his 1770 voyage, all reports had suggested that they were few in number and lived almost exclusively in the coastal areas on a diet of fish. Indeed, the size of the native population in 1788 remains contentious today with the colonial apologists estimating it at a maximum 300,000 and recent researchers preferring figures of 750,000 to one million.[8] But either way, the indigenous people occupied the entire continent and held the most profound attachment to the land and its flora and fauna.

When the gaudily dressed intruders arrived with their teams of slaves to be cruelly whipped when they disobeyed – and their four-legged creatures that might have stepped from the Dreamtime stories – they were at first nonplussed. And when the soldiers turned their magic firesticks upon them to deal death at impossible distances, the people were terrified. The Aboriginal elders tried to fit the experience into the cosmology that had served them so well for millennia. Historian Henry Reynolds caught their reality incisively in his 1981 classic, *The Other Side of the Frontier*.

'While conflict was ubiquitous in traditional societies, territorial conquest was virtually unknown. Alienation of land was not only unthinkable, it was literally impossible. If blacks often did not react to the initial invasion of their country it was because they were not aware that it had taken place. They certainly did not believe that their land had suddenly ceased to belong to them and they to their land. The mere presence of Europeans, no

matter how threatening, could not uproot certainties so deeply
implanted in Aboriginal custom and consciousness.'[9]

But individuals, language groups and nations of the Aboriginal
people reacted differently. Some were fascinated by the technical
wonders the invaders had mastered. Some would come to see
association with the newcomers as a viable alternative to the
unequal treatment they were receiving in their tribal station.
Some would seek to engage them as allies in long-standing inter-
tribal resentments. Others would fight the intruders at every
opportunity. In short, they reacted as any other large and diverse
group of humans would when confronted by the overwhelming
force of an alien invader.

The British were well schooled in exploiting those inherent
differences. For centuries they had used such tactics in nearby
Ireland which they had colonised during the reign of the Tudors.
They had refined the tactic of 'divide and conquer' in the vastly
more populous Indian Subcontinent. And while they might have
faltered in their American colony – partly through the intervention
of the French – they were presently engaged in a similar strategy
in the African continent and in the great Yangtse Valley of China.

By contrast, Australia's Aboriginal people were easy meat.

Tasmania was a special case. From the beginning of settlement,
the conflict between European and Aboriginal was unremitting
and in the 1820s Governor George Arthur, a soldier in the British
Army, ruled his fief with a gospel in one hand and a gun in the
other. And since the Aboriginal people declined the one, he gave
free rein to the other. In 1828, he declared martial law and for
three years his soldiers had *carte blanche* to shoot the indigenous
people on sight.

He organised a 'Black Line' comprising every able-bodied
colonist to sweep across the island, mustering the Aboriginal
people into the Tasman Peninsula and killing the runaways.
After seven weeks the attempt was abandoned but by 1832 it

is believed only 300 Aboriginal people remained alive. They were gathered and transported to Flinders Island in Bass Strait where they fell victim to disease, and by 1874 the genocide was practically complete. However, what has not been accounted for in these figures were the Aboriginal families living on the many islands in Bass Strait, Kangaroo Island and even on the mainland as a result of the establishment of cross-cultural communities with sealers and other settlers.

On the mainland, a steady stream of squatters with their herds of sheep and cattle followed in the wake of the explorers. And while to the traditional owners they committed a diplomatic affront to strict Aboriginal protocol in not seeking permission for their incursion, that could be forgiven since they were clearly ignorant and morally uninformed. In any case, like all journeymen before them, they would soon move on. Even when they showed no sign of moving, their presence could be excused provided they adopted the sharing culture of their hosts.

But inevitably, there came a time when the invaders went beyond the pale – when their animals destroyed the waterholes and chased away the kangaroos; when they refused to share the meat of their stock and instead kept them in their hundreds and thousands instead of eating them like any sensible person; when they desecrated the sacred sites and ruined the cave paintings with their own graffiti; when they accepted the sexual favours of the tribal women then refused to respond with food and trades of axes and other useful implements; and when they raped the women and dishonoured their husbands and the tribe, there was no alternative left but to take up arms.

Time and again, the rape of Aboriginal girls and women by European men who had ventured into the inland without women of their own was the trigger for conflict. And by the 1830s as the squatters spread from the Sydney beachhead south, west and north into well-populated Aboriginal land, the clashes became ever more furious.

Land-seekers following the trail of explorer Hamilton Hume into Victoria were initially forced to retreat from their selections. When they returned it was with loaded rifles and a determination to assert their 'rights' to occupy the country. And in 1836 they were formally supported in their demands when the British government officially declared Australia '*terra nullius*', asserting that the land belonged to *no one* prior to the British Crown taking possession of it. In a single stroke, they had nullified – to their satisfaction, but unknown to the Aboriginal people – at least 60,000 years of intimate attachment to the only country the indigenous people knew.

Unfortunately, the men who led the charge into the 'new' country were mostly fortune hunters who saw the Aboriginal people as 'animals' who barely deserved recognition as fellow human beings. They had come from a country that for the last three centuries had led the world in the slave trade. And to them, the Aboriginals were even lower on the human scale than the Africans.

They rarely had the slightest interest in their culture or their history. And in the way of warfare everywhere, they dehumanised the enemy to the point where the Aboriginals became 'vermin'. These emissaries of the 'New Albion' (as Captain Phillip had initially named his Sydney settlement) cut a swathe through the indigenous territories, spreading death and disease along the way.

In Victoria there were a series of massacres, and one in the Western Districts was dubbed 'Waterloo Plains' in memory of Lord Wellington's famous victory over the armies of Napoleon.[10] Indeed, Waterloo was a favoured label for a series of massacres. It was commemorated in another atrocity on the northwest plains at about the same time. On this occasion, a detachment of troopers was sent to the Gwydir Valley after Aboriginal people delivered payback for the rape of their women by spearing five stockmen in separate incidents. The soldiers surrounded a big tribal group of about fifty men, women and children and opened fire at 'Waterloo Creek'. An inquiry was later held into the incident but no action was taken.

The only occasion when white men suffered official consequences for the murder of Aboriginal people in New South Wales was in 1838 in response to a flagrant killing spree by convicts at Myall Creek station. Led by one John Fleming, the ten English and one South African overwhelmed twenty-eight women, children and old men at their station camp when the manager and the young men of the tribe were away from the home paddock.

They tied them together with a long rope and led them 800 metres away to a gully where they used swords to behead them. One woman was set aside and repeatedly gang-raped before she too was killed. When the young men returned, another convict on the property who had refused to join the bloodbath told them to clear out in case the killers returned. He was too late; the gang intercepted most of them and slaughtered them as well.

In the trial initiated by Attorney-General John Plunkett, the killers were acquitted to the general jubilation of the crowd. But Plunkett persisted and seven faced a second trial for the killing of an Aboriginal boy. This time they were found guilty and hanged on 18 December 1838. However, Plunkett was a rarity and the governor of the day, George Gipps, wrote that he was 'powerless in the face of the venturesome settlers whose philosophy is that the only good Aborigine is a dead one'.[11]

But if New South Wales was a battleground between the Aboriginal people and the settlers, the newly separated colony to the north, at the extremity of which the French cabin boy Narcisse Pelletier was even now finding shelter and sanctuary among the Aboriginal people, was very much worse.

Queensland, named for the British sovereign herself, supported no fewer than 35 per cent of the Aboriginal population of the continent. Nowhere is the argument of population numbers more fiercely contested, but by any realistic estimate, they numbered more than 200,000 when Cook's *Endeavour* berthed at the river mouth for repairs. And 100 years later, as Narcisse made good his recovery, their numbers had, if anything, slightly increased.

PART
Three

3

Narcisse/Amglo

Narcisse's memories of those first days with his rescuers were a jumble of images, but he would recall forever with raw clarity the desperate surge of terror when he woke to find himself alone, *abandonné* once again by the people whom he believed would save his life. He sat up and stared out across the great ocean into the rising sun, empty but for that single small island directly ahead about five kilometres off shore. The rest was bare of any human trespass – not a sail, not a wake, not a gunwale, nothing to disturb the sleeping spirit far beneath.

That was the moment he knew with his whole heart that Pinard and his shipmates would never return. He was swept by a sudden rage that knew no bounds, an all-embracing hatred for the man under whose protection he had made the journey across the world only to be discarded, jettisoned, to die a lonely death on this foreign shore. It was wrong, it was *la trahison ultime*, the ultimate betrayal.

'*Les enfoirés!*' Bastards!

The anger gave him strength and he struggled to his feet which were cut and blistered and he rested against a thin tree trunk. In the shade of a low bush he noticed a great shell brimming with water. He managed a few steps before he fell to his knees, took it in one hand and drank deeply. Perhaps the black men had left it for him, a parting gift to sustain him until . . . what? Until his shipmates returned for him? Until he starved to death?

He had been visited by hordes of insects while he slept and their bites were stinging and itching on every part of his bare skin, from the end of his tattered canvas trousers to his exposed arms and face. He walked down to the water's edge. The reef protected the long beach from the ocean swells and the sea barely rippled into the sand. He gave himself up to it and fell face first into the shallows. The water was warm and he turned on his back and bathed his feet and then the raised bites on his face and legs. He reached behind his head to the injury and his hand came away sticky with gum and when he smelt it there was a freshness to it that penetrated his nostrils. With it came the realisation that the wound no longer pained him.

His hands flopped into the water and in the deep silence from all sides the anger was replaced by a sense of utter desolation. He closed his eyes and unbidden came pictures of Saint-Gilles and its cobbled Rue du Calvaire leading to the family home. Alphonsine was in the kitchen, her arms covered in flour as she kneaded the dough for the morning *baguette*. He could almost smell the baking loaf and tears coursed down his cheeks. He brushed them away with the back of his hand and the salt water that clung to his forearm stung his eyes.

He rose and turned back towards the scrub above the beach and began to walk with the rising sun beating on his shoulders. A movement further down the beach arrested him. It was a dog, its coat the colour of crusty bread, and involuntarily he moved towards it, crying out, *'Chien! Viens!'* The animal turned instantly and retreated into the scrubby foliage. But the sight of a fellow creature somehow lifted his spirits and then suddenly his rescuers appeared from the bush directly in front of him and he was running towards them.

'Mes amis!'

There were four of them – the three women who had first found him and the shorter of the two men who had half-carried him to the resting place. When he reached them he embraced the man but the women hung back, chattering to themselves at his words and gestures. They had brought food – tubers cooked in the coals of a campfire; fruits of several shapes and sizes; and a fish baked and wrapped in a palm leaf. He followed them to the hollow behind the beach as all was quickly spread before him.

He sat and reached both hands to the feast. They watched in silent wonder as he wolfed down the offerings. Between mouthfuls he mumbled *'C'est magnifique'*, *'Formidable'*, *'Merci, merci beaucoup'* and paused only to wash it all down with cool, clean water. The man, who identified himself as 'Baroway', took a place beside him, urging him to taste each of the fruits while the women, who sat two or three metres away, whispered a running commentary to each other.

When his hunger was slaked Narcisse pointed vaguely to the bush and asked, *'Où et Maademan?'* Baroway understood and pointed to the north. There followed a cascade of words that made no sense at all. But with his companion obviously eager to converse, Narcisse touched the man's chest saying *'Vous êtes Baroway'*, then he indicated the women and asked, *'Qui sont-ils?'* Who are they?

This too released a torrent of incomprehensible sounds; and after repeating the process several times without discerning any names, Narcisse decided to name them for himself. He looked closely – they were clearly very different from each other in age and shape – and in doing so he suddenly became conscious of their nakedness. But while he could feel himself blushing beneath his insect bites, they seemed perfectly unconcerned. He tried but failed to look only at their faces which were clean and shining, their hair damp, perhaps from a morning swim.

All were well made, though one was older than the other two by a goodly margin. She had wider shoulders and heavier breasts and reminded him a little of the wife of his old teacher, Madame Palvadeau, so he silently christened her 'Marie'. The next in age was shorter and with sharper features than the others. She became 'Veronique'; while the youngest was not much older than himself and she reminded him of the shy daughter of the village fishmonger, Monsieur Mantell, so he mentally named her 'Rosine'.

He took some satisfaction in his initiative and tried to convey their new names to them. *'Vous êtes Marie,'* he began but before he could go further their angry response silenced him. He had committed some serious *erreur culturelle*. He felt himself shrinking inside and in the next moment his stomach rebelled at the great volume of food he had demanded it digest after the starvation of his travail. He fought to contain it, but it was no use; he was barely able to crawl beyond the hollow before he heaved and expelled the entire meal.

When he returned to face them, they were quietly explaining to each other the cause of his *détresse* and his social error was forgiven. There was plenty of the food left and this time he was more prudent in his selection. And once he had eaten his fill, the dog he had noticed earlier reappeared and the younger woman, Rosine, gave it what was left of the fish. It ate, he noticed, with one eye firmly fixed on himself and if he moved a muscle towards it, the animal bristled.

As he looked to his saviours, a new perception pressed itself upon him. It felt as though he had entered upon the hearth of their home. To him, the surroundings were of nature, available for the use and pleasure of all who happened upon them; but to these people it was as familiar and as personal as the Pelletier home in the Rue du Calvaire. It was no more than a passing thought, but it would return to him many times in the weeks ahead until it lost its definition, and their home and the world became one.

This time the meal stayed down and the people by word and gesture encouraged him to rest in the shade. Baroway made a small fire by speedily twirling an upright stick with its point held against another flat upon the ground. Notches on both sides revealed how often the process had been repeated. Once it caught alight they used green leaves to make smoke that kept the mosquitoes at bay. The sandy soil became a hammock and the sea breeze set it in gentle motion.

When he woke, the sun was setting. He was well refreshed and when he stood and looked along the beach he saw that Maademan had returned and was leading the small knot of people his way. They were carrying the product of a successful afternoon's fishing, and at his side was a newcomer, a boy who appeared about his own age. Narcisse hurried to meet them. Maademan seemed pleased to see him and as they met the older man placed his hands on both of Narcisse's shoulders in a gesture of greeting. Then he turned to the boy and one word among many introduced the youth: 'Sassy'.

The boy shyly averted his eyes from Narcisse. He was slightly taller than himself, slim and well-muscled. When he raised his head and looked in Narcisse's direction, there was a shy smile playing around his lips. They then broke into a wide grin revealing shining white teeth against the darkness of his skin.

Narcisse made to respond with his own name, but Maademan interrupted. His stern features and imperious manner left no room for argument, and even though Narcisse could not under-stand his words, their meaning was clear. Henceforth, the leader said, his old identity was to be left behind, consigned to a past that was gone forever. Now he was to be born anew. Maademan had decided upon a name for him. And when he pronounced it, the syllables rang strangely on his ears – somewhere between

Anglo (*anglo-*) and anchor (*ancre*) but with a rolling 'm'. He repeated the sounds to himself a dozen times, 'Amclo, Anclo, Amglo, Ancro,' before settling upon Amglo.

Only much later did he come to realise the complexity of what had gone before. The whiteness of his skin had proclaimed him the ghost of one of their people – in their language, a *Pama* – who had passed away; and Maademan had reported his arrival to the gathered clansmen he had visited while Narcisse slept. He spoke well and with authority so was given permission to adopt the boy, who would take the place of one who had passed from life to that spirit world beyond the horizon, and who was now returning, stripped of all his memories of that earlier life. However, to Narcisse at the time it meant only that he was no longer the solitary outcast, *le réprouvé*, but a member of some new fraternity, *exotique* but welcoming, *accueillant!* And a wondrous mix of relief and gratitude warmed his heart.

That evening after the fish were cooked and eaten, many words and gestures were exchanged between himself and the men. Maademan and Baroway, he learned, were brothers. And Sassy was Baroway's son, not Maademan's as he had first thought. The boy's mother had died some time ago and, as his uncle, Maademan was in charge of his training, his *formation*. It was all very complicated with no common language but it eventually became clear that Maademan was married to two of the women – Marie and the younger Rosine – while Baroway's wife, Veronique, had been stolen from a nearby tribe, the Umpila.

Their own tribe was called the Uutaalnganu, but they had other names as well. And even as Narcisse became Amglo, he would choose one of the names that sat more easily with his native tongue: *Les gens de l'île de la nuit*, the Night Island people, named for that atoll that broke the horizon in two as he had looked to the rising sun.

As the fire faded to embers, the small group found their places to sleep. Sassy stayed nearest to Narcisse and before they slept he said words whose literal meaning was beyond the cabin boy but whose tone was unmistakably that of a friend. The castaway fought back a tear. In a day that had begun in the terror of abandonment, it seemed almost unbelievable, *miraculeux*, that such a change of fortune should have descended upon him.

The spirit of Saint Narcisse, it seemed, lived on in this tropical Jerusalem.

4

Queensland

Two thousand kilometres to the south, a very different world had developed in the colony that in 1859 had just separated from New South Wales to become Queensland. On his voyage up the east coast in 1770, James Cook had named a bay of islands after Lord Morton, the then president of the Royal Society. But due to a spelling error in the publication of his account it became Moreton Bay thereafter. And that was the very least of the mistakes, blunders and downright barbarities to be made in the area that bore his name.

In 1823, the former Royal Navy officer John Oxley, who had bought his position as surveyor-general from his predecessor Charles Grimes, had chosen Moreton Bay as the site for a new penal settlement for some of the more intransigent convicts. However, when they arrived at the red cliffs of Humpybong the following year, even the soldiers sent to guard them began to die of malaria borne by the local mosquitoes. The commandant, Henry Miller, moved the operation from 'Redcliffe' to a hilly area upriver relatively free of the deadly insects and more easily defended from the Aboriginal owners.

The settlement would subsequently take the name of a New South Wales governor, Thomas Brisbane, whose only claim to fame was that he devoted himself to mapping the stars of the southern sky – registering some 7385 during his two-year tenure – from his observatory at Parramatta. This left him only one day a week – Tuesdays – to tend to his administrative duties. Indeed, Brisbane was a devotee of all matters heavenly and, like Tasmania's George Arthur, demanded that the Aboriginal people exchange their ancient beliefs for the Christianity that he so fervently embraced. His efforts were equally unrewarded and, like Arthur, he responded by setting his soldiers on what he viewed as recalcitrant natives.

Captain Miller made little effort to spread the biblical word. In any case, the local tribes were preoccupied with their struggle to defend an Arcadian territory from the intruders. Their blessings were temporal: a warm, healthy climate and an abundance of game – kangaroos, possums, bandicoots, carpet snakes, goannas, scrub turkeys, freshwater turtles, cod, eels, mussels and crayfish – to say nothing of the eggs, seeds, nuts, honey, waterlily and wild yams they dug from the earth. They even made a cordial from the honeysuckle flower. And the islands of Moreton Bay were so rich in oysters that the convicts were engaged to shovel them into boats which were sailed to the settlement where they were burned for lime in loads of eighteen to twenty tons at a time.[1]

Half a dozen separate tribes occupied the area including the Meanjin, the Ngugi, the Nunukul and the Goenpul. Their spiritual figures included Ben'ewa to whom hunters paid their respects as they set out on their daily forays. And while the women collected the daily provender of bush tucker, the children played *buro-injin*, a favourite game in which one team tried to get a kangaroo-skin ball stuffed with grass to a pole without it being touched by the opposing team.

According to historian Libby Connors, 'Boys competed in throwing and bouncing small war clubs, known as "waddies", as well as boomerangs and semi-discs fashioned from the fig-leaf

box tree. In their pretend fights, they used shorter spears with
blunted ends to avoid injuries. At the end of the day the head
man, or "komaron", called the children home using his small
bullroarer, the "gungarbi".[2]

In 1826, a new commandant, Captain Patrick Logan of the
57th Foot Regiment, arrived with a soldier's *modus operandi* of
uncompromising 'discipline' towards convict and Aboriginal
alike. Born in 1791, he had fought in the Peninsular Wars against
Napoleon and occupied Paris with Wellington's forces in 1816. He
left the army during the peace that followed and returned to his
appropriated Irish farmlands. But rural life held little attraction
for him and he re-enlisted in his regiment in 1819. Six years
later the unit boarded ship in Cork for their posting to New
South Wales.

In Sydney, Logan was put in charge of detachments guarding
convicts and his liberal use of the lash so commended him to
his superiors that Governor Brisbane appointed him to deploy it
at will to the 'villains and degenerates' of Moreton Bay. He was
just the man for the job. As the convict population rose from
77 to more than 1000 – including 138 women – he instituted
a reign of terror that involved punishments of up to 300 lashes
on the bloodied triangle.

Logan began a building program that included the notorious
windmill on a hill overlooking the settlement. When its sails
broke, he turned it into a treadmill and the convicts powered it
until they dropped. His rule was that 'convicts shall be steadily
and constantly employed at hard labour from sunrise till sunset,
one hour being allotted for breakfast and one for dinner during
the winter six months; but two hours be allotted for dinner
during the summer'. Any slacking brought forth the plaited leather
lash 'laid on hard'. So hated were the overseers drawn from the
convicts' numbers that they were quartered in separate huts as
they risked being murdered in their sleep.

The commandant's attitude to the Aboriginal people was no less intemperate. He made no attempt to reach an accommodation with them and when he expanded the settlement's farming activities into sacred places, the inhabitants responded with raids on the outlying huts and depots. Aboriginal warriors also attacked the intruders on the main islands of the bay, especially Stradbroke, Moreton and Bribie.

Logan's reprisals took a leaf from Thomas Brisbane's high-toned Christian manual and when the soldiers were not supervising the convict labour gangs, they were engaged in payback ambushes and skirmishes in the tribal lands. However, the commandant had time to lead exploratory expeditions from his riparian base and in doing so he reached what would later be known as the Gold Coast, Lamington National Park and the upper reaches of the Brisbane River.

On 17 October 1830, he was on just such an expedition and rode ahead of his team which had passed several Aboriginal hunting parties. Suddenly his 'cooee' alerted his followers that something might be wrong. When they hurried forward they found his saddle, then his dead horse and finally his body. The coroner later confirmed that he had fallen to the weapons of his Aboriginal enemies. When news of his death reached the convict quarters, according to a contemporary report, the inmates, 'manifested insane joy . . . and sang and hoorayed all night in defiance of the warders'.[3]

The Aboriginal response is not recorded.

Thereafter the settlement's convict population gradually fell as did the area sown for cultivation until the whole penal enterprise was abandoned in 1839. The Aboriginal people took this as evidence that their campaign against the *mogwi* – as they termed the white intruders – had been successful.[4]

They could not have been more mistaken. Three years later the colonial authorities in Sydney declared the entire 'northern districts' open for free settlement and a virtual landrush followed. Indeed, some settlers had 'jumped the gun' and were already making their way through the traditional lands of the Yuggera people between Brisbane and the Darling Downs. They were competing for the prize runs in one of the most fertile areas of the entire colony.

The Yuggeras fought a hit-and-run campaign to cut the settlers' supply lines, and the squatters fought back with gunfire. Despite some early Aboriginal successes in the so-called Battle of One Tree Hill, where the Yuggeras rolled boulders down on the intruders, the settlers pushed through with their flocks of sheep and mobs of cattle. However, the Darling Downs was prized territory for the Aboriginal clans and they continued the fight. Indeed, for the first time in the sorry history of the Frontier Wars, several groups combined to resist the intruders.

In 1841 about 500 spear-carrying fighters from across the Lockyer and Brisbane River valleys assembled under the orders of the Yuggera head man, Multuggerah. They attacked the newly established stations and drove off thousands of their stock. But while they celebrated their 'victory' it was decidedly short-lived. The whites organised their own mounted troupe armed with shotguns, pistols and swords. Time and again, they descended at dawn on Aboriginal camps and an unknown number were killed. The white men pursued the people as they scattered through the bush.

According to a Sri Lankan ex-convict, George 'Black' Brown, who was at the scene of one massacre: 'The young natives were making their escape to the scrub. The horsemen were riding after them; the natives were jabbing their spears at them . . . the firing was continued about half an hour. I cannot say the numbers that were killed.'[5]

Meantime, to the north of Brisbane, the Dalla people chose to cooperate with the Archer family who had established Durundur station in the Kilcoy area and offered the hand of friendship to the traditional owners. Tom and David Archer were from a Scottish family who had moved to Norway when the family timber business collapsed at the end of the Napoleonic wars. The siblings were motivated in part by the need to repay their father's debts when they arrived in New South Wales in the late 1830s.

By 1841 they had brought their stock overland to Dalla country where they immediately began long talks with 'Paddy', the *komaron* of the Dungidau, one of the tribal offshoots of the Dalla. The Archers agreed that the Dungidau people would have *carte blanche* to traverse the property while they and their employees would honour their sacred sites. And if the Dungidau worked for them in clearing the ground, lopping the heavy timber and stripping the bark for roofing the homestead and outbuildings, they would be paid in beef, sweet potatoes and Indian corn.

The agreement was the more remarkable since three of the ceremonial sacred bora rings belonging to the Dalla were within the Archers' holding. Indeed, David Archer remained troubled by their encroachment on the lives of the traditional owners. He wrote to his clergyman cousin, Edward Walker, about the propriety 'as to whether European foreigners and aliens are or are not entitled to intrude upon the Aboriginal population of this soil'. Edward reassured him that 'the intent of the Almighty [is that] we should cultivate the ground'.[6]

However, the Dalla elders had their own strategic reasons for concluding the deal. They had decided in tribal council that an association with the *mogwi* would serve them well in their perennial conflict with their enemies, the tribes of Bribie Island and the area we now call the Sunshine Coast. It proved to be a shrewd tactical decision. The Archers not only policed the interaction between their workers and the Aboriginal women, they intervened when outsiders intruded on Dalla territory.

By the time another brother, Charles, arrived in 1843 he was surprised to find that 'this tribe, so far from doing any injury, are the greatest assistance in procuring bark, breaking up ground with the hoe, carrying rations to the sheep [outstations] etc . . . While our neighbours, the Messrs Mackenzie are frequently annoyed by attacks both on their flocks and shepherds, I do not think a single sheep has been stolen from here by the Blacks since I came to the station and I believe for a long time previous.'[7]

However, the Archers' accommodating approach was not widely emulated. The overwhelming attitude of the settlers was rooted in the 'possession' asserted by James Cook on behalf of the British Crown, and confirmed by the Westminster declaration of *terra nullius*. To them, it was the Aboriginal people who were the trespassers on *their* land. Unsurprisingly, the local tribes were bewildered and offended by the concept, and at times warriors from the Yuggera and the Dalla combined to attack the outstations before retreating to the thick scrublands impenetrable to the mounted horsemen in pursuit.

By then a number of German missionaries had insinuated themselves into the community, with headquarters in the suburban Brisbane area that bears the original name of Nundah. At least three of them had taken to camping with branches of the Ningy Ningy tribe in a widely spaced area north of the main European settlement. They spent their days seeking to evangelise the children in camp while their parents were occupied hunting and gathering. But when the festering trouble between Aboriginal and intruder burst into the open in early 1842, they wisely retreated to their Nundah compound.

On Evan Mackenzie's Kilcoy station, the outstation shepherds became fearful of a large gathering in the surrounding bush. Their response, according to the missionaries and recorded in the Mackenzie papers, was a mass killing on or about 5 February 1842. The shepherds, most likely under instruction from the station owner, mixed arsenic in the flour and sugar they gave to the Aboriginal people. And since the women made bread cakes each evening 'the first victims . . . might well have been their children'.[8]

The Aboriginal people invariably connected death with the sorcery of their tribal enemies rather than any physical source. So as they continued to consume the toxic ingredients, the death toll rose to between fifty and sixty before the real cause became clear.

In the days that followed, three Aboriginal leaders tracked the shepherds 'to their usual watering place' and speared them to death. Those who carried out the sentence imposed at a tribal gathering were themselves the subject of an extensive manhunt and one of them – known by the whites as 'Commandant' was spotted at a hut by 24-year-old David McConnel, the owner of nearby Cressbrook station. McConnel later boasted in a letter to his brother Henry: 'They became desperate & being very strong men, they all broke loose; so we fired on them; killed one, Commandant, a fellow 6ft 3 high & strong in proportion on the spot, stabbed one twice with a bayonet, put four balls into him besides, & two balls into the third; the two latter got off but I am sure could not go far.'[9]

McConnel not only failed to permit Commandant's people from taking the body for funeral and mourning rites, he beheaded the man and retained the skull which was displayed to the explorer Ludwig Leichhardt on his visit to Cressbrook in 1843. Indeed, Leichhardt was able to confirm the circumstances with his missionary compatriot, Reverend Schmidt, and wrote, 'There is open warfare between the two [races].' It goes without saying that no action was taken by the authorities.

★ ★ ★

Leichhardt, at only thirty years old, was one of the earliest of Queensland's European explorers. Born in the Prussian province of Brandenburg, he had studied the natural sciences at several universities and institutes in Germany and England without ever taking a degree. He had arrived in Sydney the previous year in the hope of securing a government position and making his mark in his chosen field. Australia was a likely source of great discoveries in geology, flora and fauna.

When the government appointment was not forthcoming, Leichhardt set forth on a solo journey from Newcastle to Moreton Bay, collecting specimens along the way. After making contact with the German missionaries and witnessing the great landrush towards the Darling Downs, he decided his destiny was to mount an expedition that would explore the vast potential of the northern districts. And on his return to Sydney he was delighted to learn that just such a venture was being proposed by the colonial government under Governor Gipps.

Alas, like so many such proposals, a shortage of funds and petty squabbling within the administration meant that the plan came to nought. Undeterred, Leichhardt set about raising funds from merchants and grazing families with an eye for ever greater land holdings; and in August 1844 he led his party aboard a coastal trader headed for Moreton Bay.

Leichhardt chose his team mainly from shipboard acquaintances: a fifteen-year-old Irish lad, John Murphy; as well as Englishmen James Calvert, nineteen, and John Roper, twenty-four. They were joined by William Phillips, forty-four, a recently met Sydney ex-convict; and an Aboriginal, Harry Brown. In Moreton Bay they would add another Aboriginal, Charley Fisher, and an American negro named Caleb as the cook.

When they reached Jimbour station on the Darling Downs, they added John Gilbert, an educated English naturalist, and a young English squatter, Pemberton Hodgson. The expedition equipped themselves with seventeen horses, sixteen bullocks and twelve dogs, some of which would be used to bring down kangaroos for meat. And on 18 September, having broken-in the bullocks to work as a team, they set off for Port Essington in the Northern Territory. Leichhardt rode in a sprung cart pulled by two horses.

The Prussian's enthusiasm knew no bounds. 'Many a man's heart would have thrilled like our own,' he wrote, 'had he seen us winding our way round the first rise beyond the station with a full chorus of "God Save the Queen," which has inspired many a British soldier – aye, and many a Prussian too – with courage in the time of danger.'

Gilbert the naturalist was equally excited at the 'glorious opportunity of unmasking the hidden novelties of tropical Australia'.

However, the explorers were quite unprepared for the task they had set themselves. Leichhardt's cart collapsed within three days, several horses bolted back to their home stables and the bullocks threw their packs. But they were sustained by a countryside that overflowed with natural resources, from the creeks and rivers carrying an abundance of fresh water to the game of flight and forest. Indeed, they would exhaust their flour and sugar long before they reached their destination, but they were never in danger of the thirst and starvation that threatened other continental explorers.

They were particularly fortunate in having the two Aboriginals, Charley Fisher and Harry Brown, in their number. For despite Leichhardt's 'sable companions' becoming homesick and impatient with his pettifogging 'discipline' from time to time, they were constantly responsible for securing emus, turkeys, kangaroos and a wide range of smaller additions to the meat larder. Moreover, there were soon two fewer mouths to feed with the departure of both Pemberton Hodgson and Caleb the cook after less than a fortnight on the track.

Initially, the tribal people gave them a wide berth, but as they travelled north, keeping parallel to the coast, they became ever more aware of the Aboriginals. Almost invariably their contacts were fleeting but seldom hostile, despite the Aboriginals' shock at their sudden appearance. Whenever his party entered a camp from which the tribal people had fled on sight of the aliens, Leichhardt always left payment in the form of useful metal objects for any foodstuffs or artefacts taken. Their occasional meetings were peaceful. And it is significant that the southern Aboriginals with Leichhardt were no more able to converse with the northern Aboriginals than were the white men.

On one occasion, Leichhardt reports that, 'Charley, who had been sent for my horse, returned at full gallop, and told me that Blackfellows were spearing our horses. Fortunately, Messrs. Gilbert and Calvert had just come in; and, mounting our horses, three of us hastened to the place where Charley had seen the Blacks, leaving the remainder of our party to defend the camp. We found one of our horses had been deeply wounded in the shoulder; but fortunately, the others were unhurt, and were grazing quietly.

'Charley saw two Blackfellows retreating into the scrub, but had seen a great number of them when he first came to the place. This event, fortunately not a very disastrous one, was so far useful, as it impressed everyone with the necessity of being watchful, even when the Blackfellows were not suspected to be near.'[10]

Shortly afterwards, Leichhardt had a thought-provoking encounter which he recorded in his journal: 'Whilst riding along the bank of the river, we saw an old woman before us, walking slowly and thoughtfully through the forest, supporting her slender and apparently exhausted frame with one of those long sticks which the women use for digging roots; a child was running before her. Fearing she would be much alarmed if we came too suddenly upon her, as neither our voices in conversation, nor the footfall of our horses, attracted her attention, I cooeed gently;

after repeating the call two or three times, she turned her head; in sudden fright she lifted her arms, and began to beat the air, as if to take wing.

'Then seizing the child, and shrieking most pitifully, she rapidly crossed the creek, and escaped to the opposite ridges. What could she think but that we were some of those imaginary beings, with legends of which the wise men of her people frighten the children into obedience, and whose strange forms and stranger doings are the favourite topics of conversation amongst the natives at night when seated round their fires?'

However, on 28 June 1845 as Leichhardt's party travelled over the base of Cape York towards the Gulf of Carpentaria, disaster struck. The previous day, John Gilbert had ridden close to a large gathering of Aboriginals and fired his shotgun at a bird he was keen to collect as a specimen. And on the evening itself, Leichhardt writes that, 'We heard some subdued coo-ees not very far from our camp which I thought might originate from natives returning late from their excursions whom our fires had attracted. I discharged a gun to make them aware of our presence and we did not hear anything more of them.'

In retrospect, it's been theorised that the Aboriginals were announcing their desire for talks with cooee overtures, and took the gunshots as a sign of hostility. The truth will never be known.

According to Leichhardt: 'This was about 7 o'clock; and I stretched myself upon the ground as usual, at a little distance from the fire, and fell into a doze, from which I was suddenly roused by a loud noise, and a call for help from Calvert and Roper. Natives had suddenly attacked us.

'They had doubtless watched our movements during the afternoon, and marked the position of the different tents; and, as soon as it was dark, sneaked upon us, and threw a shower of spears at the tents of Calvert, Roper, and Gilbert, and a few at that of Phillips, and also one or two towards the fire. Charley and

Brown called for caps, which I hastened to find, and, as soon as they were provided, they discharged their guns into the crowd of the natives, who instantly fled, leaving Roper and Calvert pierced with several spears, and severely beaten by their waddies.

'Several of these spears were barbed, and could not be extracted without difficulty. I had to force one through the arm of Roper, to break off the barb; and to cut another out of the groin of Mr. Calvert. John Murphy had succeeded in getting out of the tent, and concealing himself behind a tree, whence he fired at the natives, and severely wounded one of them, before Brown had discharged his gun.

'Not seeing Mr. Gilbert, I asked for him, when Charley told me that our unfortunate companion was no more! He had come out of his tent with his gun, shot, and powder, and handed them to him, when he instantly dropped down dead. Upon receiving this afflicting intelligence, I hastened to the spot, and found Charley's account too true. He was lying on the ground at a little distance from our fire, and, upon examining him, I soon found, to my sorrow, that every sign of life had disappeared. The body was, however, still warm, and I opened the veins of both arms, as well as the temporal artery, but in vain; the stream of life had stopped, and he was numbered with the dead.'[11]

Whatever the immediate cause, the Aboriginals withdrew and after burying Gilbert and dressing the wounds of Roper – who would eventually lose his eye – the expedition slowly recovered its momentum and thereafter all meetings with the Aboriginals were either peaceful or distinctly friendly. And as they crossed Arnhem Land in the direction of Port Essington, they were accompanied by an entire tribe who offered them every assistance.

'They remained with us the whole afternoon,' Leichhardt recalled, 'all the tribe and many visitors, in all about seventy persons, squatting down with crossed legs in the narrow shades of the trunks of trees, and shifting their position as the sun advanced. Their wives were out in search of food; but many of their children were with them, which they duly introduced to us. They were fine, stout, well-made men, with pleasing and intelligent countenances. One or two attempts were made to rob us of some trifles; but I was careful; and we avoided the unpleasant necessity of shewing any discontent on that head.

'As it grew late, and they became hungry, they rose, and explained that they were under the necessity of leaving us, to go and satisfy their hunger; but that they would shortly return, and admire, and talk again. They went to the digging ground, about half a mile in the plain, where the boys were collecting *allamurr*,[†] and brought us a good supply of it; in return for which various presents were made to them.'

But having shown the expedition the way to their destination, Port Essington, the Aboriginal guide, Baki Baki, declined to go further. Clearly, he and his people had dealt with the northern colonists before.

Other European expeditions would follow, notably that led by Edmund Kennedy in 1848 which focused even more directly upon the unexplored peninsula in the north.

Indeed, the Kennedy expedition with its tragic ending is known to every Australian schoolchild since it supports and illustrates the comforting stereotypes of the dominant narrative.

The son of a colonel in the British Army and graduate of King's College, London, Kennedy at only twenty-two had become assistant-surveyor to Sir Thomas Mitchell. Seven years later he was charged with leading his own expedition when, in 1848, he was ordered to find a route to the Gulf of Carpentaria and then to explore Cape York itself. It was a daunting task. The

† A yam-like tuber

peninsula is more than twice the area of England, split by a central mountain range and with tropical rainforests and wide savannahs on both sides cut by hundreds of rivers and creeks. Moreover, it was as densely populated by its Aboriginal owners as any area on the continent.

On 28 April, Kennedy set out from Sydney by ship with twelve men, including the fifteen-year-old Aboriginal tracker, Gulmarra (known by the whites as 'Jackey Jackey'), and reached Rockingham Bay 150 kilometres north of Cairns the following month. But the terrain, a mixture of mangrove swamps, rainforest and thick scrub made progress almost impossible. After nine weeks they had travelled just seventy kilometres from the coast and less than twenty kilometres north towards the cape. Kennedy had to abandon the carts and much of their supplies in a hopeless bog.

By mid-November the men and horses were seriously weakened and he left eight of the most affected behind at Weymouth Bay while he pressed on towards the proposed rendezvous with the supply ship *Ariel*. Two more were left behind when one of them accidentally shot himself, and Kennedy and Gulmarra struggled on.

They had made occasional contact with the Aboriginal people of the area but as they progressed further into their territory the tribal warriors attacked. Kennedy was speared several times and died, according to the story retold in Queensland classrooms, 'in the faithful Jackey Jackey's arms'. The Aboriginal boy eluded his compatriots and finally reached the *Ariel* on 23 December 1848. He then guided the rescuers back to Weymouth Bay where they picked up two men, the only other survivors.

While the Kennedy expedition was designed to 'open up' Cape York for settlement, its tragic ending had exactly the opposite effect. The only other major explorer who went anywhere near the cape prior to the advent of Narcisse Pelletier was Augustus Charles Gregory in 1856. He entered the area from the Northern

Territory but remained on the western side of the Great Divide as he travelled south before turning east to Gladstone.

Gregory reported that in the Upper Burdekin, adjacent to the cape, 'the extent of country suited for squatting purposes is very considerable – water, forming a never-ending stream, [is available] throughout the whole distance'. However, he stressed the necessity of 'force' to accompany any settlers 'because the terrain and abundance of food and water would continue to allow the Aborigines to resist determinedly'.[12]

The area to the north where Narcisse arrived two years later remained untouched and unseen by white men until the cabin boy was taken in by his Aboriginal rescuers.

5

Narcisse/Amglo

By word and gesture, Maademan made it clear that they were on
their way to the assembled clan. There Narcisse would meet *les
nombreux,* the many, and he would find his place within them.
Narcisse plucked up his courage. He had slept well and the injury
to his head was fully healed. The women, it seemed, had applied
some herbal mixture on that first day while he slept and held it
in place with the sap of a tree. His feet were also quickly healing
and he felt his strength returning as the small party made their
way through open timbered country.

With Maademan leading and Baroway at his shoulder, each
carrying a boomerang – *kunkamu* – spears and a beautifully carved
woomera – *yuli* – to propel them, Narcisse settled in behind with
Sassy. His two spears seemed thinner and lighter than those of
the older men. The women followed, carrying woven dillybags,
and in Marie's case, a sharpened stick that Sassy called a *cachin* and
mimed its use to dig yams, *thampul*. And behind them, ranging
silently left to right, came the dog that attached itself to the group
while still treating Narcisse with suspicion.

'Il ne m'aime pas,' Narcisse said. He doesn't like me.

Sassy grinned. 'Ku'aaka.' Dingo.

Soon they reached a stream that flowed between high banks but was now little more than a gentle trickle over the sandy soil with smooth pebbles and clumps of bright green grass beneath the clear water. It provided a drink for the birdlife that surrounded them in great abundance. Whenever a new variety came in view, Sassy named it for Narcisse. Thus a great white cockatoo with a bright yellow crest became *pay'pa,* and the black crow *waatha.* Narcisse repeated the words aloud as Sassy grinned and nodded his encouragement. Suddenly Maademan signalled silence.

Ahead the stream had broadened to a wide pool and to one side where the sunlight met the shade of the high bank, half a dozen ducks swam and bobbed their heads into the water before raising them from the still surface and shaking bright droplets into the air around them. Sassy had moved silently forward and at some unseen signal he and Maademan launched their spears while Baroway threw the flattened and curved boomerang that cut through the air like a knife and collected one of the birds. Sassy's spear went slightly wide and just clipped a wing, but Maademan's skewered a duck just as it rose and spread its wings. The others took off in a confusion of squawks and splashes.

Sassy dived into the pool and in a flash, it seemed, he rose from the water with the duck he had wounded. He gave its neck a quick twist and then collected the other two as well as Maademan's spear. He brought them back to the side of the pool then returned for Baroway's boomerang which had floated to the other bank. The women packed the kills into their dillybags and Maademan looked at Narcisse and tapped his chest, which was lined with a cicatrix of raised scars.

'*Yalu tha'ina,*' he said. Good hit.

Narcisse felt he understood. '*Oui, oui.*'

'Maademan.' The man again tapped his chest and grinned in quiet triumph.

'*Oui, oui, Maademan.*'

He was tempted to ask about the scars which were also evident on Maademan's right upper arm, but that, he knew, would involve more words than he could command. He resolved instead to ask Sassy when they were alone together.

They resumed their progress and after an hour's steady walking they approached the meeting ground. By now the sun was hot and the morning breeze from the sea had died away. Narcisse sought the shade of each tree they passed and when he noticed the first of the children coming running towards them, he stopped and leaned against the nearest to hand. The ever helpful Sassy called it *yuku* but by now Narcisse had more new words than he could handle. Suddenly, the children saw him and stopped in their tracks. As one they squealed in fright, turned on their heels and ran crying for their mothers.

'*Pourquoi?!*'

'*Pulpu,*' Sassy said. White.

Maademan urged him forward to the wide clearing with groups standing and sitting by small bark shelters; and as they approached even the mothers became distressed. Four or five gathered their little ones and made off into the bush where they turned and stared. They seemed to be trembling in fright.

The other adults numbered about forty or fifty, the men gathering on one side, the women on the other, and even they seemed unable to fully comprehend what manner of creature had come into their midst. Maademan stepped forward and beckoned Narcisse to his side. There followed a speech from the big man that was utterly beyond the boy's understanding, particularly as he appeared to be ending his oration when both men and women began interrupting and pointing at his ragged trousers.

'*Pulthuna, paa'ayi?*' they cried. Boy or girl?

'*Pulthuna, pulthuna,*' Maademan replied.

And when the cries continued the big man suddenly turned to Narcisse, put one hand over his crutch and held his genitals. *'Ngul'uthu.'* It is true.

But still, it seemed, they were unconvinced, so with a single movement Maademan took the waist of his trousers by the hips and drew them sharply down to his knees, exposing his manhood to the entire clan.

Narcisse was mortified. He felt himself blushing to the roots of his being. He quickly covered himself as best he could. But instead of the taunting laughter that would have erupted from a similar crowd in the town square of Saint-Gilles, his audience merely turned to each other and muttered their nodding confirmation of his sex. A question had been answered. His place in the scheme of things could now be considered.

And yet . . . while the great bulk of the onlookers had treated his exposure with a confounding nonchalance, Narcisse could not help but notice that on the fringes of the crowd there were at least one or two, perhaps several, of the females who smiled behind their hands and lowered their eyes as he struggled to cover his modesty. And when he turned for support to Sassy, he could recognise a genuine *empathie* in his friend's open face.

The rest of the afternoon was given to meetings with several small groups of the men as Maademan ushered him from one place to another. Their reception ranged from barely disguised hostility to curiosity to a tentative acceptance.

Maademan's family had established their own camping place and groups of two or three men – occasionally accompanied by an old woman – came to them. The assemblage, it seemed, was made up of distinct smaller groupings, families that contained a random mix of siblings, cousins and in-laws. The words for these complex relationships in the local language would not become clear to Narcisse for many weeks; and the gradations of protocol in his dealings with them for very much longer. But that afternoon, a dozen times or a hundred, he introduced himself, 'Je m'appelle Amglo', and the response of his listeners ranged from confusion or a solemn frown, to more often a torrent of utterly inexplicable sounds.

By the time the sun was setting Narcisse was mentally exhausted, but his newly introduced clans-people were busy with excited preparations as they gathered sprigs of leaves and uncovered small caches of white and red clay with which they painted their bodies and faces. Baroway again made fire using his long stick – the *tiki* – which he spun in his hands while squatting over the flat *yuma*, firewood, surrounded by the lightest kindling to catch the first glowing sparks.

When the fire was going, the women of Maademan's family prepared and cooked two of the ducks the men had killed, together with a handful of small crayfish they had gathered in the afternoon from another broad billabong; and in the coals they set the yams they had exchanged with another family for one of the ducks.

The food tasted as good as anything Narcisse had eaten at home or on board any of the ships he had crewed since leaving France. But when he tried to express his thanks and compliment the cooks, his words were no more than meaningless sounds to accompany his elaborate mime. The *patois* of the Vendée that for all his life had been so much a part of his being, his *personnalité,* was now worthless, and he almost wept with frustration and *douleur.*

He retired to a nearby tree, seeking a moment of solitude. It was short-lived. The unfamiliar food had induced a pressing need to relieve himself. With families scattered about the area, he had no idea where he should go or what *politesse* was required. He turned to Sassy who very quickly understood and led him some distance from the encampment then dug a shallow pit for him in the sandy soil before discretely retiring. Narcisse completed his business in short order and used grass to clean himself before covering the pit.

As they were returning, Sassy stopped beneath a tree from which green mangoes hung like giant teardrops. There was clearly something he wanted to tell his new friend and, in a combination of words and gestures, the message slowly reached him. The people, he said, had agreed. Amglo would be accepted.

Narcisse bowed his head in understanding. Only much later did he realise just how grave that decision had been. And while it was well supported, it was not unanimous. If it had gone the other way, his fate would have been sealed in a shower of fighting spears.

Sassy was all smiles. One feature worked in his favour, he said with awkward gestures. Amglo's penis, *uulngu*, *wanga*, was not big, *mukana*.

Narcisse was bemused. Sassy turned serious. He explained that the most deadly insult that could be made was '*Ngono wanga mukana*'. Your penis is big.

Narcisse was wordless. Sassy took his forearm and led him out of the shade. '*Incroyable*,' Narcisse whispered, then laughed together with his friend.

On their way back came the sound of drums combined with the sharper rhythms of hard wooden clapsticks, and as they reached the cleared area a group of men – both young and old – were performing a dance the like of which Narcisse could never have imagined. They shuffled forward, stamping their feet and chanting what sounded like verses of an elaborate poem; and at a signal known only to them, they ended with a shout and moved off to the side of the clearing.

It would be many months before he learned that the Sandbeach people, which included his own Night Island group, in the long north–south arm of a great bay leading to the tip of the cape, were practically unique among the Aboriginal people in their use of the drum to accompany their dancing. It had come to them in the lifetime of Maademan's grandfather from the great island of the north and they had embraced it in their celebrations.

The dances would tell stories of the world known to some as the Dreamtime and others as Storytime, when the great spirits of the ancestors gave form to the world, the mountains and the seas, the rivers and the lagoons, all the creatures that inhabited them and their relationships with the people. But on this night, as the women took the place of the men dancing in the moonlight and firelight, and the drums kept pace with the stamping feet, Narcisse felt strangely as though he had become an alien spectator in a world that no other person of his race or kin had ever known. And while he had an eager guide to the strange wonders, *les merveilles,* of that place, in Sassy, and perhaps Maademan, he feared deeply and desolately that it would always be beyond him. As the men again replaced the women, turnabout, turnabout, slowly the drumming rhythms faded, his eyes closed of their own accord and his head bent to his chest.

When the dawn came, the camp roused itself and Narcisse heard the delighted shouts of children. Maademan had slept beneath a neat arrangement of bark bent and supported to stay firmly in place, and now he and his little group were about the day's business. Narcisse sat rubbing sleep from his eyes when Sassy came smiling across the open space with a giant white-tailed rat still impaled on his spear. His contribution was welcomed and the women went to work preparing it. Then the young man offered his hand to Narcisse who grabbed it and rose as his friend leaned back to take his weight.

Sassy pointed in the direction of the shouting and they headed there at a gentle trot. The day was already warm and Narcisse took off his shirt as they travelled. When they reached the pool there was a sudden silence as wide-eyed children and young adults saw them. Then came squeals as half the youngsters hurried to the opposite bank. Sassy called, *'Kuunama!'* Stay! And most retreated behind trees while sneaking wide-eyed glances at the *para*, the white man.

Narcisse turned away to drop his ragged trousers and left them beside his shirt, but then as he recalled Sassy's words beneath the shade tree he paused in the sunlight before immersing himself in the clear water. It was warm at the edges but as he dived towards the centre where it was almost two fathoms at its deepest, it was cool and wonderfully refreshing.

He was reminded instantly of the days when he and Élie Jean-Félix plumbed the depths of the River Vie as the tide rushed in from the Bay of Biscay. But there the water was salt and harsh to the taste, while now it was as soft and pure as an off-shore breeze; and as he looked upwards he could see shafts of sunlight reaching down from the surface. He sprang from the sandy bed and rose to the shimmering surface, breaking it with a joyous expulsion of breath and laughter.

Sassy joined him from behind and they splashed to the bank in an involuntary race with Sassy touching the dry ground just ahead of him. Narcisse drew himself out of the water and reached for the shirt to dry his face. But the stone he'd placed on both his garments was gone, as indeed were the shirt and trousers themselves. He looked quickly from side to side. Nothing. Then a little further off he saw them.

Baroway's wife, Veronique, had torn a strip from the tail of the shirt and was even then knotting it around her forehead in a headband, while Marie and Rosine were sitting with a larger group of women apportioning the trousers among themselves. A protest leapt to his throat but before he could give vent to the loss, Sassy tapped him on the chest with the fingers of his right hand, then tapped his own. *'Yapu-yapu,'* he said. Brothers.

Narcisse was suddenly overcome. *'Je suis . . .'* he began but then there were no words available, nothing he could say that would express the storm of emotions that swelled within him. A great sob escaped. He half collapsed to the ground where he sat in his nakedness. He put a hand across his face to hide the tears. And when, finally, he wiped them away and looked across the lagoon, the small children were making their way back into the water.

Amglo gave them a gentle wave. One or two smiled back at him.

PART
Four

6

Queensland

Narcisse Pelletier was not the only European to be accepted by the Aboriginal people of Queensland. In 1846, the seven survivors of the shipwrecked *Peruvian* came ashore at Cape Cleveland – later to be settled as Townsville – though four of them soon died of exposure and drowning. The remaining three – the ship's captain George Pitkethly and his wife, Betsey, as well as able seaman James Morrill – were taken in by the local people.

The Pitkethlys succumbed within two years though Morrill survived a further fifteen with several groups before making contact with white settlers and returning to a European lifestyle. Little is known of his time with the Aboriginals, though he retained some links with the people and sought to mediate between them and settlers in the region. He married a white servant girl but died of natural causes only two years later.

Undoubtedly, other castaways and escapees from the convict settlement in Moreton Bay who sought sanctuary with the tribal people were less fortunate and were either killed as trespassers or committed some misdemeanour to Aboriginal law that brought about their demise. Indeed, as the survivors of the *Peruvian* were coming ashore, Queensland was fast becoming a killing field in the front line of the Frontier Wars.

By then the authorities had instituted one of the more repre-
hensible measures in the long, shameful chronicle of the British
appropriation of the continent: the Queensland Native Mounted
Police. They were charged with the 'dispersal' of all Aboriginal
people who impeded white newcomers into this most densely
populated area of the Australian mainland.

The foundations of the Native Police Force were laid in
the sepoy and sowar armies of British colonial India, followed
by the Cape Regiment in South Africa and the Malay Corps
in Ceylon (later Sri Lanka). In each case the British employed
one group of inhabitants to join with them in suppressing their
compatriots. They used money, privilege and propaganda to
separate them from their fellows and retain their continued
cooperation.

The Australian version had its first informal beginnings in
the Hawkesbury Valley when in 1805 Chief Constable Andrew
Thompson coerced 'friendly' Aboriginals into tracking and
assisting in the eradication of 'hostile' people of differing tribal
backgrounds. Indeed, the leading British figure in the infant
colony, John Macarthur, used the power of the purse to engage
men from both rival Dharawal and Gandangara clans to become
his uniformed bodyguards.[1]

Another early exploiter of tribal divisions was the notorious
Major James Thomas Morisset, hideously disfigured by shell
fragments in the Peninsular Wars, who would later turn the
Norfolk Island penal colony into a hell on earth. Under orders
from the equally unbending Governor Brisbane, he not only
established a reign of terror among the Aboriginal people of
the Bathurst area, he spread a munificent £50 from Brisbane's
treasury to recruit outlying Aboriginals to his force.

The practice was not always successful. Aboriginal trackers
were often suspected of leading punitive detachments on wild
goose chases. This was certainly the case in the Campbelltown

region where settlers led by the extended family of Australian-born explorer Hamilton Hume formed a practical working relationship with the Aboriginal people. However, the great majority of settlers in all parts of the mainland had no sympathy for the people whose ancient tribal lands they were appropriating.

The outlying penal settlements raised different responses and Aboriginals were regularly employed around the Newcastle and Port Macquarie facilities to capture escaped convicts. On occasion, Aboriginals were recruited as 'constables' and given uniforms to establish their authority and status. However, their involvement became official when the first Native Police corps was established in the early 1840s in the Port Phillip region.

The corps was financed by Lieutenant Governor La Trobe and comprised some sixty members of whom forty-five were Aboriginal men operating under white officers, often former members of the Royal Ulster Constabulary. But once it became clear to the recruits that their duties involved the capture and killing of their compatriots, a senior Wurudjeri elder among them, one Aboriginal member, Billibellary, resigned and persuaded others to follow his lead. Nevertheless, while few remained in the corps for more than two or three years, it continued through the early years of the goldrush until it was finally disbanded in 1853.

By then the Frontier War in Queensland harboured the most effective instrument of 'dispersal' in the country. In 1848 the New South Wales government had passed legislation to fund a new operation based broadly on the Port Phillip model. They appointed an eager volunteer in a Murrumbidgee station manager and local court official, Frederick Walker, to become the first commandant of the Native Police Force. Over the next seven years, he would initiate an uncompromising campaign against the Aboriginal people of the north.

Walker's first Aboriginal recruits were fourteen men from four separate tribes of the Riverina. They would have as much relationship to the Queensland Aboriginal nations as the French to the English. He devised a *modus operandi* that would further dissociate his recruits from the northerners. He branded the hostile defenders of their lands as 'charcoals' whose status fell far below that of his uniformed troopers.

Moreover, he established a test by which the charcoals' capacity for redemption could be measured. If they accepted their 'bringing in' as mendicants to the pastoral stations, they would be tolerated. But if they defied him and insisted on following the 'old ways', the decision was theirs and he and his troopers could not be blamed for the consequences.

But while Walker was focused on the area that would become Queensland, his methods commended themselves to the New South Wales authorities under Governor William Denison. At the time, the clans around the Clarence River were following the usual pattern of retribution against settlers who had raped and abducted Aboriginal women. Denison turned to Walker to 'disperse' the troublemakers.

Denison was an Eton old boy with firm links to the English Establishment – his father had been an MP and his brother became Speaker of the House of Commons. After graduation from the Royal Military College, he joined the Royal Engineers and in 1846 was appointed Lieutenant Governor of Van Diemen's Land. By then, the 'Aboriginal problem' on the island had been resolved by the genocidal activities of his predecessors and in 1854 he would be promoted to governor-general. But to a man whose expressed attitude to convicts was that 'to everyman the full penalty which the law allots to his offence should be meted out', any Aboriginal 'rebellion' was simply intolerable.

Walker regarded the unrest in the Clarence as 'minor', but was happy to respond to the highest authority in the land. He assigned an officer with unimpeachable credentials to deal with it. Edric Norfolk Faux Morisset was the son of the notorious

James Thomas Morisset whose Norfolk Island excesses had already become the stuff of legend. Morisset the younger did his father proud with a series of savage punitive raids, usually at dawn while their victims slept, resulting in at least two massacres that caused government inquiries. In each case no findings were made against him and his career in the Native Police prospered. Indeed, he would eventually become commandant of the force.[2]

Walker then reinforced his contingent with a recruiting drive in the Deniliquin area; and with thirty new troopers outfitted in black peaked caps, green shirts and dark trousers with a single red stripe, he was able to create four divisions – one in the Wide Bay–Burnett region, others in the Maranoa and Goondiwindi areas, and one roving detachment to be deployed as required. However, the commandant had developed a dependence on strong liquor and in 1855 he was dismissed from the force 'for constantly being in a state of inebriation'.

A further parliamentary inquiry into the efficacy of the Native Police Force followed in 1857, but it found that the force was: 'absolutely requisite for the protection of life and property, and is essential as a most valuable adjunct to the pioneering energies of the extreme outlying districts . . . Previously to the Native Police being introduced into the Northern Districts [Queensland], the outrages committed by the blacks were of frequent occurrence, extending to murder as well as the destruction of stock to a great extent.'

The committee made veiled references to 'complaints' against Native Police activities that 'a more mature experience' might have avoided. But 'on the whole, your Committee are prepared to state . . . that there does not appear the least ground to question, or even indicate, a doubt of the capabilities and adaptation of the Native Police Force for the duties for which that body was originally raised; but on the contrary, that under proper provisions and judicious management and direction, such a Force is admirably adapted to protect life and property, and materially to assist the progress of the settler in the unsettled frontier districts.'[3]

In fact, the Native Police Force was quite unsuited to the protection of settlers. Its tactics were aimed at retaliation for Aboriginal attacks. But their mode of operation at least gave the settlers themselves the official imprimatur for the wholesale murder of those Aboriginal people who resisted the white encroachment on their sacred lands.

These essentially defensive actions by the Aboriginal people of Queensland were invariably portrayed as 'massacres by deceitful and treacherous savages' and were given enormous publicity, thereby setting the scene for thoroughly justified reprisals.

Typical was the so-called Hornet Bank Massacre that took place in October 1857, shortly after the presentation of the committee's report. The Aboriginal attack was itself a retaliation for the killing of twelve Yeeman people in the upper Dawson River at the very limits of northern settlement at the time. The area had been claimed by one Andrew Scott in the early 1850s when he arrived with flocks of sheep and herds of cattle. In 1854 he leased Hornet Bank to John Fraser who, with his large family, increased the stock and ran afoul of the Aboriginal owners who bitterly resented their intrusion.

Two years later Fraser died of dysentery while droving cattle to the Ipswich area in the south and his eldest son, 23-year-old William, took over the management in partnership with Scott. Relations with the Aboriginals soured further and as Yeeman tribesmen attacked shepherds' huts and speared cattle, there were deaths on both sides. The whites took revenge by shooting twelve Aboriginal men and, in an act of settler bastardry, the Frasers pretended to cement a 'truce' by offering fruit puddings which they had laced with strychnine.[4]

The effects were horrific. Strychnine poisoning produces the most frightful symptoms of any known toxic. Ten to twenty minutes after ingestion, the body's muscles begin to spasm, starting with the head and neck then spreading to every muscle in the body with nearly continuous convulsions. Eventually they increase in intensity until the backbone arches continually. The agony is beyond description. Death comes in two or three hours from asphyxiation caused by paralysis of the nerves that control breathing.

The Aboriginal revenge was well planned. On the evening of 27 October, an Aboriginal servant killed all the homestead dogs to prevent their barking the alarm and in the darkness the Yeeman attacked. They set about killing the entire family as well as the children's tutor, Henry Neagle, and two white stationhands. Only fourteen-year-old Sylvester Fraser survived after being hit on the head with a waddy and falling between his bed and a wall.

When the Yeeman left, Sylvester ran to the next station homestead nineteen kilometres away and reported the attack. The stationhands there armed themselves and went on a rampage, killing an entire community they found sleeping some sixteen kilometres from the Fraser property. It was the first of many massacres in the area over the succeeding weeks.

Meanwhile, Sylvester rode south to inform his brother William who was at Ipswich. After learning of the loss of his family, William was seized with a mania for killing Aboriginal people which found some release when he joined the Native Police Force. There, he had 'every opportunity to assuage his grief through murder'.[5]

The records show that William Fraser killed more than 100 members of the Yeeman people. But that was insufficient to quell the fires of revenge and he embarked on a career of savagery towards any Aboriginal people who came within view. He shot an Aboriginal jockey at the Taroom racetrack; and after two Aboriginal men were found not guilty of involvement in the attack on his family's homestead, he shot both of them dead as they left the Rockhampton courthouse.

His brutality became so flagrant that it was widely believed that the government had given him *carte blanche* for twelve months to wreak his vengeance on an entire people. It was even reported that he shot an Aboriginal woman in the main street of Toowoomba, claiming that she was wearing his dead mother's dress; and that two policemen on the scene spoke briefly to him before saluting and walking away. Certainly, he was never charged with any of these alleged outrages.

However, it is uncontested that in 1905 when asked by *The Queenslander* if he had such an authority, he responded: 'I never asked and never received such an authority but felt I was justified in doing [the killings].'[6] Indeed, police and public sympathy for Fraser ran so high that he was never arrested and was regarded as a folk hero in the backblocks of Queensland. And in 2008 the gravesite of the Fraser family was added to the Queensland Heritage Register.

From 1857 onward the Native Police Force was wholly engaged in 'punitive' operations, almost invariably daybreak attacks on Aboriginal camps and tribal communities. They couched their activities in deliberately deceptive terms. Aboriginal people were never 'killed' but rather 'dispersed'; and the force was always said to be responding to Aboriginal 'aggression'.

Moreover, the authorities sought to promote the fiction that no territory was being 'conquered; instead, it was all 'Crown Land' being settled and the original inhabitants – as British subjects – were committing crimes by resisting the appropriation of their traditional lands.[7] This was made the more farcical by the law which actually prevented Aboriginals from giving evidence since they could not swear an oath on a Bible whose contents were unknown to them. Their only recourse to defend their ancient territories was armed conflict, but against the rapidly improving firepower of the enemy's guns, their cause was a hopeless one.

Nevertheless, the guerrilla warfare did at least slow the progress of the Europeans and their advance stalled temporarily in a ragged front line from the coast at what would become Rockhampton, in a southwesterly direction towards the New South Wales border. All across that disputed territory the Aboriginal people were either being exterminated or subsumed into the fringes of the dominant society.

Meantime, Edric Morisset had taken his place as Commandant of the Native Police in 1857 and a new figure had arisen as 'the most sadistic and merciless officer' in the force. Frederick Wheeler was appointed Second Lieutenant on 7 December 1857. He was an odd mix – the eldest son of a London merchant and a Sicilian noblewoman, educated at London's exclusive Westminster School, and sufficiently well connected that both Morisset and the Government Resident and Police Magistrate John Wickham recommended his appointment. He was sent to the furthest northerly post at Rockhampton where shortly afterwards his detachment of troopers deserted *en masse*.

It was an unprepossessing start to his career but once back in Brisbane, he was ordered to establish a new Native Police camp on the shores of Moreton Bay at Sandgate. From there he would control the Aboriginal people who continued to harass the outlying settlers.

The camp consisted of a rough slab hut for the officer and bark humpies for the troopers. But since Wheeler's family of a wife and eventually four daughters lived in Brisbane, he no doubt spent much of his off-duty hours with his family. Most of his punitive missions were conducted in an arc from Maryborough in the north, the Great Divide in the west and the Tweed River in the south. He was soon greatly feared by the people as the reputation of 'this sadistic destroyer of Aboriginal lives continued to grow'.[8]

However, Wheeler's hatred and contempt for the Aboriginal people was by no means uniformly shared by members of the white community. Notable standouts included William Landsborough, born in Ayreshire, Scotland, the son of a clergyman. He arrived in Sydney as a seventeen-year-old in 1842 and joined his elder brothers on their New England property. When they sold up and began the big move to the Bundaberg district in the early 1850s, William took up land himself a little further north on the Kolan River.

It was here that he began his life as an explorer, starting out each year when shearing was completed. In 1856 Landsborough reached the area where Gladstone now stands and the following year extended his penetration to the Rockhampton district where he took up land. In 1858 he tracked west to the Comet River and soon afterward sold his Kolan River property to finance his northerly ventures.

Landsborough took great pains to avoid conflict with the Aboriginal people 'even if this meant changing his plans or moving on to avoid unnecessarily giving offence'.[9] But when in difficulties or in need of guidance 'he sometimes sought and obtained advice from them as to the nature of the country'.[10] His workforce was made up of former English and Irish convicts, as well as several Chinese shepherds who would turn their hands to growing fruit and vegetables on his properties. And as he extended his explorations to the north and west, he was invariably accompanied by Aboriginal trackers and guides. He would eventually become owner or part-owner of more than a million acres of Queensland grazing property. But, like most other settlers, he would zealously avoid the mortal dangers and natural hazards of Cape York.

For the Aboriginal people of Sandbeach country, the world was
as unchanging as it had always been. The rains would come and
go; the rivers and creeks would rise and fall; the turtles and the
dugong would swim into their waters to lay their eggs and feed
on the seagrass. And the hunters would be out in their canoes
with their spears poised. The women would gather the fruits
and weave their dillybags, just as they always had. And the men
would plant their seed which would grow in their wives' bellies
until a new life sprang from their loins to join the tribe; while
the old and infirm would go to that place beyond the sea, that
spirit world of Dreaming and Storytime.

Just as they always had.

7

Amglo

After the big meeting where Narcisse/Amglo had been accepted by the Night Islanders, the family groups had scattered to their favoured places at the fringe of the sandbeach. From there the daily business of the people resumed. The women fished with string lines, dug yams with their smooth polished yamsticks – *cachin* – or gathered wild apples and other fruits, some of which needed many hours of grinding and rinsing to be edible. They were always occupied, either with food or children. They suckled their babies for several years and carried them in leafy cradles while they worked. Any spare time was taken up with plaiting and weaving *yakara*-fibre bags, fishing nets and even 'cat's cradles' for their children.

For the men, no two days were the same; though Amglo always began his with a swim in the sea – usually with Sassy – and an early morning session with his spears. The men of his 'family' had given him three well-used weapons and Baroway was showing him the technique for carving his own from a branch of the special *kalka* tree. It was a long, laborious process and a hundred times a day he yearned for a knife instead of the shell-blade and stone rasps that made up the men's toolkit.

He fashioned a bark target on the beach and each day his practice followed the same pattern. To begin, he launched his *javelots*
by hand, starting from ten paces and gradually extending the range
to twenty, thirty and forty. Then he would fit the spear into
Baroway's old *yuli,* woomera, and keep practising until he hit the
target twice in a row. By then he had been joined by a regular
group of children who had their own practice routines, using
much shorter spears whose tips had been blunted and covered in
paperbark and resin. And one of their number – a little boy he
christened 'Tookie' – had become his retriever until he tired and
Amglo himself took up the task. Within a month the exercise
had made him fitter and stronger in all his limbs than he had
ever known before.

He ate voraciously – breakfasting on mangoes and leftover fish
or meat from the night before; then through the day slaking his
hunger with fruit, oysters and other tidbits. Each evening was
a feast that ranged from shellfish and turtle, to wallaby, goose,
duck, snails, grubs and much more, usually accompanied by
various tubers cooked in the coals.

Within the clan he was slowly but surely finding his way.
Sassy's constant chatter in the tribal language gave him a feeling for
the rhythm of conversation and each day provided new words and
phrases to learn. He felt himself changing, adapting, becoming.

He now knew the Night Island people belonged to a vast
territory that began with the sea and all the creatures within it,
all the way from the distant coral reef to the shore. This was
their timeless hunting ground. Then came the golden sandbeach
that stretched for many kilometres north and south of the island;
and after that the land itself, all the way back to the mountains.

Within that great estate there were huge mangrove and marsh-
land areas; beyond them rainforests, scrubland and savannahs.
These the people tended with regular fires to refresh the land

and direct the wallabies and emus to places where they could be harvested for the cooking coals.

Amglo knew that abutting their territory to the north was the country of the Kuuku Y'au people, to the south the Umpila and beyond them the Lamalama. Their languages were similar but not the same. And relations with the neighbours were always on the knife edge of conflict. Nevertheless, they traded with them and all came together for corroboree at least once a year to settle disputes, negotiate marriages and tell of their great feats of hunting the dugong and the crocodile.

These were occasions of high diplomacy and great care had to be taken since there were delicate issues of intermarriage and of differing totems in any conversation between clans. The Kuuku Y'au, for instance, claimed six totems – *cuscus* (the ringtail possum), *payamu* (the rainbow serpent), *pul'u* (the pheasant), *yuka* (the morning star), *kutini* (the cassowary) and *i'wayi* (the crocodile). The Umpila also honoured the morning star, the rainbow serpent and the dingo. While his own Night Island people's totems were *maathuy* (the pelican), *tinta* (the king parrot) and *piiwu* (the wallaby).

Each child received a skin totem from his mother even before birth and the choice depended on the spirit that came to her when first the unborn baby moved within her belly. So Sassy was touched by the spirit of the *maathuy* and all his life he would be tasked with its care and celebration in dance and song. Since his own birth took place in another world, Amglo was denied a nativity totem, but he shared fully in the clan and skin totems of the Night Islanders and was soon a devotee of the beautiful *tinta* with its flashing scarlet breast and rich green wings.

It was now a joy, *un délice*, to be joined to such a beautiful totem in this new life. When he came upon the parrot – or a pair – in the good country behind the beach, he felt blessed and reassured. When he stood quite still and let his own spirit reach out, he could not help but feel a harmony between them. And when they took wing, just for a moment he shared the thrill of joyous flight.

Indeed, the world of the spirit was strangely familiar to him. In some ways, his entire life had been a spiritual journey from the moment his mother gave him the name of Saint Narcissus. From the childhood stories of Monsieur le Curé he had come to know the spirit world of the saints. And on his own journeys across the sea, he had felt and seen the spirit of the deep in all its moods and passions.

Amglo knew the companionship of his family group. Maademan was a strict mentor, but he was full of the wisdom of experience. Unlike other older men, he seldom raised his voice and even less a hand in anger or reproof. Baroway was more distant but no less friendly; and the women were a dutiful presence, chattering endlessly in their own circle, well apart from the men.

There were other matters of tribal groupings just beyond his ken. They were called *kaapay* and *kuyan* and seemed to depend on the appearance of each person. And by parental agreement, it seemed, the children were placed in one or the other. But since he was no part of it, there was little reason to pursue it.

He knew also of the great tribal heroes of the past but their names meant nothing to him. And there were whispers of I'wai Tjilbo, the crocodile ancestor, but in words that were far beyond his understanding. So he contented himself with the thought that some small part of him would remain forever French. And that was no bad thing.

This personal privacy extended to the names of his native companions. They all had a succession of names from their birth and other junctures in their lives. But they addressed each other by the family relationship they shared, be it brother, sister, parent, uncle, aunty, cousin and in-law to the last connection. And since these didn't apply to him and because the language names were hard to remember, he secretly chose to give names of his own making to those with whom he often dealt. For example, Sassy was betrothed to a young girl whom he would marry after she reached puberty; her given name was a strange collision of syllables so to him she was 'Mimi'.

And as he grew in confidence, Amglo found himself extending his circle of acquaintances. He was instantly attracted to one man who, like himself, had been adopted by the clan. He was from the Kanidji people in the mountainous southwest and, unlike the Night Islanders, he was black as soot. So Amglo gave him the name 'Bruno' after the man who delivered coal for the fires in Saint-Gilles. Sassy joked that on a dark night he was nowhere to be seen . . . unless he opened his eyes! Or smiled, 'ngaachina,' said Amglo, making his first joke in the language of his new life. They laughed together as they pictured Bruno's white eyes and sparkling teeth in the forest of the night. When they told the joke to Bruno the next day, he joined in the laughter.

Bruno was not only darker than his adopted clan, he was round in face and figure where every other man – and most of the women – were slim and athletic. He seemed happy with his novelty. While he had never been accepted as a valued hunter or warrior, he was a friend to all and a kindly mentor to the children in their rowdy games.

His wife, to whom Amglo gave the name 'Sabine' after *la courtisane* of the Saint-Gilles docks, bullied him mercilessly. A tall, striking woman with a roving eye, she was shunned by many of the women whose husbands had been pleased to share her sexual favours in the hidden corners of the bushland. But Bruno seemed unconcerned by her wanderings.

The fondness Amglo felt for him was reciprocated by his fellow outcast and Bruno often joined Sassy and himself in their expeditions into the bush – where both the men talked with him about the plants and animals that made up that world – and occasionally to Night Island itself. It was only about five kilometres off shore but he had been curious about it ever since he had first searched the horizon for Pinard and the others who had marooned him.

There was little to recommend it – no running water and no game to feed a hungry hunter – but it was at least a place of solitude. And even as he made his new life among people whom he respected and cared for, thoughts of the captain brought a painful tightening of his belly, a breathlessness of rage that he believed would be with him forever. It was a new addition to his personality, his inner life. Perhaps it had always been there from his own people of the Vendée who were renowned for their short tempers and fighting qualities. But there were times when it rushed to the surface and banished all control.

This had happened only a few days ago when Maademan had tasked him with minding a big piece of turtle meat that had been butchered from the morning hunt. He was sitting alone in the shade of a *thanka* tree just back from the beach when the tall figure of an older boy he had named 'Yannick' approached, carrying the usual hunter's arms of spears and fighting stick. He was one of a family, Sassy said, who had opposed the adoption of Amglo into the clan. And in their several meetings since, Yannick had never responded to his greetings. Now, in a babble of shouted words and violent gestures, he accused Amglo of stealing the meat – *paalntanya* – for himself.

Amglo had no words to counter the accusation and could merely repeat that it was a lie – '*Wikamana, wikamana!*' This only enraged Yannick further and he threated Amglo with his hunting spear. The noise attracted others and Sassy came running up the beach towards them. Amglo retreated to the sand as Yannick advanced and as Sassy reached them he threatened him as well. His friend's intervention gave Amglo the chance to grab one of his old spears in the sand and once in his hand the rage took hold. He screamed and rushed towards Yannick and, as Sassy ducked aside, Amglo used it in close quarters, attempting to drive it into his enemy's belly.

Yannick knocked it down and made his own thrusts at Amglo's groin. He leapt aside just in time but the barbs struck the outside of his leg just below the knee and held the spear for just a moment. It was enough for Amglo to swipe the haft of his spear across Yannick's neck and jaw but not enough to disable him. With a roar the bigger boy returned to the fight, but by now the older men had come running and Maademan himself dashed into the melee, swinging his great arms to separate the combatants.

Amglo struggled against his mentor – *'Je vais le tuer!'* he cried. I will kill him! – until the older man ripped the spear from his hands. Maademan then pushed Yannick full in the face and he sat down hard on the sand. There followed a fusillade of words from Maademan addressed to both fighters; and though most of the words meant nothing to Amglo, the tone was unmistakeable: *S'arreter,* desist!

Both boys regained their feet. Defiance of the older man was not an option. But neither was forgiveness; only a truce and that was reluctantly agreed. Amglo and Sassy walked away together, arms about each other's shoulders. Amglo stole a glance at Yannick as he returned to his family's collection of small but well-made shelters. His expression was clear: nothing had been resolved.

That evening he bathed his cut leg in the brackish water of the creek just back from the beach. Marie sent Rosine to collect some herbs which she pounded into a mash and applied to the wound. However, she seemed concerned that the barbs of Yannick's spear might have been tipped with poison, *uupiiri.* If so, the herbs would not cure it completely.

And so it would prove.

8

Queensland

The white settlers and the British officers of the Native Police were reinforced in the rightness of their cause by events far distant from their outback stations and camps. The British Empire had come under strain from its colonial adventures in fields as diverse as India, where in 1857 a widespread mutiny broke out among the sepoys; in China, where constant British incursions were deeply resented; and even the United States, where Britain seemed likely to side with the Southern Confederacy in the forthcoming Civil War to protect the cotton supplies to British textile mills. And with the ending of convict transportation to Australia a new sense of urgency fired their determination to assert total domination over the troublesome Aboriginal people of Queensland.

Frederick Wheeler returned to Rockhampton at this time with a new contingent of his southern recruits, determined to wreak vengeance on tribal resistance. But once again they proved difficult to retain in the service. On one occasion, a young Yugambeh boy from the Nerang River district was induced to join up with five other young men from the area. They were taken by ship to Rockhampton and then to the nearby police camp to be trained. Wheeler warned that anyone who disobeyed orders or tried to leave camp would be subject to a firing squad for 'desertion'. And indeed one of the recruits was killed 'when trying to escape'.

But instead of discouraging the others, the five remaining teenagers fled the camp and set out to walk the 550 kilometres home through unknown country. They kept close to the coast with the sea on their left and avoided the dangers of detection as they passed through the tribal territories of clans with whom they shared no common language. They lived off the land for three months before one of their party climbed a tree and finally spotted *Wollumbin*, Mount Warning, in Bundjalung country. They were home.

Nevertheless, they never felt safe from Wheeler's revenge and according to one of the runaways, Keendahn, whenever they heard the police were nearby, they ran into the bush to hide until their people gave the all-clear.

Shortly afterwards, William Landsborough joined a rescue party in North Queensland led by William McKinley to search for the missing members of the Burke and Wills expedition which set out in 1860 to cross the continent from south to north. He was surprised to discover that an earlier group on the same mission had been led by Commandant Frederick Walker. He had apparently overcome – at least temporarily – his addiction to alcohol. But his attitude to the country's Aboriginal custodians was unchanged. According to historian Noel Loos, 'When Walker's party, consisting of three Europeans and five Aboriginal troopers were ordered by a large number of Aborigines to leave a waterhole to the northeast of where Hughenden now stands, Walker ordered a mounted squad to charge. Twelve [Aboriginal] men were killed and few if any escaped unwounded before they could throw a spear.'[1] Later, Walker attacked at least four other groups of warriors with a similar outcome.

Perhaps not surprisingly, when Landsborough and McKinley ranged over much of the same territory, they found it impossible to make contact with the Aboriginal people. Walker had reported that he had never seen a country so thickly populated, while Landsborough concluded that he 'could not imagine' that they were numerous. Loos says, 'It is tempting to suggest that one factor contributing to the differing estimates was the expectation of conflict and the assessment of the potential "enemy", a conclusion which Walker's military terminology tends to support.'[2]

Meanwhile, Wheeler was adding to his own egregious reputation in the southwest near what would become the town of Roma. In 1859 a German migrant stationhand, Konrad Nahrung, had travelled to Bendemere station on nearby Yulebah Creek to bring his sister back to his workplace on Cooranga. At the time, the tribal people had been aroused by the station manager, a man named Sims, who had thrown a stone that severely injured a little boy who, he claimed, had frightened his horse nearly causing him to be unseated.

About fifty Aboriginal warriors gathered near the homestead and the stationhands barricaded the building against attack. Wheeler's camp was about thirty kilometres away and one of the stockmen slipped out in the darkness and galloped to raise the alarm. Wheeler and twelve of his men set out immediately and arrived just before daybreak.

According to Konrad Nahrung, 'The blacks had no mercy shown to them. Some were shot trying to escape in the water, others before they got that far. The police pursued them till late in the day, killing all they could. And what caused this? The one rash act by Mr Sim.'

The action became known as the Bendemere Massacre.

Soon afterwards Wheeler was in the Caboolture area where, according to the *Brisbane Courier,* he and his troopers shot and killed 'at least eight Aborigines' in an action that the paper labelled 'most wanton and unprovoked'. At the time the Waka Waka people were holding a corroboree and were concerned only with their own rituals. A white eyewitness reported that, 'The Native Police surprised the camp, fired on them and killed seven men and one gin ... they had done nothing to justify the attack.' Wheeler responded that 'his instructions compel him to disperse the blacks wherever they may have congregated'.[3]

The wide and expanding area of the conflict is illustrated by the distribution of the white population. When Queensland came into being as a separate British colony on 10 December 1859, the white immigrants numbered 28,000. But only 6000 were in Brisbane; the rest were scattered on the disputed frontier over thousands of kilometres to the north and west, and they were advancing with every passing year.

The Aboriginal troopers within the Native Police Force had become utterly corrupted by their part in the murderous catalogue. They became notorious as rapists and terrorists of their compatriots. And on occasion they extended their depredations to the whites they were charged to defend and support.

This was a particularly sensitive concern to the authorities as evidenced in the fate of a white servant girl, Fanny Briggs, who disappeared from a farmhouse on the outskirts of Rockhampton in October 1860. Her partially decomposed body was found early the next month and it was clear that she had been raped before being murdered. Soon after, two troopers – Gulliver and Alma – were arrested. However, the evidence against them was so slim it seemed unlikely that a trial in Brisbane could find them guilty even in the racially inflamed atmosphere of the day. And since this would cause a roar of outrage among the settlers, Queensland's first governor, George Bowen, and his executive council gave secret orders to their officers to deliver 'summary justice' themselves.

According to historian Robert Orsted-Jensen, the prisoner Alma allegedly drowned when his leg-irons dragged him under while trying to cross a creek, while Gulliver was shot during his escape attempt. Orsted-Jensen says that if the truth were known at the time, 'It would probably have led some people to call for the resignation of the Governor and the Executive.' Moreover, 'the later biographical accounts of Governor Bowen and his ministers would have had a very different appearance.'[4]

In fact, Bowen was fairly typical of the British governors of the day. Born to the manse, he was educated at Charterhouse School and Oxford University, after which he briefly joined the navy, spending a mere sixteen days on Nelson's flagship *Victory*. Soon after, aged only twenty-seven, he was appointed president of the Ionian University in Corfu, then a British protectorate.

He returned briefly to London and was named chief secretary to the Ionian government in 1854. He married into the local aristocracy. His bride, Diamantina Roma (whose names would be memorialised in a town and later a river of the Channel Country), was the daughter of the Ionian senate president.

Bowen had insinuated himself into the good graces of William Gladstone who, as chancellor in the Palmerston government, secured his appointment to Queensland as the first of a series of vice-regal positions. He engaged Gladstone's private secretary, Robert Herbert, to his own personal staff and on arrival appointed him colonial secretary. They would operate as a duumvirate and the following year Herbert would become Premier of Queensland.

His executive was drawn from the leading squatters and funding of the Native Police Force was a priority, as evidenced by the allocation of more than £13,500 from a total budget of only £220,000. Indeed, they became known as the Squatting Ministry, not least because of the restrictive property qualifications of the electoral act.

By 1860 Frederick Walker had become a substantial grazier in the Springsure area of Central Queensland and had undergone a change of heart about the policy of Aboriginal dispersal. He advocated using them as indentured labour on properties such as his. But the heavyweights within the government remained tethered to his earlier view of the Aboriginal as not only expendable but as a 'doomed race' whose time on earth was coming to a close, and the sooner the better for all concerned.

Walker's successors in the force were similarly inclined. Commandant Edric Morisset pursued the hard line on dispersal, recruiting young officers willing to go that extra mile to carry out their brief. One of them, Second-Lieutenant Alfred March Patrick, led his troopers on to the Albinia Downs station of squatter Christopher Rolleson and ordered the peaceable Gayiri people off the premises. He then claimed they attacked him, but according to Walker 'the peace was broken by the Native Police under Mr Patrick, attacking and killing and wounding several of the friendly blacks'.

Patrick was outraged, claiming 'other police officers before they had been in the force a fortnight had shot lots of blacks' while he had been in the force for six months before he'd shot a single one. The *Port Denison Times* went to the heart of the matter: 'Many of the officers are but young, hot-headed men who from habit, and perhaps from nature, think no more of shooting a blackfellow than a pigeon. They hold a theory that an offence committed by one portion of a tribe should be wiped out by the wholesale slaughter of as many of the first party they can come across [and] as the troopers can shoot down, and they see nothing wrong in the act.'[5]

In the wake of the Patrick affair, Morisset retired from the force 'in view of my wife's ill-health'; however, it is more likely that the 'family reasons' included the publicity surrounding the murder of more Waka Waka people near Murgon, less than 160 kilometres from Brisbane, by his young brother, Rudolph Roxburgh Morisset. Moreover, Frederick Wheeler was again in the news, having shot four Aboriginal men near Ipswich, one of whom was the 'tame blackboy' of a leading squatter.

Leadership of the force then passed to the bearer of another name from the colonial past, Lieutenant John Bligh, a distant relative of the former governor. His reign would be no more enlightened than that of his predecessor.

9

Amglo

Amglo was proving an excellent student of the tribal language, particularly when speaking with Sassy, his teacher. The two boys, now in their seventeenth year, were inseparable. And Amglo's hunger for more words that would help him to understand the world of his clan was unquenchable. Indeed, he was in awe of the young and old alike who knew at least three languages and were able to employ each of them as circumstance and custom required.

Sassy was patient and positive, with an ever-ready sense of humour. And they were always on the move. At first, the abscess that had risen on Amglo's leg after his fight with Yannick slowed him with the pain. But then Baroway's wife, Veronique, came to him one day with a herbal mix.

'*Winchinya,*' she said. This will help. As she had been a member of the Umpila people, the mix was part of their medical 'secrets'. Amglo was moved. She had always seemed distant and quick to anger. And her tongue was as sharp as a spearhead. But now she applied the poultice gently and covered it with mud that quickly dried. For five days he abstained from his morning swim; and when he finally washed the muddy potion away, both the redness of the sore and the lump in his groin were gone.

After that he and Sassy returned to the pleasures of the sea, swimming and fishing in the clear, sheltered waters that lapped the golden sandbeach. They practised their spear-throwing in the same waters and paddled the family canoes out to the island and among the mangrove shallows where they caught *imuyu*, mudcrabs, to be cooked over the fires that night.

They made expeditions into the surrounding bushland. These were growing more adventurous with each passing month, even extending beyond the areas that Sassy had trod with the older men in seasons past. Maademan had warned them several times to be sure they remained within the Night Islanders' territory. If they infringed the Kuuku Y'au country to the north or the Umpila to the south, the result could be war.

Indeed, Amglo had been fascinated to watch the ritual when a pair of Kuuku Y'au tribesmen ventured into the Night Island country on a mission.

Their arrival came as no surprise. A boy had delivered a message stick to a Night Islanders' camp a day before. And when the two naked warriors arrived in the late afternoon, they made a show of laying down their arms before sitting down at least ten metres from the campsites.

They made no attempt to engage the Night Islanders in conversation and for a time simply spoke quietly to each other. Then one of the older Night Island men at his family fire spoke of the weather in a voice loud enough for the visitors to hear. At this, the visitors raised their voices slightly on the same subject. And when the Night Islander replied, they moved closer to the fireside, still without actually engaging directly.

The Night Islander women began cooking a wallaby and this was the signal, it seemed to Amglo, for a series of compliments from the visitors. These were answered by men from other fires and once again the visitors moved closer to the centre of the encampment.

And so the process continued until the original Night Islander made a joke (which passed over Amglo's head) and the visitor responded in kind. Other voices chimed in from nearby fires and in time a second Night Islander joined the discussion around the fire which continued between the four men in voices loud enough for all those interested to hear.

When it was done, and the business concluded, there was dancing from the Night Island men, and a brief appearance of women dancers, before the green boughs were placed on the fires and the smoke billowed over the campsite to ward off the mosquitoes.

Next day when the visitors were gone, Amglo learned from Sassy that the business had concerned a dugong which had entered Kuuku Y'au waters where it was captured. It had been wounded by a spearhead that had the markings of the Night Island totems. The visitors had brought a large portion of the meat with them – wrapped and buried just beyond the campsite – in payment for the gift.

'They did a good thing,' said Amglo.

'They did,' Sassy agreed. 'But they also wanted to be among the Night Island people so they could spy on you.'

Amglo was genuinely surprised. 'Why me?'

'Pama Pulpu!' A white man.

Amglo felt foolish.

'Also our women,' Sassy said.

'But they were both given wives for the night,' Amglo said.

Sassy nodded. *'Yilaamu,'* he said. Old ones.

Soon after, they prepared to leave on another of their expeditions across Night Islander territory. Sassy, who was required to provide for his betrothed, little Mimi, had caught a big saltwater barramundi the day before and delivered it to her family. Her father was tall and thin; he reminded Amglo of his mother's elder brother so 'Edmund' he became.

After breakfast they checked their *kalka*, spears, *yuli*, woomeras, *winchi'i*, fighting sticks, and since they were coming to the end of the dry and most of the creeks would be reduced to muddy waterholes, Sassy carried an *ulku*, water bag, made from a big turtle's bladder. By now Amglo was proud of his ability to make fire and took his firesticks in an old dillybag that Marie had kindly given him. They set out in the late morning and headed west through the open acacia country. Sassy's dingo trailed behind.

Just before leaving they had made 'totem talk' and Amglo was pleased – but no longer surprised – when he spotted a *tinta* on the thin branch of a tree just above his head. '*Bonjour,*' he whispered before catching himself and seeking the local words . . . '*Wulpayna!*' Happy days!

Soon they were in the more shadowed land of rainforest where the trees grew taller seeking the sun and the great ferns shivered their fronds in the light breeze that found its way into the darkening forest. He was aware of the silence. It was different from the silence of the sea, the beach or the open country. It was the hush of nature where invisible spirits abounded and from their secret places listened for the footfall of strangers. It was the silence demanded by the *wingirii*, the sorcerer, whose spirit never rested in its search for a body to make mischief.

The boys spoke in whispers. Amglo fell in behind his companion who knew the painful leaves and thistles to be avoided or held back using his fighting stick until Amglo passed. And though it was strictly against the law, Sassy wanted to show him his own sacred place and they walked at a good pace as the sun made occasional bright patterns in the gloom. Suddenly, Sassy stopped. He held up his arm for quiet then crouched so Amglo could see ahead. There, not more than thirty metres away in a tiny patch of sunlight, was a cassowary.

'*Kutini,*' Sassy said.

Amglo stared. It was a magnificent splash of colour. With its upright neck the bird stood as tall as himself and on its head was a pointed, golden crown. Its dark feathers seemed to shimmer in the circle of sunlight. Its neck was an iridescent blue, with red mottles at its base. It raised one three-toed foot, stretched its neck and turned its head to face them. It seemed quite unafraid and as it lowered its foot, Sassy quietly backed away. Amglo followed suit and from behind a big tree they both heard the deep booming sound of its call. Then came a crashing of twigs and undergrowth and when they looked again it was gone.

Until then, Amglo had only seen the cassowary chicks that had made their entrance into the world from the eggs stolen from nests. They stayed close to the families that raised them until they were big enough to eat. The idea that they had missed a great chance for a kill came and went through Amglo's mind and Sassy seemed to feel the same. '*Yilaamu,*' he said. '*Thampin.*' An old one. Not a good idea. Amglo knew that one blow from that bird's powerful foot could break a man's leg.

They continued down a slight slope between the trees until they came to a tiny clearing where a rock had become entangled in the roots of an ancient tree. Sassy rubbed his hands into his armpits then spread the moisture from them over his face. 'This is my place,' he said. He pointed to the base of the rock. That was where his mother had buried the placenta, *puuya,* of his birth. It would always be his place, he said softly, and he was pleased to share it with his friend whose own special place must be far away.

Amglo fought back the tears that started into his eyes.

They sat together in the silence until the mosquitoes and other insects found them.

More walking took them to a pool of fresh water, *maama mitha,* but because it was very muddy they drank sparingly from the water bag instead. Then Sassy walked around the perimeter of the pool, his head bent as he stared into the bank and the water's

edge, his spear poised. Amglo followed just behind his friend and
was the first to spot a movement in the water – a trail of silver
bubbles breaking the surface. He pointed and Sassy laid down
his spear and knelt on the bank; then in a swift movement he
dropped to the ground, his arm shot out, plunging his hand into
the water and returning with a small freshwater turtle, *ulkiichi*.

He grinned up at Amglo who just then spotted a second slight
swirl on the surface and this time he fell to his knees and made
to grab it. But in his haste Amglo overbalanced and splashed
into the pool. Nevertheless, he had secured his quarry – another
bigger *ulkiichi* – which immediately bit him on the tender flesh
between thumb and forefinger.

'*Merde!*' he cried, and flung the turtle on to the bank. By
now he was standing in a metre of water and Sassy was alarmed.
'*Punthana!*' Come out!

Amglo struggled to understand the order. But when Sassy
followed with '*Paltachi!*' he knew immediately – that meant
freshwater crocodile. He made it to the bank in very short order.
'*Wantuna?*' he asked. Where?

Sassy laughed. '*Nga'a.*' Somewhere in there.

They retired to a shady spot well back from the pool where
Amglo showed his newfound expertise in fire making and soon
the turtles were providing an appetising meal for the travellers.
Afterwards they dozed in the shade as the dingo – which still
treated Amglo with suspicion – finished the scraps of their meal.
The temperature rose and the silence of the bush was broken only
by the cicadas, and the occasional squeal of a black cockatoo or
the mournful cry of a crow.

In the afternoon they resumed their walkabout, reaching the
foothills of the mountains before turning south. As they made
the turn, Sassy said they would soon find a creek streaming out
of the mountains. It marked the boundary of Umpila country.
But in the turn Amglo noticed a movement on a tree to his left

some forty metres away. He touched Sassy's arm to halt him and stared at the tree. Sassy nodded. It was a big goanna, *wali,* which had flattened itself against the trunk. And the great lizard was suddenly aware of them.

Moving carefully and without haste, the boys each fitted a spear into their woomeras then, using only hand signals, they parted so that each could approach the tree from different sides. The goanna followed their movements. The tension rose in Amglo's breast as he approached. He had practised his spearing until his arm and shoulder ached and he'd been forced to sleep on his other side. But now would be the test of all that hard work.

Sassy was positioned on the other side and Amglo raised spear and woomera to his shoulder and took careful aim. But just as he launched it, the nervous goanna spun around and started down the tree trunk. Amglo's spear glanced off the trunk just where the goanna had been milliseconds before. It was a perfect shot, except that the target had moved.

Now, as the goanna reached the ground, Sassy appeared on the left of the tree, his dingo on the right, and the goanna turned and raced at full speed at Amglo, its mouth open and tongue licking the air as it loomed towards him. Amglo stood his ground. At the last second the reptile swerved to one side and that gave Amglo his chance. He ran at it with his fighting stick raised and smashed it down on the goanna's back just behind his head. It rolled over and a raw hissing sound came from its throat as it tried to raise itself to strike. But Amglo was too quick, a second and then a third smack with the stick and the creature moved no more.

Amglo's chest was heaving with the effort and the killing as Sassy reached him. He was grinning. '*Mini-mini,*' he said. Very good.

That night they feasted on the goanna and when they were done the dingo appeared for his share. When he was finished, he padded across to where Amglo was reclining against the trunk of a *thanka* tree. He lay down beside his outstretched leg.

Sassy noticed. '*Aathi-aathi,*' he said. Friends.

Amglo smiled quietly to himself. It was a good feeling. *Mini-mini.*

Next morning they continued to the south where Sassy was sure the big creek could be found. It was important for Amglo to know the limits of their country. For his part, Amglo was happy to keep going as long as possible. Back at the campsites, life with the clan was never simple. The language seemed to come from all sides. And the relationships between the people were so complex and confusing that he was continually making mistakes that made him appear foolish.

But the most unsettling part of the Night Islander world was the continual bickering, squabbling and physical fighting that often followed from the arguments. The women were just as bad as the men and it was not hard to see why. Almost every man had at least two wives, and usually one was much older than the other. The result was jealousy and accusations of favouritism that often erupted into physical blows. Indeed, there were times when the man demanded that the women stop their sniping and settle the matter with combat.

They were strong, athletic figures and even the older women could strike a fearsome blow. And when they set to with their yamsticks, blood would flow. Often the man had to intervene before one or other was mortally wounded.

The men's arguments were equally aggressive and often involved some dispute over a real or imagined insult, or the breaking of some cultural law or custom. Moreover, for a people who lived from nature's bounty of land and sea, the few possessions they acquired were as valuable as a pirate's treasure. And they were defended just as fiercely.

The evenings were crowded with activity. It seemed at times that the dancing and singing were nightly affairs, each with some meaning that Amglo grasped only vaguely and with no real appreciation of its importance – be it in memory of some lost relative, a fine hunt, a changing of the seasons or an act of devotion to one or other of the godlike creatures, the *yilami*, of the Storytime.

It was a relief to leave all that behind and roam through the wonder of a natural world where the *tinta* flashed its red and green apparel through the dappled shade and a friend was on hand to share the adventures and the confidences. In the evenings around their fire, they could talk more freely about their favourite subjects – not least the women and girls of the tribe and the urges of nature that come to all young men, particularly one like Amglo who, in another life, had already tasted the special pleasures to be found with the opposite sex.

Their talks were nothing like the endless boastings of the sailors he'd mixed with in that other life. Sassy had so many different connections within the clan that the law prevented him from even discussing the possibilities with many of the females. But that didn't stop Amglo.

In the early days after his acceptance into the clan, his nakedness had made his attraction to some of the young women embarrassingly obvious. And the laughter it produced had his ears burning with shame. But he soon found that his person adjusted to this new way of seeing the human body and to his great relief he was able to control the rising of his *uulngu*, at least in the company of others. Alone at night was a different matter. When the visions of flashing eyes from some of the more attractive girls crept into his mind as he lay face down on the warm sand of the dunes just back from the beach, he was lost. In his imagination he ravished every one of them, and sometimes several at once . . .

The scream of a white cockatoo, *kikiapa*, brought him back to the earthy present. Sassy looked fearfully about.

'*Ngaanimu?*' asked Amglo. What is it?

'*Wappa*,' he replied. Amglo needed no other explanation. He had heard tales of the *wappa* men, invisible spirits who preyed on solitary hunters. The white cockatoo was their friend.

Amglo smiled and held up two fingers. The *wappa* would never attack when there were two of them.

Sassy nodded and they made their way through an area that had been burned by the tribesmen some time ago and was now covered in a rich green layer of feed for the wallabies. But still he seemed troubled. The country was clearly unfamiliar to him. He pointed to the hill straight ahead. '*Ilka paluku*,' he said. We are on this side. He shook his head. They should be on the other side, on the north, *kungkay*.

They were near a boulder, and nearby the dingo was standing quite still, staring fixedly. Amglo walked towards it to sit while Sassy considered how best to change their course. He had almost reached it when suddenly the dingo reared back as a big snake struck at it. Amglo suddenly saw the length of it, at least two metres of copper-coloured viciousness, its head raised just above the ground as it advanced with effortless speed and the dingo retreated. Amglo threw his spear from about ten metres but it punched into the ground just beside it. The snake flung itself its entire length backwards, straight at Amglo, just as Sassy reached him.

'*Thaipan*!' he shouted. '*Waathinya*!' Run!

Amglo needed no second warning. Tales of the most vicious and deadly serpent were the stuff of campfire yarns ever since he had begun to understand the language. He instantly abandoned any thought of retrieving his spear and ran for his life. Even Sassy had trouble keeping up with him as the dingo trailed them over the open ground to the forest beyond. All three turned their heads back as they ran in a vain attempt to see whether the snake was giving chase.

Sassy was the first to stop. There was no chance that the *thaipan* would venture too far from its nest. And while the snake could cover the first ten metres in a flash, it didn't have the staying power for extended pursuit. By then they were in the fringe of the forest and the ground sloped into the thicker undergrowth that should lead them to the big creek. But Amglo could see his friend and guide was uncertain.

'*Waanthinya*,' he said. We can go home. But Sassy was determined, and they pressed on until they came to a dry creek bed.

'*Wantantu*?' Amglo asked. Which way?

They crossed to the other side.

Just as Sassy indicated they should turn left to follow the creek bed to the east and the sandbeach, a long hunting spear slammed into a tree trunk near Amglo's head. Then two more flew into the soft bank of the stony creek bed.

With a cry, both boys ran full pelt over the stones until they reached a shallow pool where Amglo slipped and fell on his side, his precious weapons and firesticks spilling into the water, just as another spear hit beside him. Sassy grabbed his outstretched hand, lifting him to his feet. No time to rescue his possessions, they ran until they were exhausted and the spears were no longer reaching them from behind.

Amglo found himself laughing at their wild escape. But Sassy's anger flared at his companion. He spoke sharply for the first time since they had met. He was not only angry, he was *yaanthankupi*, ashamed. He knew immediately what the consequences would be. The first would be Maademan's rage. But that was the least of them.

10

Queensland

In their endless quest for yet more land, the immigrants expanded to the west and north. The intrusions of Frederick Walker and his Native Police Force and explorers like William Landsborough gave promise of good grazing country. The fires of the Aboriginal people had turned big areas into savannah bounded by forest which gave cover to the hunters as they stalked their wallabies and emus.

Moreover, the government authorities were keen to establish an indisputable claim to the whole colony and to defend it against foreign – that is, French – claimants. On 9 December 1861, Governor Bowen sent a despatch to the Duke of Newcastle as Secretary of State for War and the Colonies, noting that substantial seaborne traffic was passing through Torres Strait. He suggested that from a naval and military viewpoint, a government 'station' on Cape York 'would be most valuable, and its importance is daily increasing, especially since the establishment of a French Colony and naval station at New Caledonia'.

Bowen enclosed a minute passed by the executive council declaring that the government of Queensland would be 'willing to undertake the formation and management of a station at Cape York, and to support the civil establishment there'. This, he said, was evidence of the 'liberal and reasonable' attitudes of government members and 'strong proof of their attachment to their parent state, since the station would be twelve hundred miles from Brisbane, that is further than Gibraltar is from London'.[1]

The duke, a product of Eton and Oxford like Bowen, had just returned from a visit to Canada and the United States with the Prince of Wales and was happy to accede to the governor's request. The admiralty quickly came on board and on 27 August the following year the governor, together with the Royal Navy's senior officer in the colony, Commodore William Farquharson Burnett, left Brisbane on HMS *Pioneer* to choose a site.

They reached Booby Island in Torres Strait in only thirteen days. This was where a permanent iron box was held fast to a rock. It contained letters deposited by passing ships of all nations to be conveyed to their respective addresses by succeeding vessels. Having collected and 'mailed' their own missives, the captain and crew of the *Pioneer* took their VIPs on a tour of the area, finally selecting a site at Port Albany on the island of that name facing the northern tip of the cape.

They named the station Somerset after the dukedom of the First Lord of the Admiralty, no doubt to assist Commodore Burnett's own passage up the ranks of the Royal Navy. Unhappily, it was not to be. Six months later he drowned when his ship, HMS *Orpheus*, was wrecked and sank off the west coast of New Zealand. It was carrying reinforcements and ammunition to the British soldiers in the land wars against the Maori.

Meantime, the settlers gradually pushed north from the more settled areas west of Rockhampton. And from time to time the Aboriginal owners pushed back, invariably with shocking reprisals. On 17 October 1861, for example, they attacked and killed nineteen whites at Cullin-la-Ringo station near what would become the town of Emerald. According to historian Timothy Bottoms, 'This resulted in a massive retribution where at least

370 Aboriginal people were killed. Conservatively, this equates to a ratio of nineteen Aboriginals for each of the Cullin-la-Ringo whites.'[2] Frederick Wheeler was in charge of the Native Police detachment in the area.

In the Queensland Government Parliamentary Inquiry held shortly afterwards, Wheeler was asked what he did with the bodies of the Aboriginal people he shot. He said they were left in the scrub where their people piled logs on to them and burned the bodies. He even claimed that he had seen them feasting on their dead's cooked flesh, an act the Aboriginal people would have found unthinkable.

However, in the early 1860s Commandant John Bligh directed most of Wheeler's operations to the southeast corner of the colony and plans were put forward for a new Native Police camp at the junction of the Logan and Albert rivers. The government agreed to finance it provided it cost less than £200, but the only tender received was for £300 and the plan lapsed. At the time Wheeler was having trouble recruiting and retaining his troopers and he spent an inordinate amount of effort pursuing the runaways.

Moreover, there were voices raised by graziers themselves against the depredations of the Native Police Force. In July 1860 a letter to the *North Australian,* signed 'A Squatter', had attacked the police for 'the dreadful deeds now done in the Queen's name'. The author said that their actions meant that whole neighbourhoods had become accessories in the 'cold-blooded murders' and this had debased the entire community. Another correspondent under the pseudonym 'Justice' wrote of 'that abominable feeling becoming a principle in the minds of the men of Queensland, that to kill a blackfellow in cold blood is not murder'.[3] However, it is significant that each used pseudonyms to register their protest.

By contrast, the Mortimer family of squatters in the Wide Bay district – like the Archer family of the Kilcoy area in the 1840s – were proud to make a public stand. They were strident opponents of the Native Police actions. The *paterfamilias,* John Mortimer, was a Calvinist Scot who had farmed in the United States prior to his immigration to Queensland in 1848. A decade later he and his brother Alexander were substantial landholders in the area and were running up to 16,000 sheep and 2000 cattle. They had little trouble with the Aboriginal people, though there was 'tension' between his operations and the Waka and Kabi people, particularly when they and other tribes gathered to feast on the local *bunya* nuts. Indeed, some of their neighbours believed the Aboriginals 'greatly hungered for human flesh in the Bunya season'.[4]

Nevertheless, the Mortimers employed Aboriginal shepherds on their outstations and welcomed their 'station blacks' with food, clothing and protection, while encouraging them to continue 'the fundamentals of their social behaviour and beliefs'. So, when the Native Police stationed at Yabba, less than half a day's ride from their Manumbah property, followed their standard 'dispersal' activities, the Mortimers wrote an open letter to 'The Officer in Command of the Party of Native Police who shot and wounded some Blacks on the Station of Manumbah'. They sent it as a paid advertisement to the *Brisbane Courier.*

With cutting sarcasm, they wrote: 'Sir, if in future you should take a fancy to bring your troopers upon the Station of Manumbah on a sporting excursion, we shall feel obliged if you would either bag or bury the game which you shoot, as it is far from pleasant for us to have the decomposing remains of four or five blackfellows laying unburied within a mile or two of our head station . . . As most of the blacks you left dead on our run were feeble old men, some of them apparently not less than eighty years of age, will you please inform us whether these hoary sinners are the parties chiefly engaged in spearing bullocks . . . or whether you just shoot them because the younger ones are too nimble for you.

'Besides the four or five you left dead on our run, you have wounded two of our station blacks, who have been in our employment during lambing, washing, and shearing and all other busy times for the last eight or nine years, and we have never known either of them to be charged with a crime . . . we are of the opinion that when you shoot and wound blacks in such an indiscriminate manner, you exceed your commission, and we publish this so that those who employ and pay you may have some knowledge of the way in which you perform your services.'

The letter engaged the attention of the new Premier of Queensland, Robert Herbert, who wrote to the Mortimers seeking 'more particulars and evidence of the allegations'. And though their response seems to have been lost to the proper channels, Herbert did order a 1861 parliamentary inquiry; the result, once again, fully supported the Native Police.

Other squatters such as Charles Dutton, who also employed Aboriginal people on his property, joined the protest against the force's savagery in applying 'powers which usurp the functions of magistrate, jury and judge. The exercise of these powers,' he wrote, 'is too clearly and distinctly claimed for them by the Executive, and acted upon with that measure of justice which too surely follows the possession of irresponsible power of life and death.' Herbert was unmoved. His 'inquiry', he asserted, had answered all complaints.

At only twenty-eight, the premier lived the life of a lordly overseer whose time in the colony was merely a prologue to a career in Whitehall. His living arrangements were a source of eager gossip behind the ladies' fans in Brisbane's colonial drawing rooms. He had formed a relationship with John Bramston with whom he had shared rooms at Oxford and who had followed him to Queensland. Herbert appointed him attorney-general and they set up a farm together which they named 'Herston', a combination

of their two names. It remains today as the name of the Brisbane
suburb that incorporates the land on which they farmed.

Herbert was proud of his record of legislation passed, but
made no attempt to control the ravages of settlers and police
directed towards the Aboriginal people. In his letters home to
his family in England, he was much more concerned with his
domestic and sporting life:

'We have had capital races and Herston has been most
triumphant,' he told his sister, 'my old favourite "Grasshopper"
having won the chief race in great style, ridden by Algernon [his
cousin on his mother's side], and Bramston on his "Doubtful"
having come in second As we trained our horses quietly at home,
nobody believed we should do well.

'Seeing the eight horses go by the stand, all in new and very
pretty colours, created intense excitement among the ladies etc.
It was a very pretty sight. There was immense cheering for
"Grasshopper". Algernon of course rode him exceedingly well.

'The cup is really a handsome one, with a cover, making a
considerable show on a table or sideboard . . .

'We have lately been catching quantities of magnificent prawns
in the creek which surrounds Herston,' he wrote, 'splendid large
fellows 4 or 5 inches long, and most delicate in flavour . . . One
of my imported fowls got a prize at the show . . . The peacocks
cause us some anxiety by roaming. They fly across the river and
remain absent for a whole day. I fear the blackfellows or some
white savages will get hold of them.'[5]

Herbert's civil service career would eventually be crowned
with a knighthood and the post of Permanent Under-Secretary
of State for the Colonies.

I I

Amglo

When Sassy and Amglo returned to the Night Islanders' encampment on the fringe of the sandbeach, they had no choice but to
report their encounter with the Umpila tribesmen to Maademan.
He immediately called the other elders — Yannick's father, who
Amglo had named 'Yann'; the regal, white-haired 'Louis'; and
the clan's finest dugong hunter, the tall, thin 'Edmund'.

They sat in a circle, listening in silence as Sassy described
their route and the mistake he had made when apparently
missing the boundary creek to the Umpila country. Amglo could
follow the train of Sassy's story but when the men questioned him
and he responded, the speed of their talking and some unfamiliar
words confused him, so he remained silent.

Then the elders sent the boys away while they discussed their
punishment. Sassy feared that he would receive at least a spear in
the upper leg and as the elders' voices were raised, they became
afraid that something even worse was being decided. However,
Maademan seemed to have the last word and as the meeting
broke up he headed to where the boys were sitting beneath a
paperbark tree. He gestured for them to rise and as they did he
attacked them both with open-handed slaps, delivered with such

force that both boys were knocked to the ground; and when they rose they were slapped down again.

For a second Amglo was consumed by a blazing rage but any thought of retaliation disappeared as the strength of his mentor overwhelmed him and his head spun with the blows. Sassy too submitted without the slightest response as blood spurted from his nose and he staggered back against the paperbark tree.

Then it was over. In all, the beating took no more than two or three minutes but Amglo was deeply bruised in both his head and chest. As Maademan left them with a final angry shout, both boys made their painful way across the sand to the soothing waters of the sea where they immersed themselves and let the salt water begin the process of recovery. Finally, Sassy spoke. *'Pa'an kanyu,'* he said. I was stupid.

Amglo was silent. He had never suffered such a beating before. The only time Maademan had struck him was when he had eaten a piece of dugong meat before he was entitled to partake of the creature that played such a big part in the customs of the Night Islanders. But that had been no more than a solid cuff about the ears. Now he resolved that he would never again be beaten, not by Maademan, and not by any other of his clan.

But there was at least one saving grace: they had escaped the pain of a spear in the leg. He had seen it applied to one other – a man he called 'Ivo' after the drunken sailor who spent his days cadging drinks on the quay of Saint-Gilles. This Ivo was not a drunkard; the people of his clan had no hard liquor, much less the Bordeaux wine that had brought Narcisse across the seas. But he had the same squinty eyes and the same light fingers as his French counterpart when the chance arose to steal from his friends and acquaintances.

Ivo had trembled from head to toe when brought forth to take his punishment. And he had howled like a dingo when the barb found its mark. His wife had taken him away and dressed the wound with herbs, and the whole clan heard his plaintive cries.

But Amglo had blessed his good fortune too soon. The beating he had endured was only part of the punishment meted out by the elders. Later that night Sassy told him the rest of it. If the Umpila people made foolish demands on the Night Islanders as payback for their trespass, there would be a big fight.

And if that happened, Amglo and Sassy would be in the Night Islanders' front line in the battle, the place where the spears of the enemy came flying hard and fast. Meanwhile, it had been decided that the time had come for both boys to begin their initiation, to become warriors fit to stand in the centre of their ranks when the fighting commenced.

Amglo was caught in a roiling mix of emotions. Talk of initiation had filled his ears almost from the time he joined the clan. He was at the right age for it and so was Sassy. Indeed, it seemed that Sassy had been held back from that all-important step until Amglo himself had acquired the skills with the *kalka, yuli* and *winchi'i* so they could take the initiation rituals together.

Word spread instantly through the extended clan and that evening, with Sassy sitting around his family fire, Amglo found himself alone until the dark, round figure of Bruno loomed out of the darkness.

He sat with Amglo in the flickering light and shade of the campfires. They spoke in a mixture of word and gesture, but as with Sassy, so close was their connection that the messages they conveyed were just as clear as if they had been talking together from the womb. And they were comfortable with the silences between their talking.

'Are you better?' asked Bruno.

'I am.'

'I hear that you begin the initiation.'

Amglo said, 'Tomorrow we go to the single man's camp.'

Bruno smiled in the darkness. 'The women are preparing the dance of farewell to their sons.'

'*Wantawantalu?*' How many?

'You, Sassy and three more.'

Even as they spoke, the fires of the campsite were growing stronger. The drums had started their rhythmic beat beneath the gnarled fingers of the sing man. The women were beginning their special dance, each holding the nipples of her breasts as a symbol of her motherhood. As they danced, they sang of the departure of the boy child, their fears and their pride as the lost boys faced the next great step in their lives. They sang to the *yilami* and to a new figure that Amglo had only heard about in whispers, something that filled their hearts with fear. They could not speak its name because they were women, but their fear was carried by the spirit to Amglo.

Bruno sensed the fear in his friend's manner. He reached across the space between them and placed his hand on Amglo's shoulder. '*Markuntha,*' he said. You are strong. '*Winnini.*' Have no fear.

Amglo took Bruno's hand in his. And so they sat until the sing man, the dancers and the drums fell silent.

That night, somewhat to his surprise, Amglo slept a dreamless sleep. But next morning as the sun rose over a glassy sea, he embarked on a journey that at times was made of the stuff of nightmare. There were moments when he truly believed he had entered another world, a fearful place of monsters who appeared as if by magic from the surrounding rocks and trees.

Perhaps they *were* the rocks and trees that had taken animal form. Perhaps he had descended into the spirit world itself where the sharp fingers of fear stole beneath his skin, drove through his flesh to the organs within and grasped the heart, the liver, the lungs and squeezed until they screamed as one, screamed like the white cockatoo, the herald of death, screamed and echoed in the darkness.

Amglo would endure it. And it would be the most meaningful event in all his life. Forever after he would be in its thrall.

Until this time, he had been carried along like a punt with no keel, a slave to the currents beyond his control. Afterward, he would be remade. He was his own keel, his own compass, and he travelled in a boat of his own making.[1]

* * *

It began in the heat of midday as the initiates left the encampment and walked at a steady pace the several kilometres to the single men's camp – an oval-shaped clearing in the paperbark forest. This was where they would live while the men of knowledge made preparations at the *nartji kintja* – the bora ground – deep in the jungle.

By now it was coming to the end of the long dry period; the southeast wind had blown itself out and there was a dead calm. It was the time the people called the *Okainta* and in the afternoon a breeze from the northwest might blow and provide a welcome relief from the heat and the insects. Amglo, Sassy and another boy whose wide eyes and innocent face caused Amglo to name him 'Gabriel', were put in the charge of 'Louis' whose tribal name was Chilpu, the old man, with his air of great dignity and knowledge.

Amglo noticed that Baroway was also among the elders and had taken charge of two younger boys. But neither made a sign of recognition. All Amglo's attention was directed to Chilpu who spoke slowly to be sure that he understood every word.

They sat in a tight circle and the stories he told were of the great *Yilamo* and of the adventures among the ancient spirit men. Night Island itself – *thathi maana* – had once been a hill or headland, *ilka*, on the sandbeach, he told them. It was the home

of Kanidji, a great hunter of the dugong; and the people praised
him for his strength and skill. But their praise made him proud
and in time he became so selfish that he refused to share the
meat of the dugong with the paddlers of his canoe and the men
of the clan who helped him to build his canoe. So they set out
in their canoes without him. But he chased them and threw his
harpoon so far and so well that he captured all the dugong in
the sea. And they returned empty-handed.

When the spirits learned of his selfishness, they took action.
They moved his headland out into the sea, far from his clan. And
since there were no trees on the island to make canoes or the
rope for his harpoon, Kanitji could no longer hunt the dugong.
He roared his anger through the night. So loud were his cries
that the people of the sandbeach could hear him, and so they
called it Night Island.

In the silence that followed, Chilpu encouraged the boys
to speak of the story; and while Sassy spoke, Amglo remained
silent. The story said so much about the nature of the clan and
the way that sharing was an integral part of their lives. But it
was not for him to speak; it was a time for listening and as other
stories followed, with the boys encouraged to speak and even
debate the meanings, Amglo listened and learned of the myths
and of the law that they lived by.

At night they feasted on wallaby and emu and fish that were
caught by a team of older men, led by Maademan. And in the
days that followed Amglo felt himself becoming part of the stories
and the songs and the clan itself.

The *Pama* belong to the land, he learned; they are part of it
just as it is part of them. In spirit they are one; and in each child
of the clan there is a special spirit place that lives within. The
Pama and the clan are one with the land.

As he listened it was almost as though the person that was
Amglo was slowly losing its boundaries, its *individualité*, and being

Échouage du *Saint-Paul* à l'île Rossell. — Dessin d'Hadamard.

NAUFRAGE ET SCÈNES D'ANTHROPOPHAGIE A L'ÎLE ROSSELL,

DANS L'ARCHIPEL DE LA LOUISIADE (MÉLANÉSIE),

RÉCIT DE M. V. DE ROCHAS.

1858. — TEXTE ET DESSINS INÉDITS[1].

Naufrage du trois-mâts *le Saint-Paul*. — L'îlot du Refuge. — Les naufragés sont attaqués par les indigènes de l'île Rossell. Séparation.

Au mois de décembre 1858, sept naufragés français recueillis par le schooner anglais *Prince-of-Danemark* arrivaient à Port-de-France, dans la Nouvelle-Calédonie[2]. Le chef de ces infortunés, le capitaine P..., se présenta devant les autorités de la colonie, où je me trouvais alors, et leur fit un rapport verbal dont voici le résumé.

1. L'un de nos dessinateurs, M. Hadamard, s'est rendu à Brest, où réside actuellement M. de Rochas, et c'est avec le croquis et d'après les conseils du voyageur lui-même qu'il a pu dessiner les scènes dont cette livraison est illustrée.
2. Voy. sur la Nouvelle-Calédonie notre 61e livraison, t. III, p. 129, et la vue de Port-de-France, t. IV, p. 84.

IV. — 84e LIV.

Le capitaine P.... était parti dans le courant du mois de juillet précédent de Hong-Kong (Chine), sur le trois-mâts *le Saint-Paul*, avec vingt hommes d'équipage et trois cent dix-sept passagers chinois, engagés pour l'exploitation des mines d'or d'Australie. Longtemps contrarié par les calmes et menacé de la disette par la prolongation anomale de la traversée, il s'était décidé à s'écarter de la route ordinaire, qui lui aurait fait doubler les îles Salomon, pour en prendre une qui devait l'amener plus promptement à Sydney, son port de destination, et qui l'obligeait à passer entre ces dernières îles et l'archipel de la Louisiade.

6

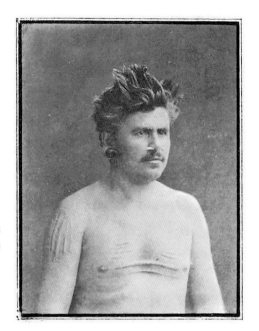

Photograph of Narcisse displaying his cicatrices and piercings from his time with the Uutaalnganu people.
From *Dix-sept ans chez les sauvages*, by Constant Merland, E. Dentu, Paris, 1876.

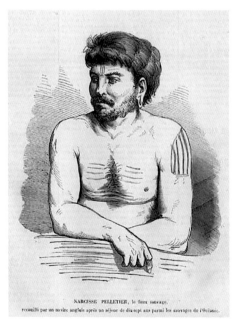

NARCISSE PELLETIER, le faux sauvage,
recueilli par un navire anglais après un séjour de dix-sept ans parmi les sauvages de l'Océanie.

This sketch of Narcisse appeared in the French newspaper *Journal Illustré*, with the caption 'the false savage', 8 August 1875. Curiously, his scars seem to have been drawn on the wrong arm.

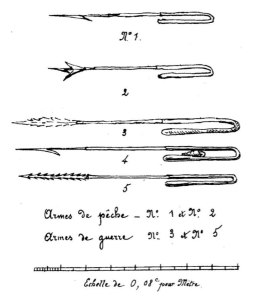

Armes en bois.

N° 1.

2

3

4

5

Armes de pêche — N° 1 et N° 2

Armes de guerre N° 3 et N° 5

Echelle de 0, 08^c pour Mètre.

Illustrations of the wooden weapons Narcisse used while living with the Uutaalnganu people. The first two would have been used for fishing, and the third and fourth for battle.

From the appendix of Merland's *Dix-sept ans chez les sauvages*.

First Lieutenant George Murray (second from left, back row) and his detachment of Native Mounted Police, 1864. Queensland Police Museum.

LA CAPTURE DE NARCISSE PELLETIER
Le jeune Français qui a passé 18 années au milieu des Sauvages de l'Australie

'The Capture of Narcisse Pelletier', illustration published in the *Journal Illustré*, 8 August 1875.

An undated photograph of Narcisse in Western clothes, after his capture. Only his earlobe hints at his time with the Uutaalnganu people. State Library of Queensland.

I

Somerset Cape York

13 May 1875

papa nanan gene seue pap nore gese
sui vivan narcise getente obore du saint
paule de boredeuf gave fee novorage
dans lur le roce du suovage de tele
les ginoi dans lile reter le onoroire
tue turoi ge suis vemire dans un
petite batou dans une ille des sovage
y gquis garcee de lau a boire le capitene
paretire dans le petite baroue ge carece
de leau dans les boua ge ve rate dans
boiex ge vais leure les sovage tuoi
viai sur sa cote venire qui nave
trove le souvage donore a boire et
onange in apa tuee ge donne la
nait in apa donne du nale ge suis
retait dans le bois bien lentain
ge tete perecee xnore gave vee o
garant fant et garant boire gavee
becoup de nale

Narcisse's letter back to his family in Saint-Gilles-Sur-Vie, written at Somerset, Cape York, 13 May 1875. Facsimile published in the appendix of Merland's *Dix-sept ans chez les sauvages.*

II

Narcisse Pierre Pelletier
le 11 juillette 1875

Mon cher Père et Ma chère mère
l manspère, je vas iesie une autre
fois. Je vous enbrase De tout Mon
cœur, ce vous ête vivant. Je suis arriver
nominé le consule De syphnay Ma
novez, je suis A bord suivir navire
se quére, ge partirait Dans un mois
bord Du autre navire que st seni
ly à trois jours ge e a Porte Bien
fige toujour mal à la gambe
Droits. Il y a Bien longtemps que gai
mal, gairait et Bien De la misère
vec eux, et mon en Personne la
gambie. Mais seulement je me
Porte Bien.
Je vous dit Bonjour
Narcisse Pierre Pelletier

III

Mon cher père et ma chère mère et mes chère frère
Je vous enbrasse de tout mon cœur ge vous iesie De mes
Nouvelles, ge me porte bien et Nous sommes arriver à
Rzogemain le 14 octobre. Je ne suis pas bien à bord.
Ivec les maitre, ge mange avec les matelots à la racien
Il n'ont pas piéte de moi De la soufrance que gai
Eut De puis le temps que gai resté avec ces sauvages.
Mais ge suis pas mal avec les matelots. il y à 2
Mois que nous étion partit de Noumea.
Narcisse Pierre Pelletier Naufragé

Two later letters to his family – from Noumea on 11 July 1875 and Rio de Janeiro in October, respectively. By then Narcisse's handwriting was decorated with extravagant curlicues, even if his French grammar and punctuation still needed work. Facsimiles published in the appendix of Merland's *Dix-sept ans chez les sauvages*.

French composer, critic and musicologist Edouard Garnier transcribed Uutaalnganu songs sung by Narcisse and set them to music. Published in the appendix of Merland's *Dix-sept ans chez les sauvages*.

Côte de St-Nazaire - Phare de l'Aiguillon   Collection A. Thuret, Nantes

The isolated Phare de l'Aiguillon, ten kilometres from Saint-Nazaire, where
Narcisse worked as the lighthouse keeper.

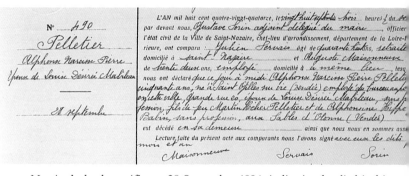

Narcisse's death certificate, 28 September 1894, indicating he died in his
house and at the time was employed as a clerk at the port office. Hôtel de
Ville records office, Saint-Nazaire.

absorbed into something larger and more encompassing. He felt uplifted and comforted at the same time. The feeling lasted all through the days until the time was right. Then the elders led them much deeper into the forest where, in the afternoon light, they came upon a cleared area, perhaps fifteen metres across, the *nartji kintja*, the bora ground, where no woman would ever venture on pain of death.

Facing them was a structure of carefully joined timber boughs roped and covered with the great flat leaves of *kali'i*, the fan palm. This was the house of the Crocodile Hero, I'wai Tjilbo, the clan's deepest secrets, and behind it were seated the men, their faces and bodies made wild and terrifying in white and yellow clay markings, who would be their guides in the approaching ordeal.

Even as they watched, the figures disappeared into the darkness of the forest and the first of many drums could be heard in sonorous rhythm from that primeval place. These drums, Amglo saw, were very different from those the sing man used in the evening dances, which were made from polished timber in the shape of an elongated hourglass. These were hollow tree trunks only ten centimetres wide with lizard skin stretched over one end and at the other the carved and painted open jaws of a crocodile.

Once they entered the bora, the initiates were held to a fierce discipline. They must remain completely silent. Certain foods were denied them and they must not even touch the food given them with their hands; instead they must use the bone of a wallaby, a kangaroo or a cassowary they received from the masters. These were yellow with age and polished with use.

They must not touch their own bodies to scratch or sooth the insect bites. Instead they were issued with special sticks made from *yungku,* the ironwood tree. They could not move unless with permission. They could not hunt as they had done each day of their short lives, unless accompanied and controlled by one of the old men.

Each one of the strictures was painful but together they were torture. And for the first time in his life Amglo made no protest. During the day, the old men gathered among them in little groups to talk or listen to 'sings' about I'wai Tjilbo, the Venerable One. But once the sun set and the breeze from the sea reached the bora, one or more masked figures would emerge from the jungle fringe to dance. Then the old men – in Amglo's case Chilpu himself – would hold the boys from behind, covering their eyes as the dancers came ever closer and the drumming rose in speed and volume.

When they opened their hands, the boys saw that the masks covered not just their faces but their heads in rounded bark and their whole bodies in black trailing fronds as they advanced in measured steps. And when they removed the upper mask they grimaced to terrify the boys. The drums reached a crescendo; and there was an unearthly scream. In the stunned and fearful silence that followed, the old men told the boys the story of the figure in the mask; and as they did so they rubbed the sweat from their armpits over the faces and shoulders of their charges.

So the days and nights followed in growing intensity until the final night, when the figure of I'wai Tjilbo himself entered the bora. His was by far the most elaborate of all the masks, for in addition to the rounded tree bark rising from his shoulders to cover his head, nine 'branches' made from spears, decorated with feathers along their length, extended from the crown more than a metre in every direction. And where his mouth might have been was the vividly painted timber replica, bristling with teeth, of the crocodile's open jaws.

Slowly he danced on to the bora and as the drums made sound patterns in the humid night that set Amglo's pulses racing, the old men and the young men began to chant the name of I'wai Tjilbo like the booming sound of the cassowary but with younger voices giving urgency and vigour to the lauding of the hero, and to the deadly danger of his lust for prey.

No one among the newly initiated slept that night. When they gathered themselves next morning for the long walk back to the Night Island encampment, not one was the same as he had been when they left it. And none would ever know how many days and nights they had spent there.

There was, however, one final ritual to complete the initiation. Each of the boys would have his right front tooth removed, except for those who favoured the left hand. They would sacrifice the left tooth. All but one knew and welcomed this outward sign of elevation to manhood; and all but one volunteered his mouth to Baroway who stood with the stone instrument of evulsion in his right hand. All but Amglo. He refused. He stared at Baroway, his mouth clamped shut, and refused.

Baroway was not happy. He knew that if Amglo died, then in the Afterworld he could drink only bad water. This was a terrible fate. But when he continued to refuse, Baroway relented. Since Amglo had no mother among the *Pama* people, perhaps it did not apply.

Amglo was relieved. He welcomed the slit to the earlobes with the razor-sharp incision of a shell blade and the cuts plugged with the first of the smooth wooden ornaments that would adorn him. And in the days and months ahead he would happily accept the bodily markings of his people – the cicatrices across his chest, raised with painful squeezing as they healed, to mark his marriages and his children; and the vertical scars on his upper right arm that numbered his enemies slain in battle.

He was pleased and proud of all things that would confirm his place in the tribe and his status among his people. For now he was a man, a Night Island, Uutaalnganu, man. His new life could now begin in earnest.

PART
Five

12

Queensland

In the 1860s Bowen's government proceeded with its plans to establish a station at Somerset and its claim to Cape York. It raised a float of £5000 from the treasury and accepted a £7000 contribution from the British government. It selected a troop of twenty-five marines to protect the establishment from the expected Aboriginal attacks and cast about for a Government Resident and Police Magistrate to take charge of the station.

The first choice was William Wiseman, the Commissioner of Crown Lands for Leichhardt since 1855. But he withdrew, preferring the relative safety of his Rockhampton base to the hazards of the pioneer. Premier Herbert and his Attorney-General Bramston took personal responsibility for the vetting and in 1863, after consultation with Governor Bowen, they settled upon John Jardine, at the time the police magistrate at Rockhampton.

Jardine was a cousin of the infamous William Jardine of Jardine Matheson, the Hong Kong Trading House that took a leading role in the opium trade with China in the first half of the nineteenth century. Both men were born in Scotland's Dumfriesshire. John's father, Sir Alexander, acceded to the family baronetcy but, as the fourth son, John was destined for the army and in 1835, aged twenty-eight, he joined the Dragoons.

Four years later Jardine sold his commission as a captain and sailed for Sydney with his wife, Elizabeth. After several unsuccessful attempts at farming, they settled near Wellington where again he took up land. Once more he was markedly unsuccessful as a grazier and by 1848 was forced to declare himself 'insolvent'. He used his connections to secure the post of Commissioner for Crown Lands in the mid-west of New South Wales. But ten years later government retrenchment left him with ten dependent children and no occupation.

The Queensland government offered Jardine a lifeline with his appointment as police magistrate and gold commissioner in Rockhampton. He arrived with Elizabeth and six of their children in January 1859. Two years later he was appointed captain of the Rockhampton volunteer company of the Queensland Rifle Brigade and on New Year's Day, 1861, he was promoted to police magistrate of Rockhampton and Gladstone.

Rockhampton had been developing rapidly as a steady stream of settlers spread out west and north of it. And in November that year the arrival of immigrant ships brought British employees for 'householders, station owners and others on the lookout for servants, while not a few men wished to choose wives from among the female passengers'.[1]

A young English adventurer, Edward B. Kennedy, was also in Rockhampton at the time and noted the arrival of the migrants. '[They were] chiefly the refuse and scum of London and the manufacturing towns,' he wrote. 'They landed on Queensland shores totally devoid of both capital and character. I think I saw the biggest lot of roughs landed in a port north of Brisbane I had ever seen in my life, trooping out of a ship. They were no sooner ashore that they formed rings in the one street of the township and stripped to fight; whilst in the bars of the settlement they relieved the inhabitants of their watches and money.'[2]

For Jardine the new appointment was an opportunity to exercise full authority and control of a government station and perhaps replenish the family fortune. Moreover, Governor Bowen himself warmly approved the appointment of 'a member of a Scottish family, brother to Sir William Jardine', who by then had inherited the baronetcy from his late father Sir Alexander.[3]

Bowen noted that the family was 'well known for its devotion to scientific pursuits' and hoped that Jardine would 'prove the means of adding largely to our knowledge of the Flora and Fauna of North Eastern Australia'. He told the Colonial Office that he'd written to Jardine, 'impressing upon him the necessity of treating the Aborigines with kindness and humanity . . . I have directed Mr Jardine to endeavour to make them comprehend, as clearly as possible, that they are British Subjects, and that, as such, they will be protected by the Government as long as they remain peaceable and well disposed.'

By then the country just south of the Gulf of Carpentaria – though not Cape York itself – was experiencing a landrush from both sea and land. The Crown Commissioner for Kennedy, George Dalrymple, had taken an expedition into the area from the Upper Burdekin in 1859 and reported good grazing country. Four years later, the Bowen–Herbert government had approved more than 30,000 square miles (7.7 million hectares) for settlement.

Premier Herbert himself joined the rush as a 'sleeping partner' with his wealthy and well-connected friends, Arthur and Walter Scott, 'believing that they would be able to sell parts of it later at a profit to the sons of wealthy English friends'. As it happened, the scheme was a disastrous failure, though it was not abandoned for more than thirty years.[4]

William Landsborough promoted the area, including at a public meeting of 3000 potential investors in Melbourne where he said he 'had never seen better country for stock than he found on the shores of the Gulf of Carpentaria'.[5] By 1863 settlers had worn a stock route from the headwaters of the Cape River – which opened to the sea at Innisfail – to the Flinders River in the gulf. According to the pioneer pastoralist Edward Palmer, 'The settlers were like an advancing army, confident in their numbers and strength; and so they advanced into the unknown land, and left the rest to fortune.'

The newcomers were accompanied by a Native Police detachment of eleven troopers under Lieutenant John Williams, and the combined forces clashed with a determined resistance from the Aboriginal defenders. They were also prey to outbreaks of yellow fever. Indeed, the population centre of Burketown was so hard hit that the government transferred its establishment off shore to Sweer's Island in the southeast corner of the gulf. Jardine told Governor Bowen that Somerset might also be used as a 'sanitorium' for the victims of the outbreak.

A further rush was triggered by J.G. Macdonald's private explorations from his station, Carpentaria Downs, which he established in 1863 and which was then one of the most northerly cattle properties. Settlers pushed out as far as the Barkly Tableland which Landsborough had discovered only three years previously. By now the wave of pastoral expansion – accompanied by the Native Police enforcers – had surged to all parts of North Queensland except Cape York Peninsula.

13

Amglo

The men were outraged on their return from the initiation ceremony to discover that a raiding party from the Umpila had stolen two women, one of whom was Sassy's betrothed, the little Mimi. Angry shouts echoed around the encampment. Threats and curses rent the air; the women wailed and some of the children began to cry. Sassy was furious. Mimi was not only his connection to the family led by a respected elder, but for two years he had supplied her wants as his future wife. He even had a certain affection for her.

The other captive was an older girl who Amglo had found attractive but who was promised to another. But he was no less enraged by her capture, and appalled that he and Sassy had caused the raid. For this was clearly payback for their trespass.

However, Amglo heard no sounds of anger or accusation towards Sassy and himself – indeed, the other men seemed to welcome the chance to parade their fighting prowess and to exact revenge on their enemies. And the women were just as eager to enter the fray.

Once the initial threats and shouting died away, they began preparations for a tribal assault. The men brought out their fighting sticks which came in several shapes, the most common being polished hardwood hooked at one end and with a grip on the other that fitted neatly into the hand. The fighting boomerangs, *kunkamu*, were not designed to return but to slice through the air at throwing height. Their spears came in several lengths but all were sharpened and barbed, while the woomeras that propelled them in the hunt were mostly used as shields in battle.

Between the tribes there was an exchange of message sticks in the days before the fight, while the men took the time to visit their spirit places and to gather the clay they would use to paint their bodies on the morning of the clash. Amglo was no less involved than the rest, but unlike the others he had never seen a fight between people with deadly weapons, let alone been part of it. Even Sassy in his young life had been on the fringes of three or four raging battles. And he was so lusting for the coming fight that Amglo could get no sense from him.

Only Bruno seemed able to talk quietly about the *ngaachi,* battle, and the prospect of death or injury. As they rested from the midday heat in the shade of a *thanka* tree, Bruno caught his mood. 'You did not have battles in your life before Night Island,' he said.

'On the great canoe,' Amglo replied, 'one man cut me.'

'But your elders went to battle when other tribes took your women.'

'There were many great canoes,' Amglo said. 'And the men fought great battles. Many were killed.'

Bruno patted his friend on the shoulder. 'You will not die in this battle, Amglo. You are too fast, too clever,' he laughed, 'too small!'

Amglo smiled. It was true. He was not as tall as many of the men of the clan. But he was strong . . . and very fast.

On the day before the battle, the entire tribe, except for a few old women who remained with the babies, walked to a hilly place, a *ngaachi tha'inyunam*, fighting ground, near the boundary of their territory with the Umpila. That night there was dancing that went on through the moonlight hours with Amglo taking his place among his compatriots and acquitting himself well. Then the men retired together and the wives slept separately.

The Umpila could be heard on the other side of the hill and their fires made a glow that lit the shadows of the treetops against the night sky. But then those sounds faded and slowly the glow disappeared; only the stars remained, hovering overhead with their tiny lights. Amglo watched them, wondering if this was the last time he would ever lie beneath them; for whenever a shooting star made its brief appearance he knew it was the soul of a Sandbeach person who had died. He or she was flying to that other place where the spirits lived. The elders at the *nartji kintja*, the bora ground, had told him so, and he believed them. He wondered whether tomorrow night he would be among them. He took heart from Bruno's faith in him.

'I am strong,' he said, 'and very fast.'

Then he slept.

★ ★ ★

They assembled in the morning. They were naked but for the string belts they had fashioned from the fibre trees that carried their *yulis*, boomerangs and other spare weapons. They had painted their bodies and their faces with *matan*, white clay, to make a fearsome sight. They hefted their spears and their fighting sticks, felt their weight, comfortable in their hands. They spoke to each other in a boasting way. They made jokes. From over the hill they could hear a bullroarer that signalled the battle and warned others to stay away.

Then as the sun reached over the tall trees to a cleared area on their side of the hill, the enemy appeared at the crest. They advanced towards the Night Islanders who spread themselves in two or three uneven lines with Amglo and Sassy at the front and centre, Maademan between them and Baroway to Amglo's left.

Maademan led the shouts of his warriors, vile obscenities against their enemies who replied in kind. And behind each of the advancing bands, the women joined in with their threats and insults and all moved forward until there was only about thirty metres between them.

Then Chilpu stepped forward from the line, a gnarled and formidable veteran of many battles, and condemned the Umpila for their crime. He was followed by an Umpila man who damned the Night Islanders for the many bad things they had done and the trespass committed by their young men.

As he finished there was a moment's silence before suddenly the air was filled with boomerangs that flew straight and deadly at the bodies and heads of the combatants. Amglo aimed his at an Umpila man directly in his line, an older man made hideous by his red ochre markings and who launched his own missile. It would have ripped into Amglo's neck had he not ducked and thrown up his woomera to send it skittering harmlessly to the side.

All around him came cries of pain and shouts of rage as the fighters brought their spears into the fray; and now Amglo could see that two or three of the Umpila had levelled their attack on Sassy and himself. He threw his own short spear and roared with a wild joy when he saw that it had found its mark, thudding into the shoulder of his opponent and sending him reeling backwards.

Baroway ginned and shouted his praise. But Amglo was too busy dodging a new volley of spears to respond.

As the tempo of battle rose, he found his reactions rose with them. He could catch the short spears as they passed and return them with all the power of his young muscles. There was even time to catch Sassy's eye and shout his joy.

As the line behind them moved forward to take their place, he looked for and found discarded weapons and threw them into the Umpila lines. Then both sides ran towards each other until, with wild cries, the two forces met in hand-to-hand combat.

Amglo clutched his fighting stick in one hand, the woomera in the other, and made for an opponent whose ugliness stood out even in this place of horrors.

The man saw him coming and threw his long fighting spear, the *kaaya*. Amglo ducked to one side but just behind him Baroway had bent to retrieve a spear and rose to fling it back. The heavy *kaaya* struck him in the neck, its vicious barbs piercing his throat and slamming into the bone behind.

The ugly one now advanced with his fighting stick and Amglo leapt forward to meet him, ripping his own stick upwards and across the head of the enemy. The Umpila man staggered backwards and Amglo was on him, driving home his advantage, smashing his skull open as a ruck formed around them with Sassy and others joining in. He was startled to see Veronique with her yamstick raised to bring it down on the ugly one, even though Amglo's blows had killed him.

Amglo skipped backwards out of the throng and received a sharp crack to the head. Blood rushed from his scalp and down his face almost blinding him. He staggered back to where Veronique and another woman were dragging Baroway out of the melee. But as he wiped the blood from his eyes, he could see that his rescuer was no more. Baroway's eyes stared sightlessly as his head rolled from side to side.

There was no time for sadness; he grabbed the spear that had felled Baroway and charged back into the fighting, But the long, awkward shaft was no weapon for close combat and the press of Umpila men wielding their fighting sticks pushed him backwards until he felt himself going down from the blows that were raining on his head and shoulders. Then suddenly Maademan and Bruno were at his side, ripping into the ruck and easing the pressure until finally there was space all around him.

In the next moment, as if in response to some silent signal, the Umpila men began to retreat from the battlefield in twos and threes until suddenly there was a general stampede and they broke off the fighting and departed over the hill.

No one followed. The battle was over. The Night Islanders were elated but they showed few signs of rowdy triumph. Two of their precious number – Baroway and an older man who suffered a short spear straight through the eye – were dead or dying. Others were wounded, though Sassy seemed to have escaped totally unscathed and Maademan, who sported a fiercely swollen nose and mouth, made no complaint. Bruno had taken a terrible blow in the groin. He was writhing in agony and unable to speak.

Amglo slumped beside him. And while other women tended to the wounds of their husbands, Bruno's wife was nowhere to be seen. Amglo could do little to comfort his friend. The skin of his testicles had been slightly torn but that would heal; the other parts looked fearfully bruised. Amglo's own torn scalp finally stopped its bleeding as the clan made their way in straggling groups back towards the sandbeach.

There were times on the journey when he felt dizzy and stopped to rest in the shade of a *thanka* tree. Each time, he was joined by two girls of the clan, sisters who had reminded him of the twins that lived in Rue Napoléon so they had become 'Evette' and 'Evonne'. They examined his scalp and told him he was *puuya kuntha,* brave, and giggled behind their hands.

He knew that the older of them, Evonne, was promised to Yannick and when he thought of it, he'd not seen him in the fight since the beginning when he was in the second line behind him. According to the girls, Yannick had been hit in the opening salvo of boomerangs and had taken no further part in the battle. He had gone ahead with his mother while his father Yann was walking with Maademan and the other older men.

The girls had heard that on their return, after a day's rest, the clan would be moving the encampment. The rains were coming soon, so new and stronger shelters would be needed. Amglo listened to their chatter and when he felt better he let them take the lead. By now the others had passed them by and the trio travelled slowly along a track that Amglo had not seen before.

While his heart was filled with the elation of victory, his leg was getting tired and at some point the little sister Evette ran ahead to bring water from a spring. When he sat, Evonne sat very close beside him. Their bodies touched and before he knew it they were making love with an urgency that overwhelmed him. She was a willing partner and just when he felt he was spent, she was eager for more, and more, until finally there was nothing left to give.

When Evette reappeared with water, they all three drank together. What had gone before was not mentioned, but it seemed to Amglo that Evette was wise beyond her years. He suspected that she had returned some time before she announced her arrival.

Evonne helped him up, then the two girls ran ahead. Amglo walked alone. It was almost dark when he arrived at the encampment where a hasty feast had been prepared. Later he danced with his triumphant comrades at arms. And when he slept, it was the sleep of total exhaustion.

In the days that followed, the Night Islanders engaged in the long and meticulous rites that attended the burial of their dead warriors. Since the entire clan was connected by blood or by marriage, they mourned as a people. But there were special duties and customs for those most closely related and while Sassy as the son and Veronique as the wife were most intimately involved, Amglo played his part in the funeral ceremonies for Baroway.

He was deeply moved at the loss of the man who had helped to save his life, to bring him into the tribe and to fight beside him. He took pride in his blow with the fighting stick that felled his killer; and he would be reminded of it for the rest of his life when Maademan made the incision on the upper part of his right arm. A herbal mixture placed upon the open cut would raise a vertical scar that was not just a signal of his deadly prowess in battle but of the man he avenged.

As the widow, Veronique's mourning was the most visible and painstaking. Amglo was surprised, once again, at the elaborate nature of his people's rituals. Even though she had been stolen from the Umpila people herself, Veronique had been a strong and dutiful wife to Baroway. And in death she followed all the requirements of the long mourning time.

Maademan cut the hair of the close family members; and when her scalp was exposed Veronique covered it with a widow's cap, *pi-pi*, made of gypsum. Meantime, Sassy had gathered the white clay that all the men used to cover their faces and appease the spirits who at the time of death were all about. He then cut the hair of Baroway's head which the women mixed with twine to make long bundles of thick strands. These were distributed to the men of the family who would wear them as a sign of great respect. Sassy showed Amglo how to make *opamaka*, wooden tablets, painted with red ochre and hung in the trees where the ceremonies took place.

They brought the fishing nets that Baroway used and as they buried the body in a temporary grave just back from the sandbeach, there was wailing from the women and the men took turns in dressing themselves in the nets and they danced in his honour. They placed long wailing sticks tipped with beeswax on the grave.

The rest of the clan showed them great respect and after three days they dug the body up and with twigs from the *yungku* tree they gently flayed the outer skin to reveal the white skin beneath. Then they wrapped it in bark, tightly enclosed by knotted twine, and Maademan and Sassy carried it on their shoulders deeper into the bush where Amglo had assisted them to build a sturdy timber frame where the body would rest until only the bones remained.

Finally, because Baroway was renowned as a dugong hunter, they would re-bury him in the sandy soil above the highwater mark, and mark his grave with a neat arrangement of dugong bones. And for many weeks after, every time Amglo saw a shooting star, he thought of Baroway.

14

Cape York

John Jardine arrived at Somerset in July 1864 with a small flotilla of Royal Naval vessels led by the paddle-wheel sloop of 818 tons HMS *Salamanda*. It was under the command of Captain John Carnegie and accompanied by the barques *Golden Eagle* and *Woodlark* carrying stores, building materials and twenty-five Royal Marines.

The newcomers had reached an area where no white person had ever previously ventured. Jardine had decided that the mainland opposite Port Albany offered a better site for the Somerset settlement and Carnegie acquiesced. The local Aboriginal people were members of several clans – now known as the Wik people – and many would have seen evidence of the alien ships that passed through the several passages of the Torres Strait. Indeed, the area had seen some notable shipwrecks, including the English merchant vessel *Sapphire* en route from Gladstone to India with a cargo of horses. Only eleven men survived after murderous encounters with island tribes in the strait.

The local Aboriginal people would no doubt have looked askance at the procession of uniformed marines to the area above the beach at Somerset Bay, where they were put to work felling trees to clear a space for their tents. The marines were assisted by the carpenters of the *Salamanda* and though the *Golden Eagle* disgorged its seven horses on the mainland, the precipitous cliffs were too steep for them to be much help to the soldiers.

Golden Eagle then moved to Albany Island and unloaded 252 sheep and 154 tons of coal reserves for Royal Navy ships. One marine was given the task of shepherd and within twenty-four hours was startled by the arrival of a two-metre brown snake exploring his tent.

By now the entire party was ashore and it included Jardine's two male assistants; the surveyor W.B. Wilson and his two assistants; J.J. Halpin, Foreman of Works, and one junior; plus Lieutenant R.J. Pascoe in charge of his marines, including Assistant Surgeon Richard Cannon. Most were helping Halpin erect the various government premises. And by September Jardine was able to move from his tent to the kitchen area of Government House. When completed the building would be an imposing structure on the bluff overlooking Somerset Bay.

Whether the Government Resident, John Jardine, followed Bowen's instructions to make 'as clear as possible' to the Aboriginal people their newfound status as British subjects is not known. But if so, the honour seems to have escaped their full appreciation. For by December Jardine wrote to Premier Herbert that he had little to report except for two 'serious aggressions by the Aborigines' in which two marines were wounded by spears, one seriously. The aggressors were repelled and 'met with severe and just punishment'.[1]

Jardine explained that on 13 September as he walked from his kitchen to the main camp for breakfast, he noticed a number of Aboriginal people, some with spears 'which were not permitted to be brought within sight of the place'. He took 'Kio, a native who usually attached himself to me' and spoke to them. They removed their spears the required distance but just as he was collecting his breakfast, his son John Robert back at the half-built house called out, 'They are spearing the gardener.'

Jardine picked up his gun and ran the eighty metres towards the garden when he met a marine running to the camp with a spear sticking out of his shoulder.

He didn't stop but ran on with his son in futile pursuit of his quarry, who stayed out of shooting range. The wounded marine turned out to be Private John Saich who had been speared through the chest into one lung and had taken a second four-pointed barb to his right upper arm.

Jardine returned to his new building where he had left two men at work and sent his son for breakfast at the camp. Finally, when John Robert returned, Jardine set out again for his own repast. However, no sooner had he sat down than he heard shots from John Robert's revolver and he hurried back to discover his son surrounded by warriors and the two workmen heading into the scrub firing their guns. A volley of spears arrived with 'one heavy four-pointed spear passing a few inches from John Robert's neck as he stooped to avoid it, and penetrated three-quarters of an inch into the hardwood post of the building'.

Moreover, when Halpin's workmen on the marines' barracks heard the shots, they fled to the camp and the Aboriginals ran off with their tools. This galvanised the marines into giving chase, but once in the scrub they too came under fire from the Aboriginal spears and Corporal Dent took the serrated barbs of a spear in the shoulder.

Nevertheless, Jardine reported, 'I cannot say positively what damage was sustained by the Natives, but I have good reason to believe it was considerable.' Since then, whenever he made his regular excursions on horseback around the settlement, he knew that 'the Blacks were running [my] trail as a pack of hounds would do to a scent'. Throughout, the letter painted Jardine in heroic terms, defending the farthest corner of the Empire against the implacable savagery of the thankless Aboriginal people.

However, unbeknown to the Government Resident, a second account of the affray was then en route to Premier Herbert's superior, Governor Bowen. Lieutenant Pascoe wrote that: 'Up to the 13th September, we were apparently on very friendly terms with the Aborigines, but on that day, Mr Jardine the Police Magistrate here flogged one of them on suspicion of having stolen a tomahawk – he had previously shot at one of them – however on the occasion of the flogging, the natives immediately attacked us and wounded two of the Royal Marines belonging to the detachment under my command [Private] John Saich and [Corporal] David Dent, the former very seriously . . . this man's life was despaired of, he has been hovering between life and death since.'

In fact, Saich would die before the letter reached Brisbane. But according to Pascoe, the flogging had led to further payback from the Aboriginal people. 'We have frequently been annoyed in various ways, and the works interrupted since the outbreak,' he wrote. 'Two of the natives were killed on September 13th whilst attacking the Police Magistrate's house.' And after that a state of scattered warfare enveloped the station.

'One [Aboriginal] was killed by one of the Royal Marines engaged in surveying with Mr Wilson on September 21st,' Pascoe wrote, 'and on October 15th at the request of the Police Magistrate I surprised a canoe on Tree Island, captured it and killed six of the natives. On October 17th two horses were speared and two stolen by the Blacks – the latter two have since been recovered.

'I have considered it my duty to assign to your Excellency what I consider the cause of these aggressions, and in justice to myself and to the detachment under my command, I can most positively affirm that none of the Royal Marines have to my knowledge, ever injured or annoyed the aborigines in any way whatever, but on the contrary have at all times treated them (previously to the outbreak) with kindness and humanity.'

Surveyor Wilson also reported to the surveyor-general that 'up to the 13th of September the Blacks refrained from any aggressions except petty larcenies'. He added that since it was not his province, he refrained from alluding to the cause of the attack.

When Bowen read all three letters, his response was immediate. He told Herbert, 'I think that Mr Jardine should be assured of the entire confidence and approval of the Government in him, and of its approval of his conduct in his difficult office.'

Lieutenant Pascoe could have saved his ink.

However, that was not quite the end of the matter. Pascoe also wrote in similar terms to his Deputy Adjutant General, Colonel G.C. Langley in London, who took the issue to the Lords of the Admiralty. Langley then wrote to Bowen that henceforth the Royal Marines would no longer answer to the Government Resident but to the commodore of the station at HMS *Curacoa* (sic), the flagship of the Royal Navy's Australian station.

Even then, there was a further coda to the event. In 1885 the Assistant Surgeon Richard Cannon, now a qualified doctor, recalled the events in his book, *Savage Scenes from Australia,* which had haunted him for more than twenty years. Jardine and his son, he wrote, together with Cannon's party of Royal Marines, hid in silence as four Gudang men were taking a spell after their turtling expedition on a sandbeach on Albany Island. They then crept down behind them as Cannon accompanied Jardine with his long rifle on his shoulder. As the Aboriginal men made for their canoes, Jardine said, 'We've got them this time, supper for the sharks, my boy.'

Jardine began firing and the marines launched their boat as the Aboriginals paddled desperately out to sea. 'We saw one of the natives topple over, grasp frantically at his paddle, and bound into the air,' Cannon wrote. 'The blue waters closed over him

and the sharks rejoiced. Now, flash, flash, flash from the marines'
boat and three black figures are only to be seen delving furiously
into the sea with frantic paddles. See the boat is on them . . .
Fancy a long dive for life! When will they come up? Never, they
are shot and drowned . . . bang, bang, bang from the boat, but
the head is down again. From Johnny Jardine, "Duck shooting
by Jove", whilst flash, flash, flash comes from our crew and far
away on the tide drifts the tenantless canoe, a melancholy wreck.'

Jardine had come to the view, expressed to Governor Bowen,
that, 'Of the aborigines at Cape York I can say little more than
has already been so often repeated in descriptions of the natives in
other parts of the Australian continent. The only distinction I can
perceive is that they appear to be in a lower state of degradation,
mentally and physically, than any of the Australian aboriginal
tribes which I have seen.'[2]

Meantime, he had brought his third son, John Robert, on
the journey, while his wife remained in Rockhampton with
seven of their children. Jardine and his two eldest sons, Francis
(known as Frank), twenty-two, and Alexander, twenty, were
even then engaged in a scheme to make the most of the new
posting's financial opportunities by droving a mob of cattle from
Rockhampton to supply the growing needs of the government
station.

15

Amglo

While Baroway's family mourned, the rains came. But not before Chilpu and another ancient were able to summon the great spirit who brought the storms and the pelting downpours almost every day. Amglo watched as the old men, the *Yintjinngga*, appeared at a sheltered place among the dunes, painted in the white clay markings of their role, the feathers and down of birds decorating their hair and bodies, the drum and clapstick giving depth and strength to the chanting of their song. It was not a long ceremony, but it was repeated each day for ten days until finally the great dark clouds that had come and gone, teasing the people and the singers, released the first of many soaking rains.

This meant that for long periods, the men could not venture to sea to hunt the turtle and the dugong; and the diet of the clan, mostly of fish and, *thampul*, yam porridge, became dull and tedious, enlivened only by the occasional wild pig or wallaby that ventured close to the encampment. And in turn the people became restless and sullen.

But for Amglo it was a time when the pleasures and pains of newfound manhood set him forth on a stormy sea. Stories of his fierce fighting on the battlefield had quickly passed among the clan and his status grew. There were even whispers from messengers that the Kuuku Y'au was prepared to offer two or even three women if the Night Islanders would agree to exchange him.

Amglo laughed when he heard that. 'Amglo the fighter!' he said to his dingo pup as he lay down one evening in his small but well-made *yutha*, with its roof of fronds over saplings bent to form a half-moon frame. The pup, little *thamanu*, was a present from Sassy whose dog had produced a litter at the beginning of the wet. Usually the pup slept outside but when the rain beat down he crawled in on his little belly. Amglo listened to the rain on the roof and wondered if Evonne – whom he now knew by her Night Islander name of Kanti (beautiful) – would come to him tonight. Since their lusty encounter on their return from the battlefield, they had shared secret smiles and flashing eyes until he had finished building his *yutha* some little distance from the family. That same night there was rustling in the bush beside it and at first he had visions of a *thupi,* white-tailed rat, or even a *kapal,* python, finding its way inside.

Then he saw her smiling face at the small entrance and in a moment she had wriggled inside. 'What of your family?' he asked.

She grinned in the darkness. 'I must be quick.'

And she was.

After that, she came several times, but it was hurried and left Amglo dazed and edgy. Twice they were able to meet at a distance from the encampment, but on the first occasion there was a powerful thunderstorm and on the second their return was cut off by a flooded creek and Kanti was nearly torn from his grasp by the swirling muddy waters. But at least there was time for talking and Amglo learned that her mother gave her a mixture of bitter leaves and roots to prevent babies. For in Night Island lore it was only the *thal'al*, the man's semen, that made the baby. And her mother had guessed that Kanti was visiting with Yannick, her betrothed.

Amglo knew that he was in the wrong. But he also knew that his sin was not a mortal one in the Night Island laws. He even took an extra pleasure that it was Yannick he was deceiving. In truth, as he came to know the ways of men and women beneath their laws, it seemed that Night Islanders were little different from the other worlds of his experience – the good, the bad, the kind, the hurtful, the mean and the lusty – they were everywhere the same.

Maademan used the time of the rains to seek another wife for Sassy. It was not a long process since most of the girls were promised soon after they were born. Amglo was happy when he settled upon Evette, but his pleasure was tempered by a worry that she would tell Sassy of his meetings with Kanti.

He was in two minds whether to speak of their *liaison* with his friend. Until now they had shared everything their language would allow. But with manhood and all its rules and duties, suddenly there were barriers. Their friendship would always be strong but now it had to take its place within their wider roles in the activities of the clan. They would both be permitted to hunt the dugong, but their place in the canoes would be decided by their skills and their worth as dutiful Night Islanders. And in a group of less than fifty souls, gossip was just as much the coinage of community as the yam damper. So Amglo hesitated.

However, once they began work on Maademan's new canoe – a task that threw them together for weeks of patient hollowing and scraping the special *tangu* tree – it just slipped out. Sassy chuckled. *'Mini-mini.'* Very good. And he responded with a secret of his own – he was 'visiting' with Bruno's wife Sabine. Now it was Amglo's turn to react and again he felt torn. Sabine was notorious and was branded *wompilgobi*, a courtesan, by the men and women alike. Yet Bruno was his friend and he felt a sympathy for him, especially since his battlefield injury.

Amglo had visited him several times and while the swelling and bruising remained, his friend made few complaints. He said it gave him the perfect excuse to stay flat on his back – *aampa kani* – and leave the hunting and gathering to others. His wife was tireless in keeping up the supplies of yams, wild apples and fish for his dinner. In fact, Sabine had a pet cassowary chick who followed her around like a dingo, and even slept in their *yutha* with them. She had sacrificed it for him; and it had made a very tasty meal.

Amglo nodded in support of his friend, though he knew there were other reasons for the demise of the *kutini* chick. It was known to attack with its little beak at Sabine's men when they were engaged in their *kuupi* activities with her. The sight of a small cut on a man's buttock, *tuumu,* was enough to have the women laughing behind their hands and the men shaking their heads.

Such were Amglo's thoughts one day towards the end of the wet as he bid farewell to his friend and headed back to the beach where Maademan and Sassy were working on the canoe. They were fitting one of the two outriggers that made the Night Islander canoes far superior to those of the Kuuku Y'au or the Umpila who used only one outrigger. The Night Islanders could hunt the turtle all thirty kilometres out to the great coral reef in far rougher seas than their competitors. And just as important, the outriggers held the canoe much steadier for the harpooner at the bow, his long spear raised to hurl at the great dugong beneath the water.

He had almost reached the men when a terrible shout arose from women and children running towards them. *'Ayntikanu!'* Saltwater crocodile. Amglo's stomach clenched when next they cried the name of the little boy, known to him as 'Tookie', who had fetched his spears during his many days of practising on the beach.

He joined the men in a mad race down the beach towards the mouth of the river where the children had been playing in the stream with their toy boats. But when they arrived there was no sign of the boy, much less of the reptile that had taken him.

The children and the three women with them were babbling with the shock of it. But eventually it became clear that they had seen the beast earlier that morning, a big male, cruising upstream to one of the three nests he kept with females in that creek; they watched it until it was gone, then returned to their play. Two of the women retired to the tide line where they worked on the intricate weaving of dillybags while the third, Tookie's mother, Pinya, fished for *talipata*, stingaree, in the shallows.

There were logs and fallen branches floating down from the upper reaches of the stream and the crocodile was among them. Tookie was furthest upriver from the rest of the group. There was a single panicked squeal as the great beast rose from the water before him, a terrible thrashing of water, and the boy was gone. Pinya saw only the sweeping tail of the beast as it plunged.

Pinya, who had carried the child beside her in a basket of palm leaves from almost the day he was born, who had suckled him for three years after his birthing, now stood with her eyes wide, her mouth agape, wailing and tearing her hair out by the roots. There was nothing that Amglo and the men could say or do to comfort her. The other women were wailing almost as loudly, but they took her just as she collapsed and helped her into the shade.

That night the men of the clan came together; and for the first time, Amglo was among them with the right to speak. He was blazing with rage and horror at his young friend's fate. The crocodile must be killed, he said. Nothing else would do.

But he quickly learned that there were other matters at stake. Some blamed the Kuuku Y'au since the crocodile was their totem so their spirit must have been behind the attack. Others said that

I'wai Tjilbo, the crocodile ancestor, was taking vengeance on the clan for their lack of respect. Still others spoke of the young crocodiles that they hunted for such good food – if the male was killed, there would be no more young. Opponents shouted that if this crocodile was killed, another would simply take his place and many more would be born. Others said that if another would take his place, where was the sense in a killing party that would put the men in danger?

As the night wore on, so many voices were raised that Amglo, who had spoken first, became so angry that he dare not speak. And when the meeting ended with no final decision, he was deeply relieved. For as the debate flowed back and forth, the vision of Pinya tearing her hair returned again and again. And in between the rough idea of a plan to kill the *ayntikanu* himself spun in his brain.

Later that night in his *yutha,* he thought back on the clan meeting where he'd learned much about the habits of the *ayntikanu*; and before he slept his plans were well formed. Tomorrow he would begin. The sun could not rise soon enough.

16

Cape York

John Jardine's sons, Alexander and Frank, were as enthusiastic as their father about turning his appointment as Government Resident at Somerset into a financial bonanza. By now there was talk that North Queensland might become a separate colony with Somerset as its capital. When that happened, the population would explode and the Jardines would be perfectly placed to supply their most basic needs.

They even used government resources to feather their nest. Jardine Senior attached one of the official surveyors at the infant settlement, Archibald Richardson, to their cattle drive from Rockhampton, on grounds that their venture would reduce government support for the station.

In May 1864, Frank set about gathering ten men for the expedition and no fewer than thirty-one horses. Once assembled, they took ship in Rockhampton and travelled north to the port of Bowen where, in July, Alexander joined them. There, Frank sought to buy some 250 head of cattle; as well as five additional horses (on the government account) for Surveyor Richardson. However, the Jardines were confronted by the first of many obstacles. An epidemic of bovine pleuropneumonia caused a severe cattle shortage in the area and Frank was forced to buy from two stations some distance to the south.

Alexander headed in the opposite direction and reached J.G. Macdonald's Carpentaria Downs, the furthest station in the colony's northwest, on 30 August. Frank was still gathering his mob before droving them north so Alexander took the opportunity for a recce of the route they might take. He set out with 'two black boys' and Henry Bode, an English migrant seeking property for himself. Alexander had acquired a copy of Ludwig Leichhardt's journal of his earlier expedition and determined to follow his course as far as possible towards his distant goal. Unfortunately, this would lead to confusion and delay, particularly as Richardson's navigational instruments proved less than useful in the variegated country that awaited.[1]

Nevertheless, Alexander and his small party travelled more than 290 kilometres before turning back towards Carpentaria Downs where he hoped to reunite with his brother and the cattle. He reached the station on 21 September but had to wait another fifteen days before Frank arrived with the bullocks and cows that would provide the foundation of the family fortune. He was pleased to see they were 'in good condition' and well fitted for the journey ahead. By now the horse team had reached forty-two, plus a mule, and the next three days were spent shoeing them in heat that reached 37 degrees Celsius.

By 11 October all were 'in excellent health and good spirits'. In addition to Richardson and the two Jardines (with Alexander as undisputed leader), the party now included employees, C. Scrutton, R.N. Binney, A. Cowderoy and four Aboriginal men with some experience in the Native Police Force – 'Old Eulah', 'Peter', 'Barney' and 'Sambo' from the Wide Bay and Rockhampton districts. They were armed with double-barrelled police carbines, while the white men carried Terry's breech-loaders and Tranter's revolvers.

The provisions were distributed in eighteen packs and included 1200 pounds of flour, 35 pounds of tea, 40 pounds of currants and raisins, 20 pounds of peas, 20 pounds of jam, plus salt, sugar and other odds and ends. They also carried three light tents designed to protect the stores.

They set the cattle going the following day, 12 October, under the direction of Cowderoy and two of the Aboriginal men with Old Eulah as 'pilot'. The Jardines left the day after, while Binney remained behind with most of the horses to feed them around the station lagoon for another day before setting out.

However, when the Jardines tried to catch up with the cattle, they discovered they had headed into the ranges to the east. Everyone blamed Old Eulah. According to Alexander, 'The Australian aborigines have not in all cases that unerring instinct of locality which has been attributed to them; and are, out of their own country, no better, and scarcely so good as an experienced white.'

Alexander was also impatient with the packhorse, Cerberus, who 'not liking the companionship of the mule, took occasion crossing another creek to kick his long-eared mate from the top to the bottom of it, to the intense amusement of the black-boys, who screamed "dere go poor fella donkit" with great delight'.

The occasions for amusement would be few and far between in the weeks and months ahead.

Their first encounter with the Aboriginals whose country they were passing through occurred on 16 October. First the expeditioners found themselves in plains that had been recently burned of all feed, then according to Alexander, 'About 50 blacks, all men, followed the tracks of the party . . . they were painted and fully armed which indicated a "brush" with the whites; on being turned upon, however, they thought better of it and ran away.'

Shortly afterwards they came upon a camp where 'the natives decamped at [our] appearance, leaving some very neatly made reed spears, tipped variously with jagged hardwood, flint, fish-bones, and iron. Pieces of ship's iron were also found, and a piece of saddle girth . . . proving that they must at some time have been on the tracks of white men.'[2]

So far they were averaging sixteen kilometres a day, but on 5 November – which they remembered as Guy Fawkes' Day† – came the first of their 'disasters'. In the morning, sixteen horses were missing. The brothers split the party, ordering most to stay behind and find them while they pushed on with the cattle. But by day's end when there was no sign of the horses, they returned to find that a grass fire had burned half their food and nearly all their equipment.

Lost were six bags of flour, 25 pounds of tea, most of the jam, apples, currants, half the ammunition, two tents, most of the harness and nearly all the Jardines' (and the Aboriginals') clothes. Alexander's favourite horse, Maroon, had died from snake bite, and a hostile party of Aboriginal men gave warning that to go further could be met with a 'shower of spears'.

After that, the expedition never fully recovered.

---

† Celebrating the foiling of an attempt by Fawkes and his Catholic associates to blow up the British Parliament in 1605.

17

Amglo

Amglo needed help for his plan to work. After his morning swim, his first stop was at Bruno's *yutha* where he confided his scheme to his friend. Bruno was happy to help and made some good suggestions. As they talked, Sabine returned with a rotten tree branch containing big land snails, *iikula*, and they made a hearty breakfast. She seemed pleased at Amglo's presence, especially as Bruno gave every indication that he would be getting up at last.

'*Yaaki wu'u*,' she said. The lazy one.

Bruno smiled and shook his head. Then with many grunts and groans he finally emerged from the *yutha* to a bright, cloudless morning.

He spread his arms. '*Kanti impana*,' he said. Beautiful.

They walked slowly at first but in time Bruno lengthened his stride as they headed for the river. Both men knew the location of the crocodile's three nests. Two were on the opposite bank that led to Kuuku Y'au country; the third was on their side where the female had recently given birth. She would guard the young against the male for several months lest he eat them; and this suited the Night Islanders very well. When they reached a certain size – about six months of age – the juveniles were game for the clan feasts.

Amglo's plan was to lure the male *ayntikanu* out of the water where he was vulnerable to a warrior's spears. He knew, of course, that even the strongest spear would bounce off the reptile's thick hide. But his plan was not to kill him but to blind him with spears to his eyes. Deeply wounded, he would be prey to a younger male or even the females he had bullied and whose young he had eaten. That was the payback Amglo wanted. That was the payback Pinya and Tookie deserved!

To lure him from the water they needed a bait, something that would keep the *ayntikanu* on land long enough for them to aim and throw their spears. Amglo had thought of a wallaby tied to a tree but Bruno had a better idea – a wallaby would make no noise but a pig would scream and the *ayntikanu* would hear it from a long way off. That meant they would have to capture the pig alive, and Bruno knew just where and how that could be done. Then, just as important, they must tether it at a time when the male would reach it before the females.

On this morning they found the ideal place for their bait. Most days the *ayntikanu* visited his nests in the same order. And as he passed by that place they would release the bindings around the pig's jaw and set him screaming. Then, if the *ayntikanu* took the bait, it was up to Amglo to make the difficult shot with his spear.

When they returned to the encampment, Bruno went to round up some of his young friends to go pig hunting while Amglo sought out Sassy who was back on the beach working on the canoe.

Sassy looked up. *'Wantumunu?'* Where have you been?

Amglo sat beside him. *'Kuunama,'* he said. All over the place. He was silent for a moment, but so filled with his plan that he couldn't hold back and told Sassy about it. Sassy's eyes lit up. Had he told Maademan?

'Ngampa!' Amglo said. No!

Sassy loved a secret. *'Mini-mini.'* Good. It should work, he said, but they must wait until the *ayntikanu* was hungry again.

Amglo turned his head aside, his belly heaving at the thought of his little friend's fate. But Sassy seemed not to notice. Waiting, he said, was a good thing. It gave them time to find the right materials for the spears – *panti,* short, thin ones with stingray barbs – and to practise their throws which had to be deadly accurate. Now his eagerness matched Amglo's own and he swore to keep the secret, even from Maademan.

It took Bruno and his little team of runners almost a week before they caught the pigs. He took a second one, he said, otherwise people would wonder why he hadn't killed and shared it. This way, one could be killed and the other kept for a while before they tied it to the tree. When he wasn't hunting pig, Bruno was sitting by the place they had chosen, watching the movements of the *ayntikanu* to learn the best time for them to spring their trap.

Amglo and Sassy used the time well. They selected spear lengths from a *chulu* tree and, in between their work on Maademan's canoe, they spent many hours cutting and smoothing the shafts and then fitting stingray and hardwood barbs so sharp that even to touch them would draw blood. And they rose early to practise, making a target of *kaaki* palm with a small eye marked on the broad leaf. By the end of seven days, at both seven and ten paces, they were hitting it almost every time.

That evening they met around the fire outside Amglo's *yutha.* There was dancing in the encampment but they were not involved. Instead, they talked quietly together as Amglo's dingo pup, *thamanu,* lay nearby, watching his master's every move.

The good news was that if the *ayntikanu* kept to his usual habit, he would pass by their chosen spot in the heat of the early afternoon when most of the people would be resting around the encampment. But you couldn't be sure. Sometimes he stayed away, other times his visits lasted longer than usual. There was nothing they could do about that, they decided. So, in the morning when the people were busy with their several occupations, Bruno would take the pig there and stay until Amglo and Sassy arrived.

That night when the people slept, Amglo and Sassy took their three spears each and hid them in the undergrowth just back from the tree where the bait would be tethered. It was a bright moonlit night and they walked around the area, thinking about the action the next day – where they would place themselves for the best angle to send their spears flashing towards the great reptile's eyes.

They would split the attack, they decided, with one on each side, Sassy upstream, Amglo below. The *ayntikanu* would come out of the water slowly, Sassy said, and if the pig tried to run and break the tough rope he would rise up on his stubby legs and run straight at the bait. He would have his eyes fixed on the pig, but to be safe they found clumps of scrub to hide themselves behind until they threw their deadly shafts.

Sassy grinned. It was a good plan.

Amglo rose before the sun and returned to the *kaaki* palm target. He had made a fourth spear, not quite as smooth as the others but when he used it that day it flew straight and true. After a breakfast of mangoes, he joined Sassy at the canoe where they had almost completed the second outrigger.

Both men were too distracted to get much work done. Sassy was excited by the fight that awaited them. So too was Amglo but as well, time and again, he found his eyes drawn to the far end of the beach where the river met the sea and where the monster had ripped little Tookie from a life that he had only just begun.

Pinya, his mother, remained in a shocking state, not helped by her husband who gave her a belting with his woomera for her moment's inattention as she fished for the family's evening meal. No one interfered. The women brought their favourite remedies for the cuts and bruises but there was no point in protest. And in truth, they believed that the punishment from her husband meant that she did not punish herself. The bruises would heal and she would heal with them.

The morning finally passed and the two young men left the camp as though to hunt an emu with boomerangs, fighting sticks and Amglo's crooked spear; and just as he expected, *tinta,* the king parrot, crossed his path with a happy cry. '*Wulmina,*' he said. Feel good.

When they reached the place by the river, Bruno was waiting. The young pig, with its jaw bound tight, was already tied to the *kampulu* tree and had rounded it so many times that the rope was shortened to half a metre. He stared at the newcomers with red-eyed rage.

Bruno rose to greet them. There had been no sign of the *ayntikanu,* he said, but if he kept to his routine he should arrive very soon.

'*Wantumunu?*' Sassy asked. Where from?

Bruno pointed to the left. '*Paluku,*' he said. Upstream.

He had found a fork in a tree overhanging the water and from there they could see it coming from a good distance, provided it cruised down the main channel rather than the fringe of mangroves growing out from the bank. With his usual grunts and groans, Bruno climbed out along the branch and they settled down to wait. Sassy's dingo and Amglo's pup found some shade beneath a nearby *thanka* tree. And as the cicadas buzzed in the afternoon heat, the men sat motionless and silent, the excitement slowly draining from their veins.

Finally, Sassy broke the silence. The *ayntikanu,* it seemed, had broken his routine. They must hunt their food before they returned to the encampment. They should try again tomorrow. Amglo was reluctant, but Bruno, who had been stuck awkwardly in the fork of the tree, was happy to agree and began to struggle back along the branch.

Amglo rose. 'Pi'ina,' he said. Wait.

Holding his shell blade, he hurried to the pig and grabbed it around the head. Maybe his squeals would attract the *ayntikanu*. It was worth a try. Sassy agreed and Amglo sliced through the fibres and jumped back as they fell away and the pig snapped at him.

Bruno stood on the branch for a better look and as the pig's squeals pierced the air, the branch started to give way beneath his feet. Bruno grabbed some thin branches above him and for a moment they lessened the weight on his platform. But the relief was only momentary as the upper twigs gave way. Then the branch itself dipped towards the river.

That was when both Amglo and Bruno saw the *ayntikanu* heading directly for the bank. Bruno cried out as he made a lunge for the tree trunk and wrapped his arms around it. Amglo and Sassy could do nothing to help their friend who by now was at least out of reach of the *ayntikanu*, with his legs as well as his arms hugging the trunk. Just as Sassy had said, the reptile only had eyes for the pig which by chance was running around the tree in the opposite direction and extending the length of his rope lead.

As it reached the bank, the *ayntikanu* rose from the water with its great jaws wide open. Amglo and Sassy both threw their first spears, but Sassy's missed entirely while Amglo's struck behind the eye and bounced off harmlessly. But it was enough to draw the beast's attention his way and for the slightest moment he seemed distracted. This gave Amglo the chance to fling a second spiked lance at the gaping *ayntikanu*. Every muscle of his strong right shoulder went into the throw and his heart leapt with joy when the razor-sharp point buried itself in the upper jaw of the open mouth.

Stung, the *ayntikanu* turned its total attention to Amglo and rushed towards him. Amglo jumped nimbly behind the scrubby

bush, but the reptile's weight trampled it down. Again, Amglo
hopped sideways and from the corner of his eye he was astonished
to see his dingo' pup racing in to join the fray. But as the *ayntikanu*
snapped its jaws shut, breaking the slender spear in half, its great
tail swept around, catching the little *thamanu* and sending him
soaring sideways.

Then Sassy was beside his friend as Amglo grabbed his third
spear in sweating hands; the *ayntikanu* turned its great head towards
the newcomer and that gave Amglo the chance he needed, the
yellow-green eye closest to him was suddenly exposed and he
rammed downwards with a cry that became a roar as it struck home.

The *ayntikanu* reared back and turned for the safety of the river.
Sassy threw his second and third spears at the departing beast
and one held briefly in the softer white underbelly just behind
his back leg. But that did nothing to slow him. He had almost
reached the water when Bruno's grip on the tree finally gave way
and he hit the river with a scream and a splash within striking
distance of the *ayntikanu*. Bruno leapt to his feet and made a wild
dash for the bank. But all the fight had gone from the *ayntikanu*
and as the sweep of his great tail took him out into the stream,
Amglo's spear rose from the water like a flagstaff from a sailing
ship or the harpoon of a dugong hunter.

The three men were drenched in sweat and river water as they
came together on the bank in a babble of words. Excitement,
pleasure, even wonder gripped them and found voice in their
shouts and laughter. Amglo was first to break away and hurried
to a grassy patch where Sassy's dingo was sniffing at the body of
his pup. He lifted it up with one hand, and as he did so he felt
the beating of its heart. He held it in front of his face and when
its eyes opened its pink tongue followed and tickled his fingers.
Amglo laughed aloud.

'Mini-mini,' he said. Very good.

18

Cape York

By the end of November 1864 the Jardines' cattle drive up the western side of the cape towards Somerset was beset with ever-mounting problems. In the last two weeks they had lost another thirteen horses and according to Frederick Byerley, the sympathetic chronicler of their expedition, 'the troubles and adventures of the party seemed to thicken at this point'.[1]

The drive came to a halt while they searched for the horses. 'Old Eulah had come in empty-handed,' Byerley wrote. 'He had seen their tracks but with night coming on he was unable to follow them.' Next day he and fellow trooper, Peter, resumed their search and by nightfall had recovered five of the runaways.

The rest were abandoned.

Meanwhile, Frank Jardine had ridden forward seeking a route around 'a barren waste of tea-tree' when he was suddenly attacked. According to Byerley, 'He heard a yell and looked round just in time to see half a dozen spears come at him, and about a dozen natives painted [and] jumping around in great excitement . . . He turned on his assailants and sent a bullet amongst them; it hit a tree instead of a blackfellow but as they still menaced him the next shot was more successful. When seeing one of their number fall, the rest decamped.

'It was now their turn to run. But before they could cross the bed of the river, which was dry, clear, and about 300 yards wide, he was able to get two good shots at short range. They dropped all their spears in the "stampede", some of which were taken home as trophies.'

In the next few days, 'the hostility of the natives was very annoying,' said Byerley. 'Only the scarcity of [ammunition] and horse-flesh prevented the Brothers from turning out and giving their troublesome enemies a good drilling, which indeed they richly deserved, for they had in every case been the aggressors, and hung about the party, treacherously waiting for an opportunity to take them by surprise.'

By now the northern spring was giving way to a hot summer and travelling conditions worsened by the day. 'What with the mosquitoes and sand-flies, men, horses and cattle were kept in a continual fever,' Byerley observed. 'The horses would not leave the smoke of the fires, the cattle would not remain in the camp, and the men could get no rest at night for the mosquitoes, whilst during the day the flies were in myriads and a small species of gadfly particularly savage and troublesome.'

Even the native birds made life difficult, particularly the crows and hawks: 'Not content with the offal about the camp, unless sharply watched, they would take the meat that was cooking on the fire!' Exhausted men fell asleep when they should have been watching the cattle and groups of ten and fifteen beasts at a time wandered off into the bush. And if that were not enough, by December they had reached an area where neither horses nor cattle would eat the grass 'which had ceased to have a trace of green in it'.

The mule, dubbed 'Lucifer', also cleared out and when they finally tracked him down, 'they headed him after a hard gallop, and tried to drive him to the join the horses, but all to no purpose;

they knocked up their horses and were obliged to abandon the pursuit. He had evidently gone mad.'

Then the rains came. Suddenly they were travelling over flooded box tree country where the going was tough and progress painfully slow. Parties of Aboriginal warriors continued to harass them until, on December 18, came an encounter they called 'The Battle of the Mitchell' after the river of that name.

According to Byerley, 'They came on to a number of blacks fishing; these immediately crossed to the other side [of the river] but on their return swam across in numbers armed with large bundles of spears and some *nullahs* (clubs). The horsemen, seeing they were in for a row, now cantered forward, determined this time to give their assailants a severe lesson.' There followed 'a flight by the savages'. But then they turned and sent their spears 'thick and fast'.

These were now coming 'much too close to be pleasant', though some of them were thrown eighty metres, so the Jardine brothers and Eulah 'galloped up to them [and] poured in a volley'. This brought other members of the Jardine party down from their camp.

Byerley recalled that, 'At first the natives stood up courageously, but either by accident, despair or stupidity they got huddled in a heap in and at the margin of the water, when ten carbines poured volley after volley into them from all directions, killing and wounding with every shot, with very little return, nearly all of their spears having been expended. About thirty being killed, the Leader [Alexander Jardine] thought it prudent to hold his hand and let the rest escape. Many more must have been wounded and probably drowned, for fifty-nine rounds were counted as discharged.'

The Jardines and their men returned triumphantly to their camp. They had 'a few close shaves but providentially not a scratch'. Byerley commented: 'This is one of the few instances in

which the savages of Queensland have been known to stand up
in a fight with white men, and on this occasion they shewed (sic)
no sign of surprise or fear at the report and effect of fire-arms.
But it is probable that they will long remember "the Battle of
the Mitchell".'

On Christmas Day, Alexander wished his companions the
compliments of the season but roused the cattle to continue
the trek. Now at last they were in good grazing country. But
almost before they could draw breath, the rain turned it into a
vast bog. The leading cattle sank to their hips and soon about
forty beasts were stuck fast, the remainder ploughing through
with great difficulty.

They were forced to haul the bogged cattle out with ropes and
some had to be abandoned altogether. Finally, all progress was
stopped by a creek twenty metres across and running a banker.
After two days Alexander determined to cross it but several cattle
and at least three horses drowned in the attempt, while the leader
himself suffered a nasty crack on the head from a floating log
which 'had it been a degree harder might have closed his career'.

Moreover, once they did reach the other side, native herbs
within the grass proved to be poisonous to the horses and five died
painful deaths. 'The rain continued to fall heavily throughout the
day,' Byerley wrote, 'which could not under the circumstances,
have increased the cheerfulness of the party.'

By now there were so few horses remaining that most of the
party had to walk and even carry some of the packs. However,
'with stout heart and naked legs they faced forward, driving the
horses and cattle before them' and by the end of the day they
had placed sixteen kilometres between them and 'Poison Creek'.
And to add to their troubles, the 'natives' were again following
them all day, 'watching with cowardly patience for a favourable
moment to attack them at a disadvantage'. Provoked beyond

measure, Frank Jardine gave vent to his frustration and fired his rifle at them with 'savage delight'.

'The two foremost fell and their companions at once they broke and fled,' Byerley said. 'This however was the last occasion on which the party was molested, their sable adversaries having probably learned that they were worth letting alone.'

But while the Aboriginal owners of the country withdrew their 'aggression', the country itself continued to exact a toll on both man and beast. In fact, their remaining horses were 'sinking fast' and for the first time there was serious rancour in the ranks. One of their number had clearly arrogated more than his fair share of the flour and suspicion fell on one of the immigrant employees. Byerley was appalled: 'It is humiliating to think that amongst white men banded together in exploring parties . . . there should be found individuals so ignoble as to appropriate an undue share of the common stock of food on which the health, and perhaps the life, of each equally depends; and yet, sad to say, such instances are not singular.'

Since the flour was now exhausted, they killed another of their precious cattle and made jerky of the beef. And when they counted the remaining cattle, they discovered yet more were missing so the 'black-boys' were sent in search of them. Earlier in the drive, they had supplemented their diet with plain turkeys, emus, goannas, pigeons and even the occasional wild pig descended from the escapees from Captain Cook's *Endeavour* during its forced sojourn on the river so named. But by now the cattle had become almost their only source of nutrition.

Two days later they returned with most of the missing bullocks and the party struggled on. By the last days of February, they were only about sixty kilometres as the crow flies from their goal. But between them and the Somerset settlement was an impassable stream and this meant they had to travel 160 kilometres to circumvent it. This was a bitter blow to the group's morale but, as Byerley said, 'On the other hand, the whole of the party were without sickness, and they had plenty of cattle to eat.'

On 2 March 1865 they were finally within reach of the settlement and as they approached, the Aboriginals who had thrown in their lot with the settlers joined them. Their motives, according to Byerley, were an expectation that the expeditioners would share their 'bacca' and 'bissiker'. Nevertheless, 'Alexander Jardine selected the three they had first met as guides, who turned out to be capital fellows.'

At last, they reached Somerset: 'At about noon the party sighted the Settlement and involuntarily pulled up to gaze at the scattered and insignificant buildings they had so long and ardently desired to see and struggled to reach. When they again moved forward their guides set up an admonitory yell which brought Mr Jardine and their brother John to the door.

'Imagining that the Settlement was about to receive another attack – for the little community had already had to repulse more than one – [Jardine Sr] seized his gun and rushed out . . . [however] but for the horses they bestrode, even a father's eye might have failed to distinguish them from the blacks by whom they were surrounded. Six months of exposure to all weathers had tanned their skins and so reduced their wardrobe as to make their appearance primitive in the extreme. Their heads were covered with a cap of emu feathers and their feet cased in greenhide. Their pantaloons were reduced to the waistbands and pockets, the legs having been matters of remembrance only. However, they were hearty and well, in high spirits and in good case.

'It must be left to the imagination of the reader to realise the swelling feelings of joy and pride in which the Father grasped the hands of his gallant sons . . . thanks to a kind Providence, they were living heroes. It is no exaggeration in praise to say that they have won for themselves a lasting and honourable name in the records of Australian exploration.'

Unfortunately, however, their accomplishments fell short of the financial bonanza of the family's vaulting ambitions. Of the 250 cattle that were to be the solid foundation of the Jardines' fortune, three-quarters were lost to misadventure – or Aboriginal spears – on the journey. There were less than sixty survivors, and most of these were either consumed or otherwise succumbed soon after arrival.

Frank later boasted that he had shot and killed many Aboriginals on the journey; on the stock of his rifle he notched forty-seven confirmed kills.

John Jardine himself departed Somerset before the year was out, a full two years before his contract expired. So too did all his sons, though Frank would return in 1866 to establish a station south of the settlement.

PART
Six

19

Amglo

In the days following their battle with the *ayntikanu*, Amglo and Sassy returned to their toil on Maademan's *tangu* canoe. Bruno was restored to his usual health and good humour; and all three kept their adventure a well-guarded secret. Any further talks in the clan about payback for the loss of Tookie faded away, and neither Pinya nor her husband raised the matter, though when Amglo saw her sitting alone looking over the water where it happened he was sorely tempted to speak to her.

At the beach the outriggers were finally attached, and in the early evening Maademan joined them. He walked around the *tangu*, stepping in to test a binding with the strong rope made from the roots of the *matula* tree or to run a big hand over the smooth inner surface. It was almost four metres long with a flat ledge at the tip of the bow, where the harpooner could stand with his spear raised. Behind him there was room for three or four paddlers.

'Ngulkuma waanana,' Maademan said. Tomorrow we test it.

The young men were pleased but nervous; they had spent countless hours on the task and the result looked and felt good. But only when Maademan approved would they be able to relax.

They ate together, a fine *thuulkuyu,* trevally, that Marie and Rosine had caught on a fishing expedition off the rocks.

That night, for the first time in many months, Amglo dreamed of his life before he came to Sandbeach country. The images were jumbled together between the great waves of the ocean as the *Saint-Paul* ran before a mighty wind, the gentleness of the China girl in that room above the café, the terrible moment when they ran aground, and those days of torment on the lifeboat when it seemed all was lost ... and then a vision came of his mother, but when he looked at her, she had no face and even when he woke in fright he could no longer picture her, or his brothers, or even Grand-père Babin ... No matter how hard he tried, they were no more than vague outlines, and they began to fade even as he fought to keep them in his memory.

In the morning, with a gentle sea and no wind, Amglo and Sassy pushed the canoe out and, with Maademan in the bow, they leapt aboard and paddled towards Night Island. The womenfolk stood on the beach watching as the young men found their rhythm and sped away.

Amglo was in the stern position and as ever he was at home on the sea. In truth, he thought, he could hardly have been more fortunate in the place and people of his new life. As they powered through the small chop and the sun beat down on his body that was becoming almost as dark as Sassy's, and as the spray splashed into his face and chest, and Maademan tested the ledge with an approving nod in their direction, the dream was gone and he was filled with a great sense of belonging.

They landed briefly on the island where Maademan lit a fire and 'smoked' the spirit place to announce their arrival. Then he led them in a ceremony that introduced the canoe to the spirits and invoked their watchfulness and safekeeping. At the end of it, he drew his hands into his armpits and rubbed their faces with his sweat. It was the sign of approval they had sought and Amglo was content.

The journey back to the beach with the wind behind them was even faster and, when they checked the bindings on the outriggers, only two or three needed fixing. This they completed before the afternoon was done. But as they prepared to return to the encampment, Maademan drew Amglo aside.

* * *

He had come to a decision, he said. With the death of Baroway, his wife was without a husband. Amglo was now a man who had proved himself in battle and in the ways of the Night Islanders. Now he needed a wife . . . the answer was clear. It was decided.

Amglo was stunned. Veronique! He opened his mouth to speak, but no words came. He lifted his eyes to Maademan's and found an elder's concern mixed with the pleasure that comes to those who bestow gifts to friends.

Still, the words would not come, but he nodded and smiled his agreement. It was enough. Maademan left him and Amglo found the shade of a *thanka* tree where he sat with his back rested against the trunk.

Veronique. Her tribal name was Mitha which meant 'sweet' in the language of the Night Islanders. But if there was a sweetness about her, it was well disguised. As an Umpila woman, her arrival among the Night Islanders would have followed the usual practice among all the Sandbeach people. For the first night – or perhaps two – she would have been visited, singly and discretely, by many of the men of her new encampment. But after that she would have slept only with Baroway. And as Amglo had seen, she had made him a good and dutiful wife.

Mitha was smaller than most of the women but she was strong and fierce when roused. He was certainly witness to that in the fight that took Baroway from them, even though it was against her native tribe. So that was much in her favour.

But Amglo remained troubled. He had no idea of her age; indeed, he had lost all sense of time since his own arrival among the clan. Was it two years or three? So much had happened; the days and evenings were filled with activities, and they ran together in an endless stream. When did the rains come? Was it once a year or was it much longer between the wet and the dry? Who could say? The Night Islanders had six seasons but no one counted the time they took or the days between them. But because Mitha had been married to Baroway, she seemed older than himself, older and much wiser. And now that her hair had regrown she was pleasing to look at, and she wouldn't take up too much room in his *yutha*.

Sassy and Bruno both visited him as he sat by the *thanka* tree but they had nothing to offer except silly grins and foolish jokes so he chased them away. The little *thamanu* came padding around and settled himself by Amglo's leg. The thigh that had taken Yannick's spear was throbbing again, and the pup licked around it with his little pink tongue. Amglo closed his eyes and tried to doze.

The marriage ceremony took place that night. Sassy built a fire in a cleared area of the encampment, while Marie and Rosine placed Mitha's possessions beside it. They included a beautifully woven dillybag, palm baskets, yamsticks, turtle and bailer shells.

When the darkness came, Amglo took his place before the fire with his spears, his woomera and his firesticks. Then Marie and Maademan led Mitha up to the fire as the clan sat quietly in a circle, just beyond the fireglow. She was naked except for a tiny grass covering of her *wuthul* and she gracefully took her place on the other side of the fire. Then the people murmured, '*Ngulkuma, paampaanya, thampul.*' Tomorrow, they look around yams. And it was done. The people melted away.

Amglo went first into his *yutha* and Mitha followed. That night they made love, awkwardly at first, but as Amglo lost his nervousness, with mounting passion ... and duration. When Mitha joined the other women the next morning to walk single file through the tea trees to 'look around yams', it was with a certain tenderness of the *wuthul* that set them giggling, Mitha most of all.

20

Queensland

In 1864, a young English adventurer, Edward B. Kennedy, arrived in Queensland to make his fortune. He had been mightily impressed with the potential of 'this grand colony' and, reading of the impending sale of Crown lands at Somerset, had booked on 'one of the grand old full-rigged clipper ships from London to Moreton Bay in 84 days'.

Brisbane itself was a disappointment. However, he had reached the town in time for the sale which took place on 4 April 1865. In his book, *Four Years in Queensland*, Kennedy recalled: 'The lots offered, seventy in number, were all town lots and were bought up with great eagerness at a very great advance on the upset [reserve] price, which was fixed at £20 per acre. It averaged £149 per acre.

'Such was the excitement that two old squatters of my acquaintance also came hurrying out from England to be in time for the bidding. For was not Somerset to be the coaling depot and chief place of call for the Torres Strait line of steamers, and to be a free-trade port into the bargain.'[1]

Kennedy and his squatter friends were all successful in their bids. However, as will be seen, his dreams of a financial bonanza would go the way of the Jardines' vaulting ambitions. And before he left the southern capital, Kennedy lost a further several hundred pounds on an investment in vineyards which made him 'a loser till the end of time'.

Undeterred, he accepted an invitation from 'a genial squatter at the Queensland Club' to stay a few days on his station west of Ipswich. There he met a young clergyman who on their return to Brisbane took him to Sandgate where he had his first meeting with the Aboriginal people. As the preacher prepared to address his audience, an Aboriginal man signalled his compatriots to be silent and told the clergyman, 'You give mine tixpence mine say lorsprer tin commands budgeree quick all same white fella.'

According to Kennedy, this translated as, 'Give me sixpence, I'll say the Lord's Prayer and ten commandments splendidly quick as a white man does in church.' Then, he reported, 'without a moment's hesitation, he rattled off like lightning, as far as we could gather, the Biblical sacraments as promised.'

After such an introduction, it seems, Kennedy's view of the original inhabitants only deteriorated. Indeed, he would write that, 'Anyone who is really acquainted with the matter . . . will bear me out in saying that there is not a redeeming point in their whole character. This is a sweeping assertion but it is a fact that there is no savage in the world so thoroughly low and degraded as the Queensland black. It will sometimes be remarked, "Look how they have sometimes befriended unfortunate explorers and shipwrecked sailors." Yes, and look how they have killed them too. The exception proves the rule.'

However, his opinion has all the hallmarks of a justification *ex post facto* of Kennedy's appalling behaviour towards them. For in at least two of his four years in Queensland, he was an enthusiastic member of the Native Police Force.

His approach was fairly typical. 'We Britons,' he wrote, 'with good reason, determined to develop and populate this magnificent island continent, and as time went on we organised a force of

Native Mounted Police for the purpose of protecting outside settlers from the raids of the blacks. As I served in the force during [a portion of] the sixties, I will endeavour to describe as accurately as possible the sort of life we led. At the same time, it will be obvious to any Queenslander of those days that some episodes connected with the doings of the force cannot be published.'

This calls into question the veracity of both author and his creation. Nevertheless, some non-controversial aspects of the book provide an important background to the Frontier War and the Native Police's part in it. For example, Kennedy revealed there were virtually no training or entry examinations required for officers of the force: 'As long as a man bore a good record, could ride and understand the use of firearms, he had as good a chance of entering the force as anyone; and he would be a poor "new chum" indeed who did not possess these qualifications.

'As for drill, beyond a few simple forms, or any sort of red tape, I never saw it, though I stayed at various barracks for longer or shorter periods. It would have been no use. The true drill belonged to the "boys", and in fact to all blacks who from the time that they could walk are naturally drilled by their tribe to track, indulge in mimic warfare, and above all to scout so as to get in first spear, waddy or boomerang. Piccaninnies swim as a puppy would – directly they can use their limbs.'

Initially, Kennedy accompanied a Native Police patrol from Townsville as an 'amateur'. But so 'fascinating' he found the 'free and independent life spiced with danger' that he applied to become an officer himself. This he secured through the good offices of Premier Robert Herbert and he began his service at Rockhampton at £9 per month plus rations.

Kennedy was given a horse named Timeringle and 'told to proceed to Spring Creek Barracks [in the] Comet and Nogoa district'. After becoming lost several times en route, he joined the only other officer, 'a pleasant Crimean veteran', and sixteen 'boys'. Their task was to patrol a list of cattle and sheep stations, 'rendering assistance to the squatters in the event of their calling on you for protection from the aborigines'.

He kept a journal of his first patrol with five Aboriginal troopers and ten horses. Their task was to locate a missing shepherd. 'On reaching the man's hut,' he wrote, 'we found everything in disorder, and as it proved, the blacks had raided most of his things, but had done no further mischief, for we ran the man himself to ground – or rather up a tree – where we found him very thirsty and frightened but with a whole skin. They evidently had no intention of hurting him, for they could have followed him up as we did if they had liked.'

Kennedy and his patrol found the camping spot where only some old women remained. 'They did not appear at all frightened, neither assisted nor disturbed us whilst we searched about for the man's things. We camped that night about a mile from the natives and next day assisted stockman and black boy to get in the cattle.'

He recounts the killings of a station owner and timber-getters in the district by Aboriginal parties led by a former Native Police trooper, 'Nicky Nicky'. A station owner named Blake tracked them down but their leader escaped and found refuge with another tribe.

Soon afterwards, Kennedy returned to London where his book, published in 1870, brought him sufficient exposure that he followed it with a 'romance' also set in the Queensland outback. It was not successful and nothing further was heard of him.

However, while Kennedy's investment in Somerset languished, much had occurred in the northern outpost of the Empire. After John Jardine abandoned his post in 1865, his place was taken by Captain Henry G. Simpson R.N. But like his predecessor, Simpson was unable to see out his three-year appointment and departed at the end of 1866 on sick leave. He retained the formal posting throughout 1867 when it fell vacant once again.

This opened the way for the return of the eldest Jardine son, Frank, the cattle drive veteran. Alas, the settlement had not lived up to the Jardines' expectations. And though the surviving cows had produced sufficient progeny to supplement the Somerset market, Frank was barely eking out a living from his property.

By now, the eager Anglican missionaries, Francis Jagg and William Kennett, had chosen the 'heathen Aborigines' of the area for conversion to the one true faith. They were learning their customs and their language. Kennett began a school of eight pupils. They made friends with the Aboriginal elders and Kennett, who had a remarkable facility for Aboriginal languages, became an adopted son of an elder named Passiwodop.

The missionaries had recently arrived from England supported by the London Society for the Propagation of the Gospel, though it was felt advisable that Mrs Jagg and her two children remain in Brisbane, for the moment at least. The Queensland government provided accommodation at Somerset and some funding for school materials.

The Aboriginal people were nervous about attending school since Jardine had banned them from the settlement. So the missionaries went to their encampments bearing gifts to gain their confidence. According to Cape York historian, Nonie Sharp, 'Kennett's gifts were not only useful and sought after, especially the tomahawks; gift-giving was the idiom with which the local people were intimately familiar – their means of coming to terms with their neighbours, of turning enmity to friendship.'[2]

Kennett made contact with all the tribes of the area, often acting as mediator in their disputes, so that by August 1867 he was able to report the ending of hostilities among all the tribes of the far north of the Cape York Peninsula.

Somerset officialdom was unimpressed. The Acting Police Magistrate, Captain Simpson, who regarded both missionaries as 'foolhardy', levelled a fierce attack on Jagg for inviting Aboriginals

into his home. Jardine took up the issue and 'disciplined' the
missionary. Nonie Sharp explains: 'This is hardly surprising since
the officials were not in touch with actions that gave expression to
a belief in common humanity, and which offered to Aborigines the
knowledge to help them adapt to new events and circumstances
. . . [they had] created a climate in which acts of violence against
local people by the settlers became harder to justify. In practice,
this meant that the missionaries were forced to leave Somerset.'

This was accomplished within eighteen months of their arrival.
As he left, Jagg said, 'The Aborigines have been described as the
most degraded, treacherous and bloodthirsty beings in existence
by the present Police Magistrate [Simpson] and those whose
only idea is to shoot them down whenever they are seen.' Sharp
concludes: 'It had become a life or death issue for the Aborigines.'[3]

In January 1868, Simpson relinquished his position and 26-year-
old Frank Jardine succeeded to the role of police magistrate. By
then, the government was having second thoughts about the
wisdom of retaining the settlement. In June they decided that
unless further support came from Britain, it would be abandoned.

When John Jardine in Rockhampton heard the news, he
wrote directly to the new premier George Palmer that unless his
government bought the family stock, his son Frank would walk
off with his stockmen on the next ship. 'The Jardines had become
the supreme power at Somerset,' Sharp says. 'The Government
needed their services and they needed the Government's mantle
of authority and respectability.'

However, in 1868 the stalemate collapsed when four of the
original 'troopers' his father had brought to the settlement allied
themselves with the 'wild' tribes and sacked Frank Jardine's cattle
station at Vallack Point. It was yet another blow to the great
Jardine quest for colonial riches. In early 1869, Frank applied
for leave of absence.

His successor, Henry Marjoribanks Chester, was equally
unsympathetic to the original owners, and from his first day he
adopted the frontline attitude: 'On arrival at Somerset, there were
seventeen horses and a mob of about a hundred cattle running
in the bush. Jardine remained for a week and showed me over
the Settlement. He impressed me never on any account to leave the
house without carrying a revolver, even if only going as far as
the stockyard, and cautioned me, in the event of a night attack
by the aborigines, never to stand upright on the verandah [of
Government House] where the aborigines could see me, but to
go on my hands and knees, the better to see them.'[4]

21

Amglo

The first year of his married life brought Amglo a sense of excitement and achievement that he had never known before. Much of his time was spent in the *tangu* with Maademan and Sassy. They needed another crew member who would join them on special hunts far out towards the great reef or if one or other of them were taken up with other duties. They chose one of the young men with whom they had shared the ordeal of initiation. He was named Markuntha (strong) and he certainly lived up to it. He was slimly built but with wide shoulders and powerful back muscles that were ideal for pushing the canoe through the chop in pursuit of the greatly prized *watayi*, dugong.

Amglo had suggested Bruno for the role and his friend was pleased to be considered. But neither Maademan nor Sassy were keen and when they gave their friend the chance to show his skills, it was soon painfully clear that he wasn't suited. He had trouble squeezing into the canoe's narrow beam and once in he wobbled the craft and barely pulled his own weight.

When they reached the shore there was no need to tell him the verdict. He walked up the beach with his shoulders slumped. Amglo followed him but when he caught up he could see that behind the disappointment his friend was actually relieved.

Hunting dugong would take him away from the youngsters who loved his stories and his teaching of the arts of tracking, throwing their short spears and hunting the small creatures of the bush and the creeks.

'Mini-mini,' he said with a sad smile. All good.

Markuntha was Sassy's choice and it needed only one trial in the canoe to realise that they would make a great team. And Maademan, who was the harpooner, *wataychi,* said that if they worked well together they had every chance of besting the clan's top hunting crew led by the man Amglo had christened 'Edmund', the father of Mimi who had been stolen by the Umpila tribe.

It was not to be; at least not in this first year. But that in no way lessened the excitement of the hunts. They began with the big saltwater turtles. There were three species – the *tukulu,* green; the *kuynangkay,* hawksbill; and the *wapun,* loggerhead. Their favourite by far was the *tukulu,* with its shell almost half a metre long and delicious meat within. They lived near the seagrass beds and by the distant coral reefs. The females laid more than a hundred eggs at a time and the clan knew exactly where they came ashore to deposit them beneath the sand. It was one of the many secrets they kept strictly within the tribe.

The *kuynangkay* and the *wapun* were smaller, but the *wapun* was easily the most dangerous with its powerful crushing jaws that could take off a man's hand. There were many ways to hunt the turtle, but all had to be handled carefully.

Amglo killed his first *tukulu* in the days after his marriage. They had spotted it in the seagrass shallows and as they drew level with it, he leapt overboard with a net attached to a rope that Maademan held in the bow. Once their prey was entangled, they paddled the twenty or so metres to shore where it was quickly upturned, killed and butchered. That night the people held a feast in Amglo's honour and he was given the best portions which he later shared with Mitha in the privacy of their *yutha* fire.

But further out to sea, the hunt was much more dangerous. A harpoon could not penetrate the tough shell of a *tukulu* and this is where Markuntha earned his place in the canoe. He was not only a strong swimmer, but brave with it. When they spotted a big turtle, Maademan, Sassy and Amglo would paddle as hard and fast as they could to overtake it. Then Markuntha would dive from the platform and grab it by the edges of the shell in both hands and with every ounce of his strength, turn it on to its back, giving Maademan the chance to drive the harpoon home.

The *tukulu* fought back and many times Markuntha was helped aboard, bleeding from cuts and deep scratches. If it was male and small enough to fit into the canoe, they would haul it aboard; otherwise they would tow the creature back while keeping a sharp eye on the reef sharks or the fearsome *chucha*, northern whaler, that also fed on wounded turtles. If the sharks swam too close, Maademan was ready with the long, finely tipped spear that he would drive home just ahead of the dorsal fin. Of course, if the turtle was female, they would bring it back alive and the eggs would be given to the wives of the hunters, and relatives would receive their share.

But the dugong hunts were the real adventures. And they were much more than that, for since time immemorial the *watayi* had been the heart and soul of the Night Islanders' spiritual world. Until his manhood, Amglo had been only vaguely aware of the importance they placed on the laws and customs that surrounded it.

He remembered that first open slap Maademan had delivered to the side of his head when he ate of its flesh all that time ago. Only now did he appreciate the depth of his wrongdoing. In his ignorance he had offended some of the most sacred observances. It was almost as if Monsieur le Curé's housekeeper, Madame Le Blanc, had fed the holy wafers and wine to her pet kitten. It was more than a sacred observance; it was the source of the Night Islanders' earthly pride. They were the *Pama Watayi*, the Dugong

Hunters, and their fame among the Sandbeach people was hard earned and well deserved.

★ ★ ★

They would wait for a relatively calm day before making cere-mony, seeking good fortune from the *yilami* then striking out just as the sun rose above the wide ocean. Their first stops were the seagrass feeding grounds of the dugong, and on such days they would even ignore the *tukulu*. The quest was only for *watayi*.

Maademan was armed with a harpooning system that had been with them since Storytime. The barbed head of the harpoon was attached to a long rope made from a special tree fibre plaited together to give it great strength. It was coiled in the canoe just below the tiny platform on which Maademan stood; and when they came close enough to the great creature he would strike forward with the shaft and leap overboard as he drove the harpoon home. He had to watch the rope carefully so as not to be entangled and dragged under as the dugong powered away from the canoe. He must also collect the shaft which had separated from the barbed head embedded in the animal and clamber back on board, all before the fleeing dugong reached the end of the fifty-metre rope.

Depending where the harpooner made his strike, a dugong could drag a canoe and crew far out to sea before it tired and they were able to pull their craft alongside, attach the rope to its tail and hold its head underwater until it drowned. And since it was far too bulky to bring aboard, the long paddle home dragging the bleeding dugong would often attract more sharks than a turtle hunt.

That had happened twice to Amglo and his team. The first time, they were pestered by a school of reef sharks and they drew the dugong tightly alongside and defended their prize with short spears and fighting sticks. But on the second they were attacked by a *thukuuru,* tiger shark, as long as Maademan was tall and as fierce as an angry *thaipan.* Among screams and shouts, their spears had little effect and they were hard pressed to keep the canoe upright as the shark's great tail smashed into the side of the canoe and the open jaws tore huge chunks from the dugong's upturned belly. Amglo had never been more afraid in all his life. They had little choice but to cut the rope and let the *thukuuru* have his feast. They were a tired and sorry crew when they finally reached home.

Usually the team butchered the dugong at a special place on the beach far from the encampment and divided the portions in line with kinship relationships – Maademan taking the choicest cuts, Sassy and Amglo the lesser, and Markuntha the remains, all to be shared with relatives. The meat was boiled in bailer shells and the cooked parts were stored on top of the *yuthas* to keep them out of reach of the roving camp dingoes.

Amglo's success as a hunter was reflected in his contented home life with Mitha, though his dog had never quite taken to her and she kept him well away from the *yutha* unless Amglo was there. He'd named the pup 'Puuya', brave, after his attack on the *ayntikanu,* and he was growing into a fine hunter himself.

After the marriage, Amglo had built a bigger place for them using thin saplings dug into a circle and bent in a half-moon shape to meet in the middle where he tied them together with rope. Once the frame was firmly in place, he covered it in paperbark to give shade in the warmer weather. Bruno helped and when it was done the extended family celebrated that evening with a dance.

Mitha laughed at Amglo's pride. After all, the clan would be moving to a new camp soon enough and the *yutha* would be left behind to be blown away by the big winds from the sea. Amglo didn't care. If he could build one *yutha,* he could repeat the process; and next time he might make it bigger.

As it turned out, Amglo's family was itself about to become bigger. No sooner had he completed the home than Mitha realised she was with child. When she told Amglo, he was struck dumb. And for two days he told no one. He spent the time alone walking in the bush or fishing with his spear in the small bay south of the encampment. A father: *piipi*. He tried to see himself in the role, but somehow the picture refused to take shape.

But when he returned and told his friends, the reality of his new role quickly became clear. Mitha consulted old Chilpu who advised that, until the baby was born, neither he nor Mitha could eat any food that came from animals with sharp claws like the possum or with spines like the echidna. The bandicoot, with his pointed toe-nail, and especially the goanna, with his claws for climbing, were also banned, lest by magic and sorcery the unborn child was harmed. Amglo made no objection; for while he didn't fully understand, it was best not to take the risk.

It was bad enough that Mitha in her new state became something different from the lively night companion and hard-working provider of their basic food needs. Some days, she stayed in and around the *yutha* and it took the other women to rouse her for the daily expedition. And when Amglo returned from his day's hunt, he was met with a surly silence that, he knew, other men of the tribe would not have tolerated. Amglo himself was tempted more than once to respond with a sharp smack. Instead, he withdrew inside himself and poured all his energies into the hunts and fishing trips with Maademan and his crew.

And so it might have continued throughout the pregnancy but for two unexpected events. First came the news that the Kuuku Y'au had discovered the tip of Amglo's spear in the big *ayntikanu* that he and his friends had attacked in their payback for the death of Tookie.

The accusation came in what was otherwise a peaceable corroboree. In fact, Amglo had enjoyed being a figure of some attention through the four-day meeting of trade and ceremony with the Kuuku Y'au and the Barunguan people who also spoke a similar language to the Night Islanders.

All had heard of the *Pama Pulpu*, white man, and the Kuuku Y'au in particular seemed very curious about him. Since he could now carry on a conversation in their language (albeit with a strange, mysterious accent), the men peppered him with questions, while many of the women and children gawked at him wherever he went. And they laughed behind their hands at his dancing.

However, on the last day as the men were seated in a circle near the dancing ground, the mood changed abruptly when Wondal, one of the big men of the Kuuku Y'au, produced the head of a spear. He claimed it had been found in the skull of a dead crocodile; and as everyone knew, he said, the *ayntikanu* was the revered totem of his clan. Everyone also knew that the Kuuku Y'au were a generous people who made no fighting when others – especially the Night Islanders – took the young crocodiles for food. If they did not, then the numbers would rise and the rivers would be filled with them. But it was one thing to kill the young for food. It was another to wound and kill *al'alanka,* over a long time, not for food but to hear *kiithal wuthaanya,* cries of pain.

He brandished Amglo's spear head. 'It is Night Islander!' he said.

There was a silence. Then just as Maademan made to respond, Amglo said, 'The spear is mine.'

All eyes turned to him. Maademan was surprised but Amglo knew that he would not back down before the Kuuku Y'au. Unless he acted quickly, the two tribes would be at war.

Amglo stood. 'I alone attacked the *ayntikanu*,' he said. 'My people knew nothing of my action.'

There was an angry murmur from the Kuuku Y'au. A *Pama* would apologise for the insult. But this *Pama Pulpu* showed no such manners. He and his clan must be dealt with.

Wondal spoke directly to Maademan. *'Maku?'* Is this true?

'Yuway!' Amglo said. Yes! He caught Sassy's eye. His friend was about to speak but Amglo shook his head and Sassy frowned as he settled back. Bruno was nowhere to be seen.

Wondal was angry. Amglo could see it in his face and hear it in his voice.

'Pama Pulpu mukana!'

It was a sentence of death by unequal combat. Amglo knew exactly what awaited him. Two warriors of the Kuuku Y'au would be armed with two spears each, while Amglo, at only fifteen metres distant on open ground, would have nothing but his *yuli* to defend himself. But he could also have a friend – also with a *yuli* – to deflect the deadly spears from their target. And Sassy would be that friend.

The meeting growled and scurried with excitement at the prospect. And in almost no time, it seemed, they had cleared the space where the contest would be played out. Maademan offered Amglo his carved and painted *yuli*. Amglo thanked him but preferred his own which was slightly shorter at about half a metre – crudely made from the *chulu* tree but strong enough to fend off all but the *kaaya*, the most powerful fighting spear. Instead, Sassy took Maademan's *yuli* and the two young men stood their ground, Sassy on Amglo's left, as the spear-throwers reached the line drawn in the sandy soil and the people crowded along the two sides of the battleground.

Wondal gave the signal: *'Waayina!'* Throw!

Both throwers made to fling their spears, but it was a trick and only one followed through with his short, thin *panti* designed to fly so fast as to clip a bird in flight. Amglo parried it in the last split second but it brushed his cheek and as he moved the second *panti* flew directly at his belly. Sassy was just able to intercept it but its barbs seemed made of metal for they stuck fast in the *yuli*. And before he could pull it out, a heavy *kaaya* was whistling through the air at Amglo.

Only his speed saved him from a deadly blow as he ducked and raised his *yuli* in the same motion. But even then he only changed its course slightly and, though the barbs missed, the shaft smashed into the side of his head and he fell sideways. That was when the second thrower launched his final spear and it came with the speed and accuracy of a silver gull diving into a shoal of baitfish.

Amglo's head was spinning. He could do nothing to defend himself. But in the last second Sassy had wrenched the *panti* from Maademan's *yuli* and he flung out an arm with the shield just covering Amglo's flank; and the great spear skidded off the polished timber and buried itself harmlessly into the ground.

Amglo went down. The blackness enveloped him. But it was only for a few seconds. When he opened his eyes the world was still spinning and the pain in his head was almost unbearable. But he was alive; he had survived. And his place within the Night Island clan was a respected one.

But that was only the first of his ordeals; and it was over in a day. The other would be with him forever.

22

Cape York

When Frank Jardine departed Somerset for his leave in Rockhampton with his father and family, the new Government Resident Henry Chester was left with only six Europeans and three Aboriginal troopers to guard the settlement which, after the first land sale, numbered perhaps fifty hardy souls. At the time they were threatened by the Yardargan people whose country was about forty kilometres south of the settlement. They were a powerful clan 'who could put 400 young men in the field'.[1] However, between them and the settlement lived the 120 Gudang people who were traditional enemies of the Yardargans, and would often warn the whites when an attack was being prepared.

Chester had little regard for the town police and had them replaced with water police in 1870. An additional five troopers also arrived but as they were still under sentence for rape and robbery, Chester wanted no part of them. A boisterous character, in 1860 he had clashed with a French swordsman with a dangerous reputation as a duellist, so when challenged Chester nominated butcher's cleavers as his weapon of choice. In his telling of the tale, the Frenchman hurriedly left town.

Born in 1832 in London's Cripplegate, the youngest of twenty children, Chester nevertheless had a primary education that fitted him for the Royal Mathematical School. Founded by Charles II, the school specialised in the study of navigation and in 1849 Chester was appointed a midshipman in the Indian Navy where he served for the next eleven years.

When the British War Office disbanded the fleet in 1862, Chester migrated to Australia and took a job with the Union Bank in Brisbane. Soon after, he joined the colonial government as Commissioner of Crown Lands and Police Magistrate in the Warrego district of Charleville and Cunnamulla. In 1868 he transferred to Gladstone, before taking up the Somerset position.

Chester used his water police and troopers in a series of 'punitive expeditions' and acts of 'dispersal' from Somerset. According to Cape York historian Nonie Sharp, he also employed 'terror tactics sanctioned by officials and carried out by Aboriginal mounted police' and a 'deliberate fomenting of the enmities between the clans of the area, as a cruel means of reducing "the Aboriginal problem".'[2]

His time as Government Resident was cut short by the return of the bad penny, Frank Jardine, who in August 1869 resumed his position as Police Magistrate to which he now added Clerk of Petty Sessions, District Registrar, Meteorological Observer and Shipping Inspector. Chester departed to explore parts of New Guinea where he managed to inflame the people of the Fly River, as indeed had others before him.[3]

While the Aboriginal people remained hostile, Jardine gradually changed the focus of his enterprise from land to sea and within two years had developed a pearl shelling operation based in Somerset with forty employees – a mix of Aboriginals and South Sea Islanders – on four boats.

Meanwhile, in the rest of Queensland the conquest of the Aboriginal people proceeded apace. The notorious Frederick Wheeler of the Native Police established his headquarters in Marlborough between Rockhampton and Mackay. In 1870 a letter published in the Rockhampton *Bulletin* from 'A Lover of Justice' claimed that Wheeler had boasted, 'The blacks only stayed in the town of Rockhampton to save their lives.' If they strayed fifty miles from town they were 'hunted down' because 'he could shoot as many as he liked without interference'.

Another said Wheeler's name 'inspired the aborigines with such a wholesome dread, that it was only necessary, when on any of their marauding expeditions, to say, "Wheeler's coming" or "Here's Wheeler" and they would go yelling pell-mell into the bush'.

He was mildly censured by the Commissioner of Police after an incident near Yaamba, north of Rockhampton, in which an Aboriginal prisoner allegedly threw himself from a horse, heavily chained and handcuffed as he was, into the river, with the intention of swimming to the other side and escaping. 'Then,' Wheeler wrote, 'after a few ineffectual struggles he sank and drowned.'[4]

These continued savageries from the Native Police were rousing some graziers to public protest. Gideon Scott Lang delivered a series of public lectures and published a pamphlet in which he declared that as a Queensland grazier he was 'no blind partisan of the blacks', but they could be 'managed' without fighting. He said that there had been more 'destruction of Aborigines' in Queensland than in any other colony. It had been 'wholesale and indiscriminate and carried on with a cold-blooded cruelty on the part of the whites quite unparalleled in the history of these colonies'.[5]

While many northern settlers were men of benevolence who wished to 'save' and 'civilise' the local people, there were others who were 'cowardly cold-blooded murderers'. They were able to do as they pleased because 'it was the rule and custom to arrange the black question by killing them off'.

Lang said that without the Native Police the squatters would have been encouraged to come to terms with the Aboriginal people; but with the force available to 'crush them out like so many ants, any more tedious way of quieting them is seen as a useless risk and a waste of time'.

The grazier accused the Queensland government of adopting a policy of extermination. According to historian Henry Reynolds, 'Like many other humanitarians, Lang looked to the [British] Colonial Office for deliverance. And if the British failed to intervene "on their head be the blood". But no assistance came from Britain.'[6]

Reynolds recounts the tragedy of Morinish, a small mining community just north of Rockhampton:

'In 1867 Morinish learnt the meaning of the term dispersal. Townspeople were woken a little before sunrise by a volley of shots coming from the town [Aboriginal] camp a few hundred yards down the main road. Those who were already up rushed towards the camp where a scene presented itself "brutal on the part of the perpetrators and revolting to the feelings of those who saw it".

'The camp was deserted but around the fires were remnants of blood-covered clothing and trails of blood leading in every direc-tion. Eventually, the bodies were discovered in the surrounding bush. The wounded staggered into town – including a [Aboriginal] girl with a bullet through her thigh and a little boy with a similar leg wound. Horrified townspeople were told that the attack was a reprisal for the murder and mutilation of a shepherd on a nearby station. But it was eventually learnt that the outrage had amounted to no more than the theft from the shepherd's hut of sugar and tea. That was the only justification for the horrible tragedy and disgraceful butchery.'[7]

After the massacre, a miner wrote to the Rockhampton *Bulletin* in protest and his letter was republished in London and sent to the Secretary of State for the Colonies. The secretary's office forwarded it to the new Queensland government of Premier Robert Mackenzie. Nothing further was heard of it.

By now most of Queensland had been either explored or settled by the British colonials. They had populated the body of the colony from the southern border to Townsville, west across the Barkly Tableland to the Northern Territory border, and north to the Gulf of Carpentaria. The Jardines' cattle drive had followed a rough course up the western side of the peninsula to the tip of Cape York. Virtually the only area untouched by the whites was the eastern coast of the cape, the home of the Sandbeach people.

23

Amglo

Amglo's second shock arrived with the birth of Kanti's child. In the time since they were lovers, she had married Yannick, the union made all the more urgent when it became clear that she was already pregnant. She could only hope that Yannick would believe the child was his.

When she was due, she made her way to the *tabu* area and there, in the care of her aunties, she gave birth to a *pulthuna*, a little boy. When the head appeared she must have been greatly relieved because at first Yannick might well have been the father. The baby had dark eyes and hair, as did both Yannick and Amglo; his skin, purple and pink, covered in blood, could have been that of a pure Night Islander; and his face was all scrunched up with a flat nose and a well-shaped mouth.

The aunties cooed happily, cut the umbilical cord and wrapped the placenta around it for burial in the little boy's sacred place. Then they carried him to the nearby stream where they washed him and inspected his toes and fingers to see there were the right numbers of each. That was when their first puzzlement began. For while all babies had mottled skin when they were born, when they laid him in the *ulku* basket made of palm leaves, his facial features seemed sharper than usual.

At the time, they merely sighed and chattered about babies they had known. At least his lungs were in good order – he cried loud enough to wake the evil spirit Awu lurking in the forest. And when he attached himself to his mother's teat, he held on so tight that tears came to Kanti's eyes and the aunties chuckled, laughed and gave each other friendly slaps.

It was the custom for the mother to remain in the *tabu* place for at least two weeks before she returned to the encampment. Once a birth name was chosen – for a *pulthuna* it would be that of the mother's brother – the baby would be presented first to his namesake who traditionally accepted it while lying prone upon the sand. By then, its skin would be darkening to the colour of the tribe. When that ritual was complete, the mother would return to the *tabu* place to prepare the child for presentation to its father.

However, in this case, there was only a little darkening of the baby's skin, and worse, as Kanti looked closely, there was an unmistakeable resemblance to Amglo. An awful fear gripped her. The ritual of deciding a baby's skin name was one for the parents and it depended almost completely on the child's appearance. It was a matter of great moment since it affected his relationship with all members of the clan for the rest of his life. So Yannick would be examining him with great attention. If he suspected the truth, both she and the baby would either be banished or, more likely, slain by the husband she had offended.

Unless . . . unless it was the work of the Awu!

That was it; Kanti had found the answer. So she told her fears to the aunties: Awu had come in the night while she was sleeping and had worked his magic on the *pulthuna* after he had been released from the mother. The aunties had seen the baby when it first appeared; and it was a true Night Islander!

Yes, they agreed, there was no doubt, they had seen the birth and it was just like any other. If the baby was slightly pale, Awu was the culprit, the mischief maker. And he was here among them. They must leave immediately, even before the customary time was up. They must return to the safety of the encampment.

The women gathered their belongings and even though Kanti was still very weak, she was buoyed by their support and set out carrying the palm-leaf basket with her precious bundle sleeping in the soft foliage. They had to help her the last few kilometres but she insisted that she carry her child all the way to the beach where her brother Markuntha was waiting, stretched out upon the sand.

When he saw the baby, he opened his mouth to speak but before he could utter a word the mother had laid the warm little body on his chest and the young man's hands rose from his sides to hold him steady. Little Markuntha made small, mewling sounds and closed his dark eyes with their long lashes and slept.

Big Markuntha looked at his sister as the aunties crowded round, chattering their story of Awu and his wicked ways. They were preparing a ceremony that would chase the spirit out of the child and when it was gone, he would be just like all the other Night Islanders. At that, the baby gave a mighty cry and the aunties laughed. With *puchal,* lungs, like that one, he would chase the wicked spirits far away!

When they left the beach, word of the sorcery spread like a cloud of insects through the community. But before the child was presented to Yannick, the aunties departed to a sacred place, *puula waya,* to make smoking and secret ceremony to remove the spirit and return Little Markuntha to his rightful colour.

It was no simple task. They walked beyond the boggy place where Bruno had caught the pigs for the attack on the *ayntikanu* and, among the great trees of the rainforest where the spirits sheltered, they made their mission known to *Yilamo.* The smoke told of their arrival and cleansed the place of the evil spirits. Then, as the sun disappeared into the mountains and the darkness thickened in their small circle, they lit a fire and danced, all five of them, beating their clapsticks and chanting their song.

For seven days they made ceremony. They slept in the open air. And each morning they inspected Little Markuntha and each morning he was the same. Kanti became silent. She would not eat the yams, the fruits or the honey they gathered; and by the seventh night it seemed that her milk was drying up. Little Markuntha cried in his hunger and as the aunties sat around the fire they comforted Kanti before, one after the other, their eyes closed and they slept deeply.

Kanti gathered Little Markuntha in her arms and left them. She travelled by the light of the moon through the rustling shadows far from the camp. She was gone a long time. Just before dawn, Kanti and the baby returned and she sang to him in his soft basket of palm leaves. And as if by magic her milk filled her *nyuunyu*, breasts, and she suckled him deeply.

She kept a watch over him and when the aunties woke they were surprised and happy to see that the child was dark skinned. They wanted to hold him but Kanti kept him close before she lifted the basket's palm strings over her shoulder. She carried him all the way back to the encampment.

The aunties ran ahead and spread the good news. Most of the Night Islanders, Amglo and Mitha among them, heard their shouts and they gathered for the presentation. Yannick took up his position, sitting at the shady fringe of the sandbeach. Kanti came forward with her child still in the basket. This was not the custom. She should have carried him in her arms and made the presentation to his father's lap where he would take the child in his hands and lift it to show the people the new member of the clan. However, once the basket was beside her husband, she knelt and drew him out.

Yannick opened his big hands to hold him. He looked the baby full in the face. His arms shot out from his shoulders with

the baby hanging between them; and all could see that Little
Markuntha had dampened his basket with his *kampu,* his urine.
It had wet his little backside which was streaked and stripy, dark
and light, like the markings of a cassowary chick. Then Yannick
turned him back and around and where he had held the child,
two big, light-coloured handprints remained on the little body.

'Pul'il', he said. Mud. The word rippled around the onlookers.
Yannick stared angrily at Kanti who reached for her child.

'Pul'il!' he shouted.

His eyes swept through the onlookers until he found Amglo's.

'Pulpu!' White! There was a terrible silence. Yannick broke it
with an angry shout. 'Palmpana!' I will throw away!

And with that he jumped to his feet and ran towards the
sea. When he reached the water, he took both feet of the baby
between the fingers of his right hand, swung his arm and hurled
it into the waves.

Kanti screamed.

Amglo hesitated only a moment, then rushed towards the sea.
Yannick tried to intercept him but Amglo was too quick. He
dodged aside then charged into the chop where the baby had
entered the water. He was nowhere to be seen. Amglo searched,
his panic rising. Then, as a small wave rose, he spotted the body.
In four or five great leaps he was with him. He reached down
and drew him out of the water.

Now Yannick was heading for him, determined to take the
child and drown his shame. Amglo had only one hand to defend
himself from the raging Yannick and by placing his body in front
of the baby he was open to Yannick's wild swings. Amglo was
going down into a metre of water, blood streaming from nose
and mouth as Yannick's fists struck his face and head.

Suddenly from the crowd on the beach Big Markuntha came
running and roaring to his aid. By the time he reached them,
both Amglo and the baby were under the water, Amglo fearing to

raise the child lest Yannick get his great hands upon it. Markuntha closed on them and leapt above the water, throwing himself at Yannick, knocking him down into the swell then thumping his head with a closed fist as he rose from the water. A second punch full in the face knocked all the fight out of him and Yannick raised his hands in surrender.

Amglo stood with Little Markuntha in his arms, the mud from the wild pigs' bog swept clean from his small body, which was a shining light tan. His eyes were closed and there was no movement of his chest, no breathing, no cries, no life. Amglo held both hands beneath him and as he reached the shore, Kanti took the baby and clasped him to her chest. She squeezed as though to expel the water and begin his breathing, but knowing even as she did so that it was too late. As his skin dried, it was becoming waxen, his little limbs hanging loose.

She turned to walk away but Amglo stopped her. *'Pi'ina!'* Wait!

There must be something he could do. Chilpu was coming down the beach towards him. Perhaps he knew the ceremonies that could bring the life back into his lungs. But no, the memory of that other time, that distant time and place when they almost lost his little brother Alphonse in the River Vie . . . the memory was drifting back to him. He took the child, lowered his little body face down on the warm sand and gently pumped his hand on his back.

Nothing. He turned him over and pumped the chest. Still nothing.

He picked him up. Then suddenly the vision of a desperate Élie Jean-Félix blowing his breath into little Alphonse's mouth burst into his memory and without a thought he pressed his lips to the baby's, then blew in short spurts while his hands squeezed his little body . . . until suddenly his own mouth was filled with the water expelled by Little Markuntha.

Amglo fell to his knees, choking on the salty liquid, still holding the child upright as he opened his mouth and cried with such force that his small body, his tiny arms and legs, seemed to shake with the strain of it. Kanti ran forward and snatched him from Amglo's grasp. He made no attempt to stop her; he turned away and vomited into the wet sand.

The aunties formed a circle around Kanti and they half-carried her to the shade where they cast frowning glances at the men gathered in groups on the sandbeach. The men looked from Yannick to Amglo. They shook their heads. Most were silent; others murmured gruffly. Blood would be spilled.

The following day Yannick's father visited Maademan and made the family's demands. His son, Yann said, was no longer married to Kanti; and was no longer responsible for feeding the child. As payback, Maademan must surrender his new canoe to Yannick's family.

Maademan listened in silence to Yann's strong words. He made no promises. He sent Sassy to bring Amglo to him.

At his *yutha*, Amglo welcomed his friend. His camp was not a happy place. When Mitha spoke at all, it was in her Umpila tongue and he knew she was doing it from anger and jealousy. Another woman had produced his first-born boy – *paanthu* – while she herself was big and awkward with the life growing in her belly.

Amglo left her without a word.

When the two younger men heard the demand that Yannick's father had made for the *tangu*, they were as one: it would not happen. Maademan nodded his agreement. But if not the canoe, he said, then what would they offer in return?

Amglo protested. Yannick deserved nothing. He had tried to kill the child! Surely he had broken the law. Maademan and Sassy were silent; and in the silence Amglo felt once again that sense of difference between himself and the *Pama,* the people he had come to think of as his own. They seemed to know the ways of their world that came as naturally as the sunrise. Whereas he was forever like the boy sailor in *Le Jeune Narcisse* with Grand-père Babin, learning the ways of the wind and sea in their little craft.

Sassy broke the silence. Instead of the canoe, perhaps they could offer the first *watayi* of the hunting season. And if that was not enough, then they could add a *tukulu*.

Maademan agreed. It was a fair price.

Amglo felt he had no choice. '*Pitaanchi,*' he said. I understand.

Maademan addressed him directly. Something else had to be settled – the future of Kanti and Little Markuntha.

Amglo knew that once again there was no choice. No other man of the clan would take Kanti as a wife when she was burdened with another man's child, and certainly not one who looked so different from the rest. Even her family would lose the respect of the clan if they took her back. They might even drown the child themselves. And Kanti would become a *woin pigoli,* a harlot, going with men in return for food and favours.

'*Punthina.*' It was decided. Amglo would take her as wife.

Maademan was pleased. Sassy took one look at Amglo's fear-filled face and burst into laughter. It was catching. Soon Amglo too was holding his sides with wild guffaws.

* * *

Yannick's family dropped their demand for the *tangu* but insisted on a second *watayi* as payback. Maademan offered a second *tukulu* and that part of the payback was finally agreed. However, they would not forgive Amglo his *ngathana,* his copulation, with Yannick's promised wife. For that he must pay in the traditional manner with a spear in the thigh.

'*Ngampa,*' Amglo said. No. '*Nuntunya!*' I refuse!

Once again, Maademan and Sassy were silent. It was the way of the *Pama.*

But this time Amglo would not relent. He still bore the scar of Yannick's poisoned spear from the first occasion they had fought. And from time to time the infection returned to pain him in the night and in the hunt. Even when Maademan told him that he would personally inspect the spear-tip before it was used on him, Amglo was adamant.

But then, with quiet words, the two men told him that unless he agreed, Little Markuntha himself might well become the target of the family's revenge. Only then did Amglo finally accept that he would have to undergo a punishment. But even so, the memory of that searing pain he had felt in another life when the first mate of the *Reine des Mers* had slashed him with a knife returned to haunt him.

Was there no other way? He asked his companions.

More silence. He looked from one to the other. Finally, Maademan nodded. There was one option, but it was much more dangerous. Since Kanti had also offended the law, she could also share in the punishment. If he chose, then both he and Kanti could be brought to the *puula waya*, the place of ceremony, where they would be tied by the wrist with rope of the *kupuy*, hibiscus tree. And with three short *panti* spears, Yannick would be free to take his payback. Their only defence would be Amglo's woomera.

Amglo considered. '*Wantila?*' he asked. When must he decide?

'*Ngalulu*,' Maademan said. Very soon.

Amglo left them and went to find Kanti. She had been banished from Yannick's fire and from her family whom she had shamed. He found her sitting in the shade of a *thanka* tree, feeding her baby. He stood in the shadows watching them. Once again, there was no choice. He could not put her through that ordeal. Instead, he stepped forward and sat beside her; and in the way of the Night Islanders he told her with little ceremony that she would be his wife. He would hunt for her and the child would be safe in his *yutha* and with his family.

She looked down upon her first-born boy child at her breast. When she nodded her head in reply, her tears fell upon his head and for a moment he stopped his suckling and drew breath, before going back to the teat with renewed gusto. Only then did she meet Amglo's eyes.

He left them and returned to Maademan. The day was passing and there was fishing to be done. Sassy had heard of a big school of *thapanamu*, young whiting, in the southern estuary and Maademan had some new nets they could use to bring back a feast.

As they walked to the fishing place, Amglo told them his decision. He would not put Kanti in danger. Her son needed her. Nor would he submit to Yannick plunging the spear into his thigh. Instead, he would offer two men of that family – Yannick and one other of his choosing – three spears apiece with only his woomera to defend himself.

Maademan and Sassy stopped in their tracks. They turned on him. They raised their voices. He was *pa'an wu-u*. Insane. Mad. By tomorrow he would be *kath'akuma*. Stone dead.

Amglo walked on. They followed, shouting their anger at him. He ignored them.

They reached the estuary and soon they were hauling in more fish than their extended family could possibly eat. Others were also fishing there and Sassy borrowed a big dillybag from a friend to carry the fish back. When they reached the encampment, they divided the fish and gave some to the owner of the dillybag. By then Maademan had persuaded Amglo that six spears was certain death. He would speak to Yannick's people; he would hold out for four.

That evening, Amglo made a second rough *yutha* a short distance from the one he shared with Mitha and set a fire before it. He took his meal with Mitha. She knew what his preparations foretold and she spoke only the language of the Umpila. But she spoke it softly and she cooked the fish with care and with the tasty greens she had gathered.

When that was done, Amglo moved to the other fire and after a while Kanti emerged from the darkness, the baby sleeping in his palm leaf basket. She placed the basket to the side of the fire, knelt beside it and lifted the child by his upper arm, the Night Island way. Then with her other hand beneath his little rump she passed him to Amglo before taking her place on the other side of the fire.

Little Markuntha slept on, cradled in his father's lap, the firelight making flickering patterns on his small, naked body. As Amglo held him, there was a moment when the constant chatter of the clan was silent, the only sounds reaching him were those of a gentle breeze in the *thanka* trees and the lolloping rhythm of the sea curling its single wavelet on the sandbeach.

He was a father.

The baby squirmed a little in his lap and Amglo handed him back to Kanti. Then they rose and she followed him to the *yutha* he shared with Mitha. Tonight the two women and the child would sleep there.

Mitha spoke to Kanti in the language of the Night Islanders. She took the baby in her hands and all three moved back into the shadows. Amglo left them and made his way to the new *yutha* where this night he would sleep with only his dingo, Puuya, as company.

★ ★ ★

The place of Amglo's ordeal was only a stone's throw from the encampment. And by the time the clan gathered there, it was mid-morning. Amglo had not slept well – dreams of lightning-fast spears flying in his direction made for a restless night. But he was up early and his morning swim with a breakfast of *ngaalu*, shellfish, cleared his head and raised his spirit.

At his *yutha*, Mitha produced the *matan*, white clay, and Amglo made the markings on his face and chest that would declare his readiness for the trial. And as he made his way from the encampment, he was suddenly overjoyed as he saw the scarlet and green flash of a *tinta*. His totem was in the vicinity; his spirit rose further in his chest.

Maademan and Sassy joined him in the short walk to the clearing. They gathered by a *kampaapa*, a banksia tree, where his mentor reported yet another change in the conditions of the encounter. Yannick's people had agreed to the four short *panti* spears but they knew how fast and nimble Amglo had shown himself to be. So Yannick would also have his *winchi'i*, his fighting stick, to beat him with.

Maademan had spoken long with Yannick's father. They did not desire the death of Amglo. The *panti* spear was for hunting small creatures and would only wound a man unless by some misfortune it struck an eye; and Amglo would have his woomera to ward off the spear points. Maademan had seen the fighting stick which was not much bigger than a woomera; and the people would be witness that the punishment was fair.

Amglo agreed; and when they reached the place he was pleased to see that both Kanti and Mitha were sitting together with Little Markuntha at Kanti's breast. Already, Chilpu had carried out the smoking ceremony and the clan was ready to see him take his punishment.

Yannick readied himself at the other end of the oval clearing. Amglo saw that the second spear-thrower was Yannick's younger brother, Banjilaka, one of the boys who was initiated at the same time as Sassy and himself. And because they had endured together, he and Amglo had been on friendly terms, despite the bad blood between Yannick and himself. Nevertheless, he knew that Banjilaka would do his family duty; he could expect no favours from that quarter.

Without further warning, Chilpu made a gesture with his hands and called, *'Waayina!'* Throw!

The spear-throwers quickly took aim while Amglo crouched to make a small target of himself and raised his woomera beside his head. Both spears flashed towards him, one at his thigh, the other – from Yannick – at his chest. He skipped to one side so the lower one missed easily but Yannick's grazed his upper arm and drew blood. Then almost immediately Banjilaka's second spear was upon him, this time at the other thigh, forcing him to try to move his weight in the other direction; and while he was focused on that he was totally unprepared for Yannick's next move. Suddenly, the bigger man was running at him, his fighting stick raised; then he flung it with all his strength straight at Amglo's face. As he turned his head aside, the cudgel clipped him across the temple and as flashing lights exploded before his eyes he felt his legs giving way beneath him. Without thinking, he raised his woomera in defence but by now Yannick was upon him, slashing him across the face with the thin shaft of his spear.

Amglo went down, the blackness on the fringe of his vision threatening to overwhelm him. As he looked up, as if through a tunnel of light, there was the fearsome sight of an enraged face, lips drawn back over teeth with one great incisor missing. He felt he was being drawn into that empty space as his *yuli* fell from his hand. He tried to move but time had slowed and moment by long moment his spirit was leaving his body.

The spear rose, and rose, its tip pointed directly at his eyes. He opened his mouth to cry out but suddenly the vision disappeared as a body came between the spear and his face and its weight drove him down against the hard earth. It was a woman's body; it was a tangle of limbs and naked trunk and as it rolled over him he caught the familiar odour of Mitha. Then other limbs, other sweat and smells – Kanti's – joined with shouts of *'Ngampa!'* No! were upon and around him.

He pushed himself into a sitting position and saw Yannick, still with his spear raised but moving backwards before the combined force of Mitha and Kanti and the support, stepping from among the onlookers, of Sassy and Bruno with spears of their own held loosely by their sides.

The weight of the clan was with them. Amglo had taken a terrible blow; the blood streamed all over his face and down his body. It was enough. The law was upheld. The spirits were satisfied. And as the sound of the people faded, Amglo gave in to the encroaching darkness; and it carried him away.

PART
Seven

24

Cape York

By the late 1860s the grazing industry on the cape had come to a standstill. In some parts it was even retreating. According to historian Noel Loos, by then the northern pastoralists faced so many problems that 'they not only sapped their finance but their enthusiasm and confidence as well'. Chief among them was Aboriginal resistance. The defence of their lands meant that immigrant workers were reluctant to expose themselves to attack and those who did so demanded high wages.[1]

Grazier and explorer, Edmund Palmer, wrote, 'The march of settlement was instantly checked, and the outflow of civilisation turned backwards.' Between 1868 and 1870, some 300 runs covering 18,000 square miles (4.6 million hectares) in North Queensland were deserted by their owners. Their cattle were abandoned or driven to the coastal settlements where they were either sold or boiled down for tallow. The Gulf Country became virtually valueless. Those few pastoralists who stayed had invested everything in their properties and had 'no hope for the future'.

But at the same time there were early indications that across Queensland the Frontier War was being resolved in favour of the colonists. Loos writes that after 1868, the period of 'uncomplicated frontier conflict' was giving way to a new accommodation. 'By February 1869,' he says, '[Henry] Bode of Strathdon, near Bowen, had established communications with Aborigines on his station and admitted them. The *Port Denison Times* reported that the "blackfellows" were anxious to be let in and were appearing openly on the outskirts of the towns, to which they were soon admitted. By May of that year the process had spread so far that one squatter claimed they were wholly admitted between Bowen and Townsville. The Aborigines and European colonists in many areas of North Queensland were entering into "a new relationship".'[2]

However, it was by no means an equal one. On the stations the Aboriginal stockmen and their wives worked for little more than rations; and the 'Blacks' Camps' on the fringes of towns were the forerunners of a devastated people's only recourse to subsistence – odd jobs for the men and prostitution for the women. In any case, it was only a temporary respite.

From Brisbane, the leader of the Aborigines Protection Society, Alfred Davidson, was reporting to its parent body in London. 'I am trying to do something for the Aborigines,' he wrote, 'but it is a very difficult and discouraging subject . . . and during the last two years I have struggled much.' He scanned the local newspapers, wrote letters to them himself as well as to the government. He lobbied politicians and governors but was 'forever frustrated, fobbed off, rebuffed'.[3]

The Queensland Premier Arthur Palmer was dismissive. Indeed, the Far North Queensland river that bore his name would provide a powerful magnet to a non-Aboriginal population of gold seekers. And when the 'rush' was at its height, it would repay the faith – or perhaps the endurance – of the remaining cattlemen of the Gulf Country. Suddenly their beef was in high demand from the thousands of prospectors lining the banks of the river and eventually extracting an astonishing one million

ounces of rich alluvial gold. Those who had earlier walked off
their properties returned at the gallop.

In October 1873 a Queensland government party disembarked
at the Endeavour River to journey to the Palmer River to proclaim
the goldfields. The group included Northern Roads Engineer
James MacMillan, Gold Commissioner Harold St George, around
ninety prospectors and a detachment of Native Mounted Police
led by veteran officer Sergeant Armstrong.

The officials were mounted, others were on foot; many in the
party were armed. Charles Heydon wrote to the *Sydney Morning
Herald* in 1874 questioning the methods used in this crucial period,
at which point 'permanent relations between the two races were
to begin'. He asked: 'Can it be possible that the leaders had
received no instructions as to the treatment of the natives, and
the importance of establishing friendly relations and treating
them with kindness?'

Apparently not. Whenever the party met Aboriginal groups,
they opened fire.

On 3 November 1873 a group of miners camped on the
Normanby River were visited by the local Aboriginals. On
their arrival, twenty-five of the miners' horses took flight. The
Aboriginals rounded them up and returned them. They then
attempted to 'parley' with the intruders and though communi-
cation was difficult, according to some participants the meeting
began peacefully.

But as so often happened, misunderstandings and the
Europeans' total ignorance of the local people's fierce sense of
territorial possession meant that relations quickly deteriorated.
Shouts turned to confrontation. A member of the party, William
Webb, later recalled: 'Messrs MacMillan and St George advanced
towards them. I noticed that they fired over the heads of the
blacks, but some of the men fired straight at the blacks, some of
whom fell. Thereupon the blacks ran away and were pursued as

far as a large lagoon, and all that went there stayed there.' All eighty were killed.[4]

The place became known as Battle Camp.

The party moved on towards the goldfields and word went out among the clans. Up to 500 Aboriginal men and women followed in their wake. In the early hours of 5 November, the miners spotted them in the bush around the camp and once again the Europeans charged with all guns firing. 'Spears were no match for powder and bullets and the blacks were handicapped,' Webb wrote. 'When all their spears were thrown their opponents threw none back for them to carry on the fight. Hundreds of blacks were killed in this encounter.'[5]

The Aboriginals were devastated. The shootout became known as the Battle of the Normanby.

Later at the Kennedy River, Webb commented: 'A lot of blacks were shot while we were at this camp. I do not know why, as they had not interfered with us.' Another expedition member, J. Hogg, also recalled an attack on 'a big mob of blacks' on the Kennedy River.[6]

Proclamation of the goldfields was followed by the rapid development of roads and settlements to support the diggings. MacMillan's hastily surveyed route became the rush track. A mail station established at a crossing on the lower Laura River, halfway between Cooktown and the Palmer River (a distance of some 225 kilometres), became an important staging post. One Harry Jones occupied land there at 'Boralga', and opened a public house and butcher's shop.[7]

According to historian Mark McKenna, arms and ammunition formed as much a part of a digger's outfit as his pick and shovel or his blanket: 'Many of the [European] miners saw the experience as an opportunity to hone their military skills; rifle and revolver practice became an "institution" in the camping grounds.'[8]

Meanwhile, the gold commissioner St George was complaining of inadequate police protection on the goldfields where fifty to eighty new prospectors were arriving every day. The *Cooktown Herald* called for more police detachments to prevent attacks and the 'atrocious murders by Aborigines' along the routes to the Palmer. Police Commissioner David Thompson Seymour complained that these had 'considerably increased as civilisation has advanced and the country became occupied for pastoral, mining and other purposes'.

The *Cooktown Herald* editorialised, 'When savages are pitted against civilisation, they must go to the wall. It is the fate of their race.'[9]

25

Amglo

Amglo's scalp had quickly healed and there were no after-effects from the side-swipe of his enemy's fighting stick. The ministrations of two wives saw to that. In fact, the active life of a Night Island warrior and the splendid array of fresh food from the hunt and the women's gathering kept him in robust health.

Mitha delivered a tiny girl–child – they called her Chuchi – and in the months that followed Amglo was at the peak of his strength and vigour. His days were spent with his fellow hunters – Sassy, Markuntha and Maademan – harvesting the sea of its dugong, turtles, lobsters, crabs, fish and rays; the land of its kangaroos, wallabies, emus, bandicoots, possums, goannas, snakes and young crocodiles; and the billabongs of their geese and ducks.

Every day was different; for as the seasons changed, so too did the relative abundance of the various animals, and the skills needed to hunt them. By the time Little Markuntha was walking, then running, in his footsteps Amglo had become a hunter of fine repute. His throwing arm was as strong and accurate as most in his tribe; his swimming outpaced all but one or two; and his speed and ferocity in battle were unmatched among his Night Islander compatriots.

Time and again he was in the front lines as conflict with one or other of the neighbouring clans erupted in battles. And he wore with pride the markings on his upper right arm that counted the men he had slain in combat. They joined with the *pithuy*, cicatrices, across his chest that numbered his wives and his healthy children. All told of his exploits, his standing and his spirit. And the bamboo plugs in his earlobes lent a dashing air to his appearance.

His children brought him pride and pleasure. Little Markuntha, bright-eyed and filled with an eagerness for life, never walked when he could run, never played when he could compete. He learned to throw his toy spear almost from the moment he could stand; and according to Bruno who tutored him with the other children, he practised harder than all the rest.

But it was Chuchi who brought Amglo his greatest happiness. She might have been darker than her brother, small-boned and shy, but she was always first to see him returning to the *yutha*, and from the time she could walk she would hurry to him, calling *'Piipi!'* Father! She would sometimes fall over in her rush to reach him and Amglo would pick her up, laughing, from the sandy soil, and carry her to the campsite.

Amglo was not alone in his open devotion to his children. The Sandbeach men found great enjoyment in the care of their sons and daughters. But his obvious affection for Chuchi was consolation to Mitha, at least in the early months when the presence of the younger and more beautiful Kanti caused the fear and jealousy that so often pained the older wives of the clan. In Mitha's case, the pain was not just of the heart but of the head. And there were times when even Amglo could see that it made her daily life difficult to bear.

She followed the usual practice of tying a string around her head just above the ears to relieve the worst of it. She boiled the leaves of the *kaykata*, the white gum tree, and sipped the water.

She walked the many hours to pluck the fruit of the *maniiti* tree in the rainforest and then spent days crushing, grinding and rinsing its powder. But still the headaches persisted.

She even consulted Bruno's wife, Sabine, who was said by the other women to know love potions that, if properly prepared and consumed, could work wonders in attracting a husband and raising his *uulngu,* penis. Sabine was willing to share her remedies – in return for yams and wild honey – but while Amglo favoured her from time to time, it was clear that he preferred his sex with Kanti. Mitha was often left to mind the children as they disappeared into the bush, or to endure the grunts and muffled cries at night.

Then came the time when Mitha again found herself with child and the headaches flew away on a spirit wind. She happily joined in the foraging by day and the dancing by night, even singing the simple melodies of her own childhood to Chuchi in the late afternoon beneath the *thanka* tree. She and Kanti renewed their friendship, and Amglo returned from his hunting to the smiles and chatter of a happy fireside.

Alas, it ended with a bleeding and a loss in the sea below the sandbeach as she squatted in the shallows and wept for the *kaa'i,* the baby, that never was.

It was Sabine who found her there, sitting on the wet sand at evening, watching the thunderheads approaching from the east, the lightning foretelling the fury of *Matpi,* the spirit of the storm.

Sabine helped her up and walked with her back to the encampment. Kanti had cooked the lobsters Amglo had caught that morning. Mitha said little and took Chuchi with her into the *yutha.* There she listened to the heavy rain on the paperback shelter and watched her daughter as she slept.

* * *

The time of the big rain, *Ngurkitha,* was the first of the six seasons that Amglo and his Sandbeach people recognised. It was followed by *Kuutulu* when the storms faded to showers and a cooling wind came from the southwest. It gave way to *Kaawulu* and a wind change to the southeast and good fishing on the outer reef. After that was dry time, *Kayimun*, then *Matpi paa'inyan* to be endured as the storm clouds built up but seldom gave up their bellyloads, until *Malantachi* when the storms roared in and the fishermen guided their canoes among the nearby lagoons, ever-ready to make the dash for shore. They moved the encampment then, preparing for the big wet; and when that was over and the *Kaawulu* wind was in the southeast, they moved again and made the canoes ready for the open sea.

Amglo built his own canoe with Big Markuntha and a little help from Bruno. It was a sturdy craft, if a little heavy in the bow and lacking the elaborate outriggers of the Night Island dugong craft. Still, Amglo was proud of it and named it *Tangu Chuchi*. It carried him to the inner reefs where the brilliantly coloured fish swam among the coral rainbow and to the haunts of the *palkuri,* lobster, and *pawa,* gummy shark. He nosed it among the shallow seagrass beds and, with Sassy or Markuntha holding the canoe steadily on course, he slipped over the side to capture a *tukulu,* green turtle, or on one memorable occasion, a young *ayntikanu,* saltwater crocodile.

Markuntha was in the rear when Amglo spotted it swimming straight ahead of the *Chuchi* near the mangroves in water perhaps half a metre deep. He took his razor-sharp *kuyuru,* turtle spear, from the bottom of the canoe and stood in the bow as they closed on the crocodile. *'Wanta mukan?'* asked Markuntha. How big?

Amglo half turned and raised his arms, indicating a little more than a metre. Markuntha nodded and put an extra effort into his paddling as they silently cut the distance to the reptile. When they were almost upon it, Amglo signalled to go a little left, closer to the mangroves. Markuntha obeyed and from his perch Amglo caught a glimpse of the white skin beneath and behind its front leg. He stood poised with the spear raised, timing the beast's lazy paddling motion, then plunged it directly into the target. But so great was the force of his movement that it carried him over the side of the canoe and into the water.

The crocodile reared backward; and that was when Amglo realised it was bigger and stronger than it had seemed when mostly submerged. He grabbed its tail as Markuntha fought to keep the canoe upright. But when he saw his friend in danger of being torn apart, he rose from a crouch and leapt into the water, grabbing the crocodile by the head and pushing its deadly jaws together.

Amglo pulled out his spear and as the crocodile twisted and rolled in its attempts to escape Markuntha's grip, he plunged it back into the underbelly again and again until it pierced the heart and the crocodile's body went slack.

By then the canoe had drifted ten metres away and Amglo swam to retrieve it. His first thought was to wonder whether there were other crocodiles in the area, but then he recalled the wise Chilpu's words – 'If you think of the crocodile he will come; so think other thoughts and he will stay away.'

Amglo thought other thoughts.

Tangu Chuchi was not suited to the long journeys to the outer reefs or the dugong hunts that were the highlights of the seasons. They were the times of greatest camaraderie with Maademan and Sassy who had both become bound to him. They were as close as brothers for the spirits themselves embraced them.

He had promised little Chuchi to Sassy when she came of age. And Maademan, who had taken a third young wife, had promised Amglo that the first daughter of that union would become wife to him to care for him in his later years. Amglo was deeply moved but made no mention of it in his family camp. For as time passed he learned the wisdom and authority of silence.

He learned too the value of diplomacy in all his dealings with his Night Island compatriots. For while there would always be squabbles and fights among them, the complex bonds of the law would ease the way around the jagged reefs that threatened tribal harmony.

He was careful to observe the delicacies. He would never approach Kanti's mother, for the law forbade it. If he spoke badly or swore, he knew to wave a lighted bark torch across his mouth, crying 'kama katta' – my mouth is foul. He knew the rituals to be observed before setting out on the dugong hunt. He knew it was forbidden for him to take any food from Markuntha, for he was his wife's brother, and though he (and Markuntha) occasionally broke that law, he realised it was part of the spider's web of custom where every strand gave strength to the whole.

He knew of the 'joking' way of speaking between relatives to overcome the formal language where offence might be taken; it was, as Maademan said, 'to make everyone happy'. He knew never to approach the fireside of another family when women were present, but to carry on his talking with other men by raising his voice.

But it was the system of sharing that lay at the foundation of Sandbeach custom and it became second nature to Amglo as he entered ever more deeply into the life of the Night Islander. He came to know instinctively the boundaries of possession and sharing that bound the clan as a single people, the *Pama Uutaalnganu,* with the Kuuku Y'au to their north and the Umpila to the south. And he was proud to be numbered among them. He was also proud to be part of the I'wai Tjilbo, the crocodile cult that opened its mysteries to him at the time of his initiation.

And so it was with great satisfaction that Amglo told his 'brothers' of his battle with the *ayntikanu,* and brought them shares of the meat that he and Markuntha stripped from its body. That night they danced and in the firelight they retold the ancient stories of the *yilami* and the spirits who were bested by the crocodile god. And it was through such meetings that he made an uneasy peace with Yannick. Such were the social rituals and links that helped to rein and curb the fighting spirit of the warriors.

★ ★ ★

Amglo loved the sea. His days were spent in its company. And in the dugong season when the great mammals came in-shore to feed on the seagrass, his nights were also devoted to its bounties. But from time to time, when the storms of *Malantachi* season brought danger to the sea hunters, he often ventured into the hinterland where in the early days his and Sassy's adventure had caused such trouble with the Umpila people.

Bruno was his constant companion on these ventures. His friend had never been a seafarer; his people were mountain born and bred. There were even times when he headed out on his own, ignoring the tribal warnings of the *wappa* man who attacked lone hunters. But nothing pleased him more than for Amglo to join him in these expeditions. And of late he had pestered his friend to take a longer journey. He spoke with an air of mystery. There was something *kachi kachi,* far away, that he wished to show him.

As Little Markuntha grew towards manhood, they sometimes took the boy with them. He was a good companion, if overdosed with an energy that had him running ahead until Amglo spoke firmly and raised the woomera that the boy had felt across his backside more than once. He had always been Bruno's favourite pupil and Amglo could see that he took advantage of his mentor's fondness. When Amglo scolded the boy, Bruno made sure he was somewhere else.

Usually the journeys lasted no more than a day or two since Amglo had a growing family to feed; and after Maademan made good on his promise to betroth the first daughter of his new bride, his days were filled with the hunt. However, on this

occasion, schools of young *kapikam*, sea mullet, had entered the
sandy estuary and half the clan descended on the area with nets
that captured enough fish, eels, tortoises and freshwater snakes
to feed everyone for several days.

So it was with a sense of newfound freedom that Amglo led
Bruno and Little Markuntha – whose new name, Yapu, older
brother, reflected the approach of puberty – into the hushed
silence of the bush. Amglo carried only his lightest weapons,
while Bruno took the firesticks and Yapu shouldered the spears
and boomerangs that would let them live from the country that
provided all their needs. Amglo's dingo, now limping with age
and encounters with one too many kangaroos, trailed after them
while Yapu's pup capered around his sire's heels.

As they entered the rainforest, Bruno drew Amglo aside and
for the first time told of the long walk ahead. Amglo questioned
him at length, but his portly companion would not be moved. The
destination must remain his secret, Bruno said, with a firmness
that Amglo had never seen before. All would be revealed when
they arrived.

Amglo couldn't help smiling at his friend's earnest frown and
accepted the bargain. The day was good for walking; his son was
dutiful; and at any second, he was sure, the familiar green and
scarlet flash would signal the watchful presence of *tinta,* his totem.

Soon they found a familiar bend in a creek bed where they
had camped before. As the sun set they speared a tasty dinner of
cuscus, possum, while Yapu foraged a great handful of wild honey
from a hive in the fork of a *pulay* tree. And just before they set
the fire, a rumble of thunder signalled a short, sharp downpour
that slaked their thirst and chased away the mosquitoes.

It was indeed a long walk, and by the third day Amglo was
losing patience with Bruno's secrecy. They had reached the foothills of the mountain range that marked the western boundary
of the Night Island territory. He had no desire to trespass into

the tribal areas of the Wik people. They defended their country as ferociously as the Sandbeach clans themselves.

Bruno pointed. *'Kuuchaanya,'* he said. Look. *'Piingkana ilka.'* We climb this mountain. He strode ahead, excitement lighting his shining face. *'Ngi'iku.'* This way.

Amglo followed but Yapu, whose burdens now included the rump of an emu they had speared the day before, called to his father, *'Piipi',* and indicated his load. *'Kuunama,'* Amglo said. Stay. Yapu needed no second offer. He settled himself in the shade of a *yungku* tree.

The climb began easily but then the going suddenly steepened. Bruno was showing unexpected strength as Amglo struggled to keep him in sight through the thickly wooded rise with boulders blocking his path at almost every turn. It was a losing battle and only the occasional cooee from above gave Amglo a point to aim at. The sweat was pouring off him and small, black bush flies were swarming in a cloud around his head. He wiped them away with his right hand while his left clasped a sapling to pull himself upwards. And while his bare feet were toughened by the years since his arrival among the Night Islanders, the sharp stones of the mountain found tender creases. He cursed the day he'd met Bruno and berated himself for listening to him.

Finally and unexpectedly, there was a small plateau to his right and behind it the shadowed slit of blackness leavened by a faint, flickering glow. A triumphant Bruno stood beside the narrow opening, a wide excited grin on his round face. Amglo's chest was heaving as he breathed in the cool mountain air.

'Ngaanimu?!' What is this?!

Bruno's face creased into a grin. *'Kuuna,'* he beckoned. Here.

Amglo waited until he caught his breath, then with a surly, impatient air, he walked the dozen paces to his friend who stood aside and ushered him into the slit.

Once inside, Amglo could see nothing but the tiny kindling fire that Bruno had made in what seemed a corner. Beside it he had placed a pile of twigs and sticks. They rested on a much larger pile of old rotted timbers covered in dust. And as he watched, Bruno bunched both handfuls together and held the cluster over the tiny flame, blowing it to catch the larger firewood. Then suddenly it caught and the light of the torch spread like magic until Amglo found himself standing in a cave the size of a rainforest clearing beneath a domed roof almost four metres above.

As he slowly turned around he saw the walls were covered with the white and red clay outlines of all the animals of Sandbeach country and more – over-sized kangaroos, rock pythons longer than any he'd ever seen or heard of, giant fish, turtles, sharks, and strange feathered creatures he couldn't identify, all swarming together like some mass escape from a great wind or a giant wave racing in from the sea.

He took a second firebrand from Bruno and stood beside the wall to his left. Close up he could see that some of the images had been painted over others, some had been scored into the rock with a sharp flint or shell. And some of the painters had proudly left their handprints, their identities, in outline on the surface . . . or were they simply telling of *Pama Malngkama*, Mankind, as just another part of this distant world? There was no way to tell.

As he stared around the chamber and held the torch high, Amglo felt as though he was part of that endless time, that never-ending world where all the animals of the earth and sea and air were connected by the spirits that surrounded them. And in that moment he felt a great comfort and belonging.

It warmed his bones and brought him the kind of the peace that comes when a storm has passed and all the world begins anew as it always has and always will.

But then another thought intruded: for while he was Amglo and that was his world, there was another from long ago – and there he was Narcisse, a cabin boy from France, and that was another place, another world, far, far away . . .

They made other torches when the first ones burned away, and though they stayed in that place for a long time, eventually the emotions it raised exhausted him. And as he left, it was almost as though he was retreating from the power of it, the strength of its all-embracing spirit.

When they emerged, the wind was cool on his skin and they spoke softly. And as they made their way back down the mountain, two questions troubled Amglo's mind: did the other men of the clan know of this place? And if so, why had they kept it secret from him?

Bruno was in no doubt. When he discovered it there were no tracks anywhere to be seen, no fires had been lit for the longest time. If any of the Sandbeach people knew of it, not a single word or whisper had ever come to his ears.

So, Amglo wondered aloud, should they tell of it when they returned?

Bruno had no answer for that. He would follow Amglo's lead.

When they reached Yapu at the base of the mountain, neither spoke to the boy about the cave and that, it seemed to Amglo, was a good guide to their final decision. Indeed, in the two days it took to return to the encampment, they barely exchanged a word about it between themselves. It was as though it was too great a secret even to share with one another. And if the boy was curious, he never once crossed the bounds of formality to ask either man of that lost time on the mountain.

Amglo was welcomed home by his brood. His daily adventures of the hunt resumed, and when the time was right, he married the very young daughter of Maademan's third wife and took her in to his family. Mitha treated her like a daughter as was proper for their ages, but Kanti was less welcoming.

And so the seasons passed, until there came a time when Bruno's wife Sabine disappeared. Some said they saw her at the northerly limit of Night Island territory. They said she climbed into a boat that carried a group of strange men. Some called them ghosts from beyond the sea. Others said they were from the same place that fathered Amglo. They said another boat lay far off shore, with sails like the clouds of the sky.

26

Cape York

As the great colonial invasion continued, the South Seas also provided a stream of newcomers destined for the infant sugar industry on the northern coastal plain. Their arrival was part of the expansive plans of the English shipowner Robert Towns to engage island labourers, Kanakas, in the development of agriculture throughout the state's arable land.

A native of Northumberland, Towns had arrived in Australia in 1827 as master of the brig *The Brothers*. Six years later he entered the 'bunyip aristocracy' by marrying Sophia Wentworth, sister of William Charles, whose Toongabbie estate provided the foundation for a career as politician, lawyer and press baron to become one of the most influential men in the colony.

Towns established a shipping business in Sydney and in the late 1840s when convict transportation ended, he sailed his ships to China and brought back indentured 'coolies' to work as shepherds. More than 3000 of them were landed in Moreton Bay and assigned to graziers appropriating Aboriginal land north and west.[1]

Towns was elected to the New South Wales Legislative Council in 1856. He expanded his own agricultural enterprise to Queensland where in the early 1860s, with the American Civil War raging, he attempted to start a cotton industry using

Kanakas as labourers. He made some progress in the area north of Bowen where the port he developed was named Townsville.

When the local cotton market collapsed with the end of the Civil War, Towns turned to coffee and that also failed. However, by then his pioneering of the Kanaka trade was well established and other European colonists would eventually bring some 62,500 islanders to work the Queensland sugar fields. But those operations also remained well to the south of Sandbeach country.

However, on the northern tip of the peninsula, the *bêche-de-mer* trade, which began in the 1840s with the Chinese market for the trepang delicacy, was flourishing anew. A processing depot had been established on Green Island off Cairns and another on Lizard Island to the northeast. There are even reports that Night Island itself was considered as a possible depot site, and that the one ship that visited at that time was attacked by the local Aboriginal people. But there is no suggestion that it occurred during the period that Narcisse Pelletier was resident in the area.[2]

Towns entered the trade in the 1860s, supplying the Australian market at a time when many thousands of Chinese miners were prospecting in the eastern states. Towns's *bêche-de-mer* boats occasionally put in to Somerset from the mid-1860s, as did other ships' captains engaged in the trade. In 1868, one of these independents, Captain William Banner, in his brig *Julia Percy,* happened upon an extensive pearl-shell bed in the Warrior Islands of the Torres Strait.

In fact, the presence of pearl shell on the Australian coast had been revealed by William Dampier in the Shark Bay and Roebuck Bay waters in the late seventeenth century. A viable industry was pioneered in that area after the explorer Francis Gregory visited in 1861. Banner's Torres Strait discovery led to the establishment of a separate pearl-shell industry based at Somerset and later Thursday Island. By the end of 1870 some 160 Kanakas were working from five vessels in the area.

The ever-adaptable Frank Jardine also discovered the advantages of South Sea Islander labour when he joined in the collection of pearl shell from his Somerset base. His association with the islanders brought him in contact with the King of Samoa, whose seventeen-year-old daughter, Sana Solia, he married in 1873.

Coastal people joined the trade and the shell was gathered by 'swimming divers' in waters up to fifteen metres deep. Boys of twelve to fourteen years old were employed and much of the diving was done at low tide for between two and three hours at a stretch. By 1874, eighteen vessels and forty luggers crewed by 707 men raised 137 tons of live shell valued at Somerset at £200 a ton. The divers received the equivalent of ten shillings a month, paid in 'trade goods'.[3]

According to historian Henry Reynolds, 'Sea-based industries were probably less disruptive of Aboriginal life than either mining or pastoralism. The Europeans who harvested the sea had no need for land other than small plots for bay-whaling stations and bêche-de-mer processing depots . . .

'Though there were violent skirmishes on every part of the Australian coast, peaceful contact may have been more common on the shore than it was inland. Both parties stood to benefit from amicable meetings – the Europeans could obtain water, local intelligence and perhaps sexual release; the Aborigines access to white man's goods without the disadvantages of permanent European settlement.'[4]

However, by the mid-1870s the most easily accessible shell in Torres Strait had been exhausted and pearlers began to use German diving suits supplied with air by hand pumps on the lugger decks. This allowed divers to collect shell at much greater depths. Fleets of luggers sailed on regular shelling operations over several days, and sometimes weeks when accompanied by mother ships to receive their harvest for sorting and packing.

Soon they were expanding their operations south to the eastern coastal areas of Cape York.

On 11 April 1875 the pearler *John Bell* was sailing off the coast of what would later become known as Sandbeach country. The ship was named for its owner, a Sydney shipwright, publican and pearling entrepreneur who had bought it from the Marsden family the previous year. It was part of Bell's pearling operation headquartered on Jervis (later Mabuiag) Island in Torres Strait and was crewed largely by men of the Mabuiag clan. Until the early 1870s the islanders, who like the Sandbeach people hunted the dugong, had a reputation for hostility to outsiders, but as German missionaries converted them to Christianity, they became much more amenable to the European traders and pearlers.

The ship itself began life as the *Iserbrook* in 1853, a general cargo and passenger brig built in Hamburg. It had brought hundreds of German migrants to Australia in the intervening years before becoming a South Sea Island trader in the early 1870s. Its captain Joseph Frazer had been involved in the Kanaka trade for several years before taking command and was well experienced in handling an islander crew.[5] He anchored and ordered a small team of Mabuiag crewmen to row the longboat ashore in search of fresh water for the journey back to Jervis Island.

They landed on a sweeping U-shaped beach of white sand just north of Night Island. Only a headland to the south separated them from the spot where Captain Pinard and his shipwreck survivors reached the shore seventeen years previously. Shortly after they landed they spotted a group of Aboriginal men and women. As dark-skinned islanders, they made friendly and respectful gestures in the hope that the owners would direct them to the fresh water they needed. But as they approached the group, they were astonished to see what appeared to be a European among their number. His skin had been browned almost to the same colour as his native companions, but he was unquestionably a white man.

Once the Night Islanders had sent their women away, they were content for the Mabuiags to fill their casks with the water from a nearby creek, particularly as they were prepared to barter for it in the traditional Aboriginal manner. And they saw them off in an equally friendly manner as they returned to the *John Bell*.

However, when they reached the ship and told Captain Frazer of their encounter with the 'white man', the master was intrigued. In the spirit of the day, he would naturally have assumed that any white man would welcome being 'rescued' from the savages among whom he had fallen. In short order he decided to send his men back to the mainland with 'trade goods' of knives, mirrors and blankets. Their task was to entice the natives to allow the European to come aboard the *John Bell*.

Once more, the Mabuiags took their places in the longboat and made for the shore.

27

Amglo

Since the sudden disappearance of Sabine, apparently with a group in a white men's boat, the Night Islanders had seen and heard of several foreign vessels passing beyond the outer reef. Amglo himself had not been among the witnesses but when he heard the reports his first thought was of the treachery shown to him by Captain Pinard.

It was a memory that had lain dormant beneath the numberless experiences he had endured and relished in the lifetime since his abandonment. It was hard for him to think of time. He had lost all sense of the European 'years', but he was conscious of the passing of untold seasons, and especially by the ageing of his extended family. Maademan's hair had turned grey. Old men like Chilpu and women like Maademan's first wife, Marie, had all died and been mourned in the elaborate Night Island ritual. Surely he had spent far more time as a Night Islander than those distant days of his childhood. But the sudden thought of Pinard made his body tense and his lips draw back in anger.

However, on that day of *Kuutulu* when the big rains had passed and the wind came from the southeast and the islanders came ashore in the longboat, the image of Pinard lived only in the fringes of his mind. The Mabuiags were people like his own

Night Islanders, if darker skinned, and some with the frizzy hair that he had seen occasionally in corroboree with the Kuuku Y'au and the clans to the north. And when they departed with their water casks filled from the nearby *alanthi,* creek, he was happy enough to see them go.

The idea that the sailing ship might somehow link him with that long ago life passed through his mind and out again. As he walked back to the new encampment after the rains with Maademan, Sassy and Markuntha, followed by several of their wives, the talk was not of the ship but of the old worn machete the islanders had left behind. Maademan used it on practically every passing tree, grinning his delight as it sliced through the bark to the bright sappy wood beneath. Everyone wanted a go. Even Amglo himself. But to his great surprise, for the first time since he had known him, Maademan was reluctant to share.

They were not long back in the encampment when Yapu came running. The black men had returned – with a white man – and they were promising more machetes, and knives and even sharpened splinters harder than timber for spear-tips. *'Kalmaana!'* he said. Come, come to the beach!

Maademan led the rush; the women came after and hung back on the fringes of the sandbeach. Amglo took his time. He was suspicious. Ships' captains gave nothing for free; and he had noticed the islanders' interest in him. They had tried to disguise it, but they were simple people, not clever like his Night Islanders.

When he reached the small crowd gathered around the long-boat, his suspicions turned to fear. The white man hung back; the main speaker was a tall man of the Mabuiags. He had a big mouth and he yabbered in a language that no one understood; but when he combined it with the mime that came so naturally to people whose neighbours jealously guarded their own unique tongues, his message was clear. The knives, machetes and nails on display were just samples of what awaited them if Amglo came aboard the big ship to choose them. The captain would then pass them over to the tribe.

But why Amglo?

The speaker was well prepared. The captain was a white man, he said, and everyone knew that people always want to deal with their own tribesmen. The captain insisted on it. But once Amglo had made his choices, he, the speaker, would personally return Amglo and the goods to the Night Islanders.

Amglo's fears rose another notch. He turned away. But from where he stood he could still hear the Mabuiag who made his appeal directly to Maademan. The knives, the nails and the machetes, he said, could make spears and fighting sticks in half the time; and the weapons would be stronger and more deadly. This would make the Night Island warriors more powerful than any other clan. And more – the dugong spears would be so sharp and solid that they would kill a beast in a single throw. He knew this because his own people were dugong hunters. There would be food aplenty for the whole tribe; the Night Islanders would be the envy of all. His own people were the perfect example – look at the longboat: compare that with the small Night Island canoes drawn up on the beach . . .

Maademan listened, looked and nodded his head. The other men murmured their agreement.

Maademan left them and walked across the sand to Amglo. The speaker's words were true, he said. With these weapons the Night Island people – his people – would defeat the Umpila and the Kuuku Y'au. They could take their women. They could hunt so well that every man could have many wives and children. And all that was in Amglo's hands. Surely he could not refuse.

Still Amglo hesitated. He had met those frizzy-haired black men before when the *Saint-Paul* was wrecked. They had tried to kill everyone, he said, and worse, they were from the place of cannibals. Perhaps that was why they wanted him – to eat the white man's flesh.

Maademan listened. If that was true, he said, then as soon as they tried to hold him he should leap from the ship and swim away. He and Sassy would follow the longboat in their canoe. They would be waiting to help him ashore.

The silence grew between them. Amglo knew that if he refused, his friends and family would not easily forgive him. He would have stood in the way of a new life, a better life, for the men of his clan.

He was torn. He too wanted to abandon the shell-blades and sharpened rocks and be reunited with the steely cutting edges of knives and machetes and nails for spear-tips. He too wanted to overpower the Umpila in war, to pierce the hard shells of the turtle with his spear and drive it deep into the heart of the dugong. And he knew that if he leapt from the ship and struck out for the shore, none of the islanders could swim as fast as he . . .

Finally he agreed; and with nerves tingling the skin of his shoulders and neck, he climbed into the longboat with the white man and the Mabuiags.

Soon after they pushed off, he glanced back at the crowd gathered at the edge of the water and the women who only now were coming down from the fringe. His little Chuchi was with them, not quite so little now as her puberty was approaching, running ahead of the others and calling something to him. Alas, the sound of the oars in the rowlocks and the brisk southeaster carried her words away before they reached him.

The big ship loomed ahead and when they reached its side, the Mabuiags held him steady until he began to climb the rope ladder up the side of the vessel. Once on deck, the captain and another white man came forward and spoke to him in a language he had never heard before. The men's gestures seemed friendly enough but there was no evidence of the promised treasures. And when he responded in his own Night Island language, neither the captain, the other white men nor the Mabuiags understood. He thought of using that other language of his childhood but despite his best efforts no words of it would come to mind.

There was a sudden tension in the air. It was time to leave. Amglo looked back to the distant shore. One or two canoes seemed to have just entered the water. He made a dash for the safety rail but the captain signalled to the Mabuiags and they barred his way. Then came the order to raise anchor and set the sails. He struggled with the Mabuiags and almost broke free when the captain and the other white man came at him with pistols drawn. These were shorter and more metallic than Pinard's dagger pistol but undoubtedly just as deadly.

He looked around wildly. A great cry escaped his lips. *'Ngampa!'* No! *'Walkina!'* Stop!

But the *John Bell's* sails filled with the southeast breeze and as the crewmen wrestled him below, Captain Frazer set a course for the passage that would take them to the open sea and then north to the tip of Cape York and the settlement of Somerset, to civilisation.

PART
Eight

28

Somerset

By 1875 Somerset was a busy settlement; there was so much activity in the Torres Strait through the pearling and *bêche-de-mer* industries, and such a constant flow of commercial shipping both ways, that Thursday Island was also developing as an entry port. Indeed, within two years it would replace Somerset as the official government station. So when the *John Bell* arrived and Captain Frazer told of his remarkable passenger, a crowd of settlers surrounded the small boat that brought him to shore.

The officials and the curious equally craned their heads to catch a glimpse of him. No more than middle height, he had been clothed by the sailors in light seafaring gear and it was not until he came close that they could see the deep tan of his skin, the well-muscled shoulders, the wild hair that stood upright on his head and the moustache that decorated his upper lip, the steady gaze of his dark eyes, the narrow white shell of a pearl oyster through his nose, the cicatrices on his chest and the big extended right earlobe carrying a wooden tube some six centimetres long.

If any called a greeting he gave no cheerful response. On the contrary, he seemed quite unappreciative of his rescue from the savages who, the settlers agreed, had obviously held him against his will. And according to Frazer, when he did speak it was in 'the mumbo-jumbo of the blacks', or in a few stumbling words of French! Either way, no one could make much sense of it.

Frank Jardine was serving his last few weeks in the settlement's principal official posts. He would again surrender his duties to Henry Chester who had returned from his New Guinea adventures. Chester would remain as Government Resident at Somerset and on Thursday Island until well into the 1880s.

But with the stranger's arrival Jardine gathered what few details he could and sent a report to the Colonial Secretary, Arthur Macalister. And until he could be transported to wherever the government decided, he was housed in the base's naval quarters under the command of Lieutenant Edward Connor and permitted to wander with only a single naval 'chaperone'. In fact, for the first fortnight of his stay in Somerset he was described as 'restless and uneasy, sitting like a bird on a rail watching everyone in a frightened way'.[1]

Even when it became apparent that he was French and Lieutenant Connor and one of the settlers with some of the language spoke with him, his only words were *'Je ne sais pas'*, I do not know. But then on 14 May, he was taken on board the mail steamer *Brisbane* for the journey south and as fate would have it, the great bulk of passengers were again more than 300 Chinese from Hong Kong, bound for the Australian goldrush. However, on this occasion they reached their destination of Cooktown safely before confronting the hazards of the riverine goldfields.

Of greater moment to the rescued 'castaway' was the presence of one Lieutenant John Walter Ottley, a 33-year-old British Royal Engineer who would serve for many years in India where eventually he would be knighted and appointed the Inspector-General of Irrigation. His mother was among the early settlers in Rockhampton and Ottley had also invested in cattle stations in Central Queensland. He would make himself known to the young man soon after he came aboard and would spend much time in his company until Ottley disembarked in Rockhampton.

Writing some forty-eight years after the event, Ottley says: 'As it happened, I had been educated for some years in Paris and consequently I possessed an exceptionally good knowledge of French, whereas no one else on board could speak that language really fluently. It thus came about that Pelletier became, as it were, my special charge . . .

'By constantly talking to him in French, I succeeded in opening up the floodgates of Pelletier's memory . . . I found him a serious nuisance owing to the fact that he had no notion of private property and seemed to think we ought to hold things in common. Coming down to my cabin he used calmly to annex anything that struck his fancy and shewed his annoyance when I took things from him and locked them up in my trunks.

'On the whole he was fairly good tempered though occasionally there were indications that his temper might be easily aroused. On one point I was quite satisfied – namely that it would be an exceedingly evil day for his old captain, should he ever have the misfortune to come across the cabin boy he had deserted so many years before. Pelletier never disguised his intention of killing him if he ever had the chance . . .

'When steaming off part of the coast he knew so well, he suddenly pointed out some apparently minute specks on a distant island and said they were canoes or dugouts belonging to a certain enemy tribe of blacks that he named. We were quite unable, even with our most powerful glasses, to make out what those specks really were; it was not until we had steamed much closer that [we saw] the objects really were canoes of some kind . . . I am now inclined to think that if the canoes had belonged to his own instead of to an enemy tribe, he would very likely have gone overboard there and then and made a dash for freedom.'[2]

29

Amglo/Narcisse

The sight of the Kuuku Y'au canoes was a sudden vision of that other world, that place of the people he loved, *his* people. Their faces danced in front of him – Maademan, Sassy, Bruno, Kanti, Yapu and little Chuchi as she ran down the beach waving to him, calling to him. What had she said? What were the last words she had called to her father? He might never know. He might never see her again. And what of her life without a father? The family would care for her, Sassy would take her for his wife, but her father would be somewhere else, far, far away . . .

He turned away from the ship's rail. That world had been lost to him the moment he'd been so roughly grabbed by the Mabuiags on orders from the English officer and bundled down to the wardroom of the *John Bell*. The captain and the other white sailors had come to look at him, to raise their voices with words that meant nothing. The one they repeated again and again was 'rescue'; and they said it with wide open eyes and clever grins. And when he stared them down they became angry, as though he had stolen their purses.

He hated the sailor's slops they dressed him in. They were rough against his skin. And when they sat him down and put before him a bowl of grey porridge, it smelled so vile he almost vomited.

They put him in a tiny cabin off the galley where the smell of burning fat turned his stomach but at least they kept him from the Mabuiags and the lying words of the speaker who avoided his eyes whenever they were on deck together. For the first few nights of the journey, they had locked his cabin door and kept it so until the morning watch. He had taken a mirror from the bathroom and he kept it hidden in the room. He had been so long without one; he stared at the unfamiliar face from every angle he could manage, and he searched the reflection for the man within.

Each day the captain had spoken to him, and though they shared no common language, he was shocked beyond words to learn that by the British calendar, *le calendrier,* the date was 1875, only seventeen European years since he had been abandoned by Pinard and taken in by the Night Islanders.

Only seventeen! It meant that he was just thirty-one years old. How could that be? His mother, Alphonsine, might still be alive. He had thought that the whole family would have long gone to their graves, that he lived on in the Sandbeach world only because the babies grew and the elders aged more slowly there than in this other world that now surrounded him. Père Martin might also be alive; his brothers Élie Jean-Félix and *petit* Alphonse would be grown men!

That night in his bunk, he took the pen and ink the captain had given him and on a sheet torn from the mate's logbook, he tried desperately to recall the words of his childhood and to write them as Monsieur Palvadeau had taught him. After several false starts he managed, *'narcisse peletier of saingile the captain left me among savages. i was a boy on board i do not know how to speak French i know how to speak savage i am not dead but alive! they would not give me to drink'*

He threw the pen aside. The French words were hiding in a shadowed rainforest of images and sounds . . .

As they tacked into Somerset Bay and hauled down the sails, he went on deck. The settlement was a scattering of old timber buildings on a headland, while on the slopes and the flat were rough huts and white painted barracks with men in uniform; and to the left a pier leading to big sheds filled with men carrying great baskets of pearl shell. They anchored in the bay and he climbed into the longboat with the captain and crew. As they approached the shore, he was confronted by the strangest collection of people of all shades and shapes that he had ever seen. They watched his every move for fear that he was some murderous savage to be bound with rope while in their company. Only when the naval officer and his sailors in their smart white uniforms took him in charge did they suffer him to be among them.

The officer whose name was Connor treated him kindly. He advised him to take the shell from his nose and the bamboo from his earlobe. And while in their conversations Connor's French was almost as halting as his own, he found that the words gave him a strange sense of comfort, a return to childhood when all care and responsibility was in the hands of others.

Each morning he swam in the bay, just as he had at the Night Island sandbeach. And on the night before boarding the ship that would take him on the first long leg of his journey back to France, Lieutenant Connor suggested he try once more to write a letter to his family.

He accepted the challenge and in the bare barrack room he set to once more with pen and ink. His lettering was firmer now and while the rules of punctuation and grammar escaped him – as they so often did in the classroom – the words were heartfelt. As he composed them in his head, that first terrible memory returned in force and he wrote:

papa maman i am not dead i am living narcisse I was on board the saint paul of Bordeaux and I had been shipwrecked in [?] the rock of the savage of the island the chinese in the island stayed and died [?]

killed i came in a little boat to an island of savages i had looked for water to drink the captain left in the little boat i looked for water in the woods i stayed in the woods i then see the savages who live on its coast come who had found me the savage gave food and drink he did not kill i give my hand he did not hurt me i stayed in the wood for a very long time i was almost dead i had o great hunger and great drink i was in a lot of pain.

He gave it to Connor who addressed it, added a note that Narcisse had begun his long journey back to France, and passed it to a sailor who would take it to the Torres Strait mail box for the next ship heading for Europe. He could only imagine the face of Alphonsine and Père Martin when it arrived.

Next morning the officer took him aboard the steamer SS *Brisbane,* the first fully steam-driven ship he had seen. It was travelling from Hong Kong to Sydney, and the news of him had already swept the ship. The people stared.

But at least he had a cabin to himself.

Below decks the Chinese were crowded into their quarters, forced to live, he said, as *'de sales cochons'*, dirty pigs, so unlike his own people. And as he stood on the deck with the English soldier Ottley, with his schoolboy French and his *tres mauvais* accent, he knew that beyond those Kuuku Y'au canoes the Night Island women would have left for their daily tasks of gathering and the men for the excitement of the hunt. He stayed at the railing, staring through the slight haze of mist and woodsmoke until it was no more than a smudge at the limit of his view.

Once the Chinese were unloaded at Cooktown, there was plenty of room for him to move around the ship. But he was troubled by the return of the infection on his leg, the legacy of his fight with Yannick. And with no Chilpu to ward off its evil spirits, nor Mitha with her herbs and poultices, he feared it would torture him forever.

When Ottley disembarked at Rockhampton, others from among the passengers and crew sought him out. One rich

Englishman named Gordon sent his servant to invite him to
meet his master who he said was 'Governor of Fiji'; and another,
named Muchell, bought him tea and cakes with his fat wife
and his thin daughter. The men spoke loudly their few French
phrases while the women – especially the daughter – stared
without blinking the whole time he was with them. Nevertheless,
despite the embarrassment and the heavy food, he did his best
to make himself agreeable. Back in his cabin, the words of his
mother tongue were returning, though at times the language of
the Night Islanders stood like fierce *gendarmes* between his brain
and his mouth.

When the ship stopped at several towns on his voyage down
the coast, he remained aboard until they reached Brisbane on
19 May. The place was hot and humid, the streets rough and
ugly among the scrubby hills. So he made but a single foray into
the town then stayed aboard until the ship found its way back
through the muddy waters of the river and out to sea.

As they drove south through the deep blue water, Narcisse
stayed mostly in his cabin, practising his writing and making lists
of French words as they returned to him. When he joined his
fellow passengers at mealtime, he was warmly welcomed and he
gradually mastered the cutlery and the manners of his companions.

But with every passing day he felt the cold seeping into his skin
and bones. It was a sensation that had been no part of his life for
the entire seventeen years of his sojourn with his people of the
clan. He hated it. The clothes they had given him were no help
at all. In fact, they seemed to make it worse. He tried staying
in his bunk with blankets up to his chin, but still he shivered
and his leg hurt.

He rose and roamed the vessel, finding the engine room where
black men shovelled great chunks of coal into the roaring furnaces.
The air was thick with dust and the raw smell of sweating stokers
but at least it was warm. He would have slept there but the noise

and the smells drove him out in search of the pure air that his lungs had known on the sandbeach.

Finally the *Brisbane* sailed through the Heads into the magnificent Sydney Harbour and as he watched from the bow the captain expertly nosed his ship into its berth. News of his arrival had obviously arrived before him, because there was a crowd waiting. They stared at him as though he was some animal released from a zoo. When the French consul himself, M. George-Eugène Simon, arrived with a small *escorte,* they ushered him through the reporters who shouted questions at him in English. He shook his head and uttered the familiar phrase, *'Je ne sais pas.'* I do not know. But this time he added another, *'Je m'appelle Narcisse Pelletier.'*

Yet even as he heard the words, he knew in his heart that they rose through the throat of another who lived within, a man named Amglo.

★ ★ ★

He remained with Consul Simon and his family for almost two months before suitable arrangements could be made for his return to France and his home in the Vendée. Fortunately, the consul reported, there was a wave of public sympathy shown to Narcisse Pelletier. His fellow travellers on the *Brisbane* had started a fund to assist his return to France. And members of the expatriate community were anxious to speak with him.

The 'rescued' castaway had much to learn from the consul and his staffers, for in the years of his other life France had undergone a political epiphany. When he left on the *Saint-Paul* in 1858, the land of his birth rejoiced in the Second Empire with Louis-Napoleon, the nephew of the great Bonaparte, firmly on the imperial throne. Now, the deposed emperor had died in exile in England two years ago.

To Narcisse, such matters were of little moment and M. Simon would report that his interviews with the castaway were from the beginning *rempli de difficultés*: 'I told him the name of his village and then I witnessed quite some of the strangest and most painful spectacles, I think, that one might see: this man made extraordinary efforts to remember. He wanted to speak to me and all that came to his lips were inarticulate sounds.

'He felt that I was not able to understand him; one might have thought that he himself did not have much idea of what he was saying or wanted to say. His face and eyes expressed a terrible anxiety and anguish, and something like despair which was painful. I suffered with him and almost as much as him. Sweat was breaking out on my brow as on his.

'Involuntarily, I remembered the tale of Hoffman's of the man who has lost his shadow and his image. I would have done anything to give him back then and there his identity, which clearly he was trying to grasp hold of again.'[1]

Narcisse was in for a further shock when the consul opened a box of letters received from his family seeking news of their lost boy. They had been written over the entire period of his life with the Sandbeach people. When M. Simon handed him one of the letters, Narcisse stared at it, unable to read anything but the signature, 'Pelletier', and quite unable to speak.

Nevertheless, as the weeks passed he was able to find some foods that he found edible – mostly fresh fruit and lightly cooked meat – and he was able to meet with several of the expatriates. M. Simon arranged for studies to be taken of him by a distinguished French photographer, Alexandre Henri Lamartinière, who sold them to the *Sydney Morning Herald*. The newspaper no doubt offset its costs by supplying copies to French and British journals when the story spread to Europe.

The fund started by his shipboard acquaintances was quickly filled and donated to the consulate. M. Simon was properly gracious in accepting the funds and early in July he personally escorted Narcisse aboard a French warship that had called into

Sydney on its way to Noumea. There he would await a second vessel bound for France.

Once again, his story preceded him and on arrival a compatriot, Charles Marchand, a young soldier who had served in the South Pacific for two years, sought him out. By happy chance, he too was from Saint-Gilles-Sur-Vie and he was able to assure Narcisse that when he departed the town both his parents and his brothers had been very much alive. Indeed, he said, Madame Pelletier had worn black every day for the whole seventeen years in remembrance of her eldest son.

On 11 July 1875, Narcisse again wrote to his parents, and on this occasion, after all his practice, his words crossed the page in a flowing hand:

> *My dear father and my dear mother and my brothers, I am writing to you again. I embrace you with all my heart if you are alive. I have arrived at Noumea the consul of Sydney sent me. I am on board a war ship. I will leave in a month on board another ship which came three days ago, I am well I still have pain in my right leg. I have been in pain for a long time, I had much misery with them. They poisoned my leg. But even so I am well.*
>
> *I send you greetings*
> *Narcisse Pierre Pelletier*

The two men of Saint-Gilles boarded the *Jura* on schedule to begin the journey across half the world via Rio de Janeiro. On the way the ship's doctor treated his painful leg and was frustrated when all his pharmaceuticals failed to heal the tropical ulcer which his patient insisted had resulted from 'a secret poison from his enemy among the Aboriginal tribe'.

Indeed, Narcisse spoke at some length to the doctor who later reported that he was 'endowed with above average intelligence, now writes very well, does some rough drawings taught him by his friends the savages and devotes himself to quite complicated arithmetical sums'. Moreover, his patient insisted that he had not abandoned his Aboriginal family willingly but had been taken 'almost by force'.[2]

When they reached Rio, he wrote again, and by now his script was handsomely decorated with extravagant curlicues (even if the grammar and punctuation still needed work):

> *My dear father and my dear mother and my dear brothers I send you*
> *all my love, I am writing to you with my news, I am well, and we*
> *have arrive at Rio de Janeiro. On 14 October, I am not happy on*
> *board. With the petty officers, I eat with the sailors on rations They*
> *have no sympathy for me. For the suffering I have had since the time*
> *I stayed with these savages. But I do not get on badly with the sailors.*
> *it was 2 months ago that we left Noumea.*
>
> *Pelletier*
> *Narcisse Pierre Castaway*

Whatever resentment he felt towards the petty officers, Narcisse was at least on the great ocean again and the spirit of the sea sped him homewards. In conversation with Charles Marchand and the sailors, he learned more of the great events that had roiled his nation in his absence.

Emperor Louis-Napoleon, it seemed, had put aside France's traditional enmity with Britain and joined her in the Crimean War which was a great success. However, the emperor's most fateful decision came in 1870 when he declared war on the rising power of Prussia. His forces were not only defeated in the battle of Sedan that September, but Louis himself capitulated to the enemy in person.

France collapsed into chaos. The Prussians held Paris under siege and conditions in the city became increasingly desperate. The people, it was said, were reduced to eating rats and even the animals from the Paris Zoo. The Minister for War, Leon Gambetta, escaped the city in a hot air balloon and established the headquarters of a provisional republican government at Tours on the Loire River.

A new republican regime was formed and when France surrendered early in 1871, Paris came under the control of a rebellious Commune and the French government, now in Versailles, attacked the Commune to devastating effect: more than 25,000 of its members were killed; those Communades who survived *le châtiment* were imprisoned with trials at Versailles still continuing in 1875. More than 4000 people were sentenced to transportation to the penal colony of New Caledonia.

Some Australian politicians, including the Premier of Victoria, Sir James Service, warned of mass escapes and said that Australia 'would never willingly submit to have the off-scourings (sic) of any other nation cast upon her shores'.[3] Consul Simon himself was drawn into *le conflit* when in 1874 six leading Communards escaped and made their home in Sydney.

Simon had rebuked Sydneysiders for their 'generosity towards the refugees', and the *Sydney Morning Herald* outraged him when it editorialised that there may have been some 'intended negligence' by the French authorities to allow the men to escape.[4]

But as the *Jura* crossed the Atlantic and headed north to *la belle France*, Narcisse was occupied with matters much closer to his heart. The journey was both a departure and a homecoming and the nearer he came to his waiting family, the more excited his anticipation; the further he travelled from his other life, the more those bonds were stretched. And when the *Jura* passed through the Gates of Gibraltar and the port of Toulon hove in sight, the prodigal gave himself up entirely to his *resurrection* from that other life and to the embrace of his family of childhood. For the moment at least, Amglo was no more.

PART
Nine

30

Saint-Gilles-Sur-Vie

When that first roughly penned letter from Somerset arrived at the family home in Saint-Gilles, Alphonsine was stunned. She had, indeed, worn black ever since Narcisse was lost. The letters she and Martin had sent seeking news of their son were a chronicle of hope and fear turning slowly to heart-broken despair. So the few words scrawled on a page torn from a logbook struck like an emotional thunderbolt.

She found it difficult to believe. He had been living with *les sauvages* and would soon return to France! It sounded like a miracle, but was it? How could it be, after all these years?

But the very next day the journal *Bulletin Français* carried a story headed, *Dix-sept ans chez les sauvages,* 'Seventeen Years Among the Savages'. It not only declared that her eldest son was very much alive but touched upon his life with the Aboriginal people and his return to what passed for civilisation on Cape York. Moreover, he had already sailed for France.

Père Martin contacted the authorities who kept him in touch – as best they could – with the progress of the *Jura* and in the days before the ship reached Toulon, he sent his son Élie Jean-Félix to meet her. And when she berthed on 13 December 1875, he was on the wharf to greet the prodigal.

The brothers embraced. Both had changed almost beyond recognition. Élie, only a year younger than Narcisse, was now an imposing figure. He had not only followed Père Martin into the *bottier* trade, he had surpassed him to become a *cordonnier,* a shoemaker of substantial means. He had grown a beard and wore fashionably cut suits. He looked remarkably prosperous to Narcisse whose possessions throughout his adult life had been confined to a canoe, a few spears, two fighting sticks and a fishnet. And he had risen to be a leader among his people. What's more, Élie had plans, soon to be realised, as proprietor of *Maison Pelletier – haute fantaisie pour Dames* at Sables d'Olonne, a few kilometres south of Saint-Gilles.

Nevertheless, the bonds of childhood were strong and when Élie broke the news that the government required his brother's presence in Paris, they travelled together on the steam-powered train at speeds reaching fifty kilometres per hour! It was a revelation.

Narcisse held a series of meetings in gilded salons with representatives of the republican government. They were not only anxious to hear his story and welcome him home but, fearful that he might take legal action over his callous abandonment on Cape York, were quick to assure him that he would be looked after.[1]

In truth, they told him, when his mother had written to the French consulate in Noumea seeking details of his fate, the Ministry of the Navy and Colonies had paid her a small pension without asking for proof of *sa disparition,* his demise. What's more, they assured him with bureaucratic magnanimity, they would not be requiring its return.

By now the French press had dubbed him *'le Sauvage blanc',* the white savage, and he was easily recognisable in the streets of the capital. On 22 December he was admitted to the Beaujon Hospital overlooking the Seine to ensure that he was free of any virulent tropical disease that might pose a threat to his compatriots. It was a very thorough examination and meant that he spent Christmas in the infirmary.

His visitors included Dr Arthur Chevin, a physical anthropologist who was best known for his claim that he could cure stuttering by forcing his patient to read aloud for several weeks.[2] He had been commissioned by the French Defence Department to adapt his cure for military recruits, but the results were *peu concluants*, inconclusive. However, he took it upon himself to interrogate Narcisse and proclaimed him a 'fraud'. 'I have to say that this individual has left me with a rather sad impression,' Dr Chevin wrote. 'He was very mistrustful, sly and probably a liar; and besides not very intelligent but speaking French perfectly well.'

Narcisse was certainly intelligent enough to take a dislike to a pompous ass like Dr Chevin and it's quite possible that he played dumb just to annoy him.[3] In any case, he was discharged from hospital with a clean bill of health – his leg abscess apparently healed – on 28 December.

For the next two days the brothers toured the city, its magnificent boulevards recently redesigned and built by George-Eugène Haussmann on commission from Louis-Napoleon. Then Élie bought tickets at Gare Montparnasse for the train journey to Nantes in Loire-Atlantique. There they transferred to the horse-drawn coach that would take them further south to the Vendée.

The countryside could hardly be more different from the 'kingdom' of the Night Islanders. In place of the rainforest, the shady creeks, the lagoons, the mangrove forests and the white sandy beaches, he was passing through snow-capped hills, tall hedgerows, imposing chateaux and fallow farmland. And it was cold. It seeped into his bones; it numbed his lips and face; it turned his fingers into icicles; his breath into steam. It was torture. He fell silent. He forced himself to think of his mother, of the reunion to come.

They reached the outskirts of Saint-Gilles in the afternoon of 2 January 1876. They left the coach at the crossroads and walked the last 800 metres down the Rue du Calvaire towards the village. Ahead was the church spire and at the bottom of the street the bridge over the River Vie. The streets were curiously deserted.

News had arrived by telegraph that the brothers were on their way and some 3000 villagers from both Saint-Gilles and the adjoining Croix de Vie had assembled in the Place du Baril next to the church. As the two men approached, cries of *'Vive Pelletier!'* rose from the crowd, among whom was Marcel Baudouin, a fifteen-year-old schoolboy who would later report the occasion and dub Narcisse *'l'enfant sauvage de Vendée'*, the wild child of the Vendée.

The brothers reached the crush at the bridge. Narcisse was thrown into confusion until suddenly his mother, Alphonsine, emerged from the press of villagers, his father a step or two behind. She had at last abandoned the mourning black of those seventeen years and had donned the first brightly coloured silk dress of her new wardrobe, with a bonnet to match. Narcisse, whose thirty-second birthday had fallen only the day before, swept her into his powerful arms. The crowd roared and laughed their delight. And when he finally released her, he repeated the embrace with his father.

Little Alphonse, now a well-built young gentleman of twenty-seven, kissed his brother on both his suntanned cheeks and stood back in wonderment as he gave way to the baby of the family, the teenaged Benjamin Hippolyte Jean, born well after Narcisse had departed and who stared at the man whose name was so familiar but whose personage was so different from anything he had imagined.

Then an angry voice from the crowd called out, *'Taisez-vous!'* – Be quiet! – for someone had stepped forward and waited to speak. *'Silence pour Monsieur le Curé.'*

The crowd hushed and the man in black waited until the silence was total. It was the priest, Monsieur le Curé. Speaking with all the gravity of the cloth, he thanked an Almighty God who had preserved his young believer through all the travails, all the horrors, of his exile in the wilderness with the heathen savages. And now He had brought him safely home, like the prodigal son, to a loving family.

Narcisse was dumbstruck. He tried to speak but nothing came.

No matter. By now the mayor of the town had taken charge of the occasion and with a flourish of waving arms he swept the crowd aside to reveal a mighty bonfire ready for Narcisse to ignite with a burning torch. As he clasped it, he could not help but recall another firebrand he had clutched in wonderment as it illuminated another sacred place. But it was no more than a wisp of memory and when he set the bonfire alight, the crowd cheered and Narcisse smiled his pleasure. He joined with the villagers as they toasted his return in strong, red Vendean wine.

That night the family told him their news and it was a record of unblemished success. Père Martin was now a *commerçant,* a businessman of repute, while Élie had forged ahead with his successes, and Alphonse had been apprenticed to a woodworker and furniture maker. The devout young Benjamin was still at his studies. But when they turned to Narcisse in expectation, they found only a stuttering confusion. When they praised God and good fortune for releasing him from the savage barbarians, they found a sullen silence, almost a resentment at their joy in his deliverance.

The next day, the anniversary of Narcisse's baptism, the priest celebrated a thanksgiving mass in the church that the young Narcisse had attended those many years ago to hear the stories of the saints. But now, in the intimacy of the sacristy when he and Monsieur le Curé spoke, there was a great gulf between them. The priest, his face now thin and furrowed, listened with astonishment then growing anger as Narcisse told him how the spirits of the saints and the Church had opened his heart to those of the Night Islanders.

'C'est un sacrilège!' he spat; and when he demanded confession, Narcisse was bereft. He knew that as the words travelled from his mouth to the ears of his confessor, they would only enrage him further. And so he said nothing . . . at least nothing the priest would understand. When he spoke at all, it was softly and in the language of that other world. Amglo's world.

* * *

He was surrounded by the family of his childhood, eager for his company, as were the people of the town whose streets and buildings and waterways he once knew so well. Yet he felt utterly alone. Everything and everyone were different, and not just from the way he remembered, but foreign, alien, and even hostile.

They didn't mean to be. They cared for him. Or rather, they cared for the person they had known as young Narcisse, the child they raised, the boy they played with, the young mousse, the one they kissed and waved bon voyage as he began his life at sea. But not the man who returned. Not Amglo. Never Amglo, nor any part of him residing in the body of Narcisse Pelletier.

He wanted to respond, to care for the family, to love them as a faithful son and a dutiful brother. But they too had changed. Mother and father were older, just as he expected, but now there was the self-satisfied conceit of la bourgeoisie that was no part of his memory. And in the life he had led, everything was shared. He struggled to accept this new and selfish way of living.

They were good people, he told himself. They had done well. He could not blame them for that. And they were generous. Alphonsine had kept the small pension the navy had paid her in a special place; and now it was his for the taking. His father had promised to match it to give him un nouveau départ, a new start, in life. No haste, no *urgence,* just when he was ready. And until then, a room in their home was his for as long as he wished.

The brothers too were as kind as they could be, but even with Élie, it was the kindness they would give to a distant relative, one who had suffered an injury or fallen on hard times. Or worse, a crazy uncle, *l'obsédé,* an obsessive whose words and actions were an embarrassment, a humiliation to the family.

The youngest, Benjamin Hippolyte, was polite but distant. There were times when he seemed to be observing Narcisse, the way a Night Island child watches a *punkupinta,* a tortoise, in a bush pool. Alphonse had no memory of him at all. And neither he nor Élie could recall that desperate time when he nearly drowned in the River Vie. Narcisse wanted to tell them of the way the memory saved his own child, but the words froze in his mouth. Where to begin? What to say . . . about any of it? A lifetime . . . another world.

He tried. He rehearsed the words in his room at night. He spoke them to the mirror he had taken from the *John Bell.* The little he had told Élie on their journey had been reported to the parents, and they said they wanted to know more. But the moment he began, they interrupted with questions. Were they cannibals? Was there a king? Did they really wear no clothes at all? Did he pray to God, to the Virgin, to the saints . . . ?

When he yearned for the silence of the church and a little sympathy, the power of the priest's sudden flash of rage – *'Sacrilège!'* – sent him reeling back to the sandbeach, the encampment, the initiation, the hunt, the *ayntikanu* advancing up the riverbank, its jaws stretched wide, its tail sweeping his little dingo pup into the air . . .

As the days became weeks, his words to the family dribbled to a close. He became restless. The chairs and tables of the house became objects to be avoided and he returned to his postures of the *'sauvages'* – squatting, shoeless, standing on one leg, the other bent at the knee, his foot resting on its opposite number. The cold had migrated permanently to his bones; his skin itched beneath the woollen clothes; he muttered the language of the Night Islanders; and at the slightest provocation, it seemed, reacted with barely suppressed rage.

When he walked the streets of Saint-Gilles, people spoke to him, asked foolish questions, made foolish remarks. When he made his way along the Promenade de la Vie to the wharf and watched the fishermen heading into the great bay, he tried to recall the departed Grand-père Babin and while his face was a blur he could just smell the sweet pungent tobacco of his pipe. And when he went further along to Le Boulevard Oceanique and an uninterrupted view of the North Atlantic Ocean, his imagination sent him flying across the blue water towards that other place, that other world, and he saw it in his mind for just an instant before he snapped back to reality.

He took his visions to his room at night where Alphonsine had warmed his bed with river stones heated in the fireplace and carried in a metal pan beneath a heavy lid and placed between his linen sheets. Unfortunately, when it was taken away the bed would cool and in his dreams he would be adrift on a rising sea until his boat upturned and he floundered in the icy water and woke with a cry.

It was exactly six weeks after his arrival that his father came into his room and told him the decision the family had taken. The suggestion had come from Benjamin Hippolyte Jean, he said, and it had been made in love. They had discussed it together then consulted with Monsieur le Curé, and he in turn had spoken with the bishop in Nantes. So, he insisted, it had not been taken lightly. But the Holy Catholic Church had an answer to his woes. It would not be an *expérience agreeable,* but they, his loved ones, would be with him throughout.

And when it was done, he would be returned to them as the Narcisse they once knew.

How, Narcisse asked, could this wonder be achieved?

Père Martin hesitated. Finally he said, *'C'est le nite de l'exorcisme.'*

Narcisse stared. *'L'exorcisme?'*

His father nodded and when he left the room he gently closed the door.

For a long time, Narcisse stared into the darkness. When the first waves of shock rolled away, there came a sense of relief. His situation had passed into other hands; it was no longer his responsibility. Now it was up to others, to Monsieur le Curé himself, to grapple with the spirit world, to defeat the spirits that raged within and give him peace. And he carried that thought into a dreamless sleep.

The morning told him a different story. In the light of day he was bereft. But since his family were unmoved, he would endure it. *Peut-être un miracle* . . . Perhaps a miracle . . .

* * *

On the day of the exorcism, there was a great bustle in the house. It would be conducted in the spacious living room. Careful preparations were required. Young Benjamin Hippolyte appointed himself the *organisateur en charge* and on his orders all curtains were drawn; seating for the witnesses was arranged before a solid oak *dressoir* upon which two silver candlesticks held long white candles. Narcisse, dressed in a white shirt and black trousers, was seated on a hard wooden chair facing the makeshift altar in profile to the small congregation of the extended family and one or two elders of the town.

The priest entered wearing the purple stole of the exorcist; and after a silent prayer began a ceremony that would last for more than an hour and would remain indelible in Narcisse's memory for the rest of his days.

First came the accusation: *le diable,* the devil, had entered his soul and there he now resided. The signs were unmistakeable. The host refused to eat the food of his mother's table; he scratched at his skin; he complained of the cold; he adopted unnatural body postures; he lost control of his normal personality and entered into a frenzy of rage; he spoke in another language known only to the devil; and when he spoke in French it was of subjects far beyond the apprehension of men.

Evil things. Sorcery.

Sacrilege.

An unnatural silence fell. Until then, the priest's tone had been almost conversational; now his words became more respectful, *très serieux,* as he addressed the Holy Mother in prayer:

'Beneath your compassion,' he intoned, 'we take refuge, O Mother of God, do not despise our petitions in time of trouble, but rescue us from dangers, only pure, only blessed one.'

'Amen,' responded the congregation.

Then he turned to the Archangel Michael, who in the Book of Revelations led the armies of God against the forces of evil.

'Saint Michael Archangel,' he cried, 'defend us in battle. Be our protection against the wickedness and snares of the devil. May God rebuke him, we humbly pray; and do thou, O Prince of the heavenly host, by the power of God, cast into hell Satan and all the evil spirits who prowl through the world seeking the ruin of souls.'

'Amen.'

He then confronted Narcisse directly and holding before him the hand-sized wooden cross that many said had been fashioned from a relic of the One True Cross itself, he opened his lungs and shouted:

'Depart then, transgressor! Depart, seducer, full of lies and cunning, foe of virtue, persecutor of the innocent! Give place, abominable creature; give way you monster, give way to Christ in whom you found none of your works. For He has already stripped you of your powers and laid waste to your kingdom, bound you prisoner and plundered your weapons. He has cast you forth into the outer darkness, where everlasting ruin awaits you and your abettors!'

The congregation was shocked to silence. Flecks of white had formed at the corners of the priest's lips and in the divine fury of his *cri passionné* some had spattered on Narcisse's unblinking gaze.

Narcisse was unaware of it. His eyes had lost their focus. He was in another place.

Monsieur le Curé, his chest heaving, wiped his face then in quieter tones began the long invocation of the saints to wrest the lost soul from the evil grip of Satan and return him to the bosom of his loved ones. And as he read the names of the blessed ones, from the Virgin and the angels, the patriarchs and the prophets, the apostles and disciples, the martyrs, the bishops, the priests, the religious and the laity, and finally all the saints of God, Narcisse stared silently ahead. And so the sacrament drew to a close and the congregation said, 'Amen.'[4]

Narcisse remained mute. The sea was lapping on a distant shore.

31

Queensland

The hand of the Christian God was much in evidence as the colonial occupation spread through land named for its sovereign defender. The missionaries were enthusiastic collaborators in the appropriation of Aboriginal land and the obliteration of its owners' ancient culture.

When the official government station at Somerset was transferred to Thursday Island, Henry Marjoribanks Chester took up his new appointment as Police Magistrate there on 20 July 1877. And the missionaries arrived hard on his heels. They were led by the London Missionary Society's Reverend Samuel MacFarlane, who had earlier been in Somerset and now established a school on nearby Murray Island. He would continue his evangelical mission in the area for the next sixteen years.

The London Missionary Society was 'non-denominational' but the ministers were usually trained in the Anglican faith. They were quickly joined on the cape and the islands by other proudly assertive denominations, notably the Lutheran and Presbyterian evangelists. According to historian Noel Loos, 'It was the aim of all invading Europeans to control the Aborigines they came in contact with. The missions aimed at probably the most total control, for the belief that Christianity was the only true faith produced the imperative to convert; that is, to change how Aborigines thought, felt and acted. [They] believed literally that they were confronted by the devil.

'Missionary Nicholas Hey of Mapoon [on Cape York] wrote: "We could not help feeling the Satanic power arrayed against us, and we realised as never before how completely he was holding sway in the heathen world".'[1]

Loos says, 'Countless manifestations of Satan were seen in the behaviour of the Aborigines, especially in Aboriginal polygamy and the role of women in Aboriginal society, but also in Aboriginal child rearing practices, women, fighting, nakedness, Aboriginal standards of cleanliness, and most particularly in Aboriginal mortuary practices.'

In his book, *The Other Side of the Frontier*, Henry Reynolds writes: 'The reaction of local clans [on the Cape] to the sudden appearance of missionaries appears to have followed a common pattern. After cautious surveillance from a distance, one or two men ventured to meet the white people. Gradually the numbers visiting the missionaries increased and when mutual confidence had been established women and children followed their menfolk into the embryonic stations.

'Individual visits were prolonged until eventually semi-permanent camps developed on the mission reserves and young children and old people were left behind while their kinsfolk faced the rigours and dangers of the bush. The greatest advantage of the missions was that they provided a sanctuary from the depredations of white pastoralists, miners or pearl fishers and from those of traditional Aboriginal enemies as well.'[2]

Loos says the reaction of the first generation of Aboriginal adults to have contact with the missions was interesting: 'Initially there was a rejection of Christian ideology and morality. It was thought to be irrelevant to Aborigines. Indeed, the white man's religion often produced scorn and hostility.'

However, he says, in a surprisingly short time, 'Aboriginal leaders emerged to assist the missionaries. With few exceptions they were young Aborigines with little or no experience of traditional Aboriginal values and religion. The young Aborigines soon lost the ability or desire to fend for themselves in the bush as their eating habits changed.'

The missionaries used many well-tested strategies to bring the people under their control. Once they had established food distribution, for example, the clans would quickly become habituated to handouts. Loos cites the Lutheran missionary Pfalzer of Hope Valley who recommended: 'The simplest way to reduce them to compliance is not to give out food for a day. In no time at all they are willing to cooperate again.'

According to Loos, 'Aborigines flocked to Hope Valley when there was no work to be done but avoided it when there was. In difficult times they brought the old, the sick or the very young to the mission. The missionaries tended the sick with great dedication and enough success for some Aborigines to seek their aid. All tried to convert the adults but soon diverted most effort to the young.'[3]

The Sandbeach people were, in their largely inaccessible location from the land, at least for the moment, spared the attentions of the missionaries. While the grazier-cum-explorer William Hann led a thoroughly disorganised expedition on the southern fringes of their country in the early 1870s, the Lockhart River, which cuts through the Night Island territory, would not be discovered and named by a white man until the fleeting visit of government geologist Logan Jack in 1880. Their connection to the European world came from the sea.[4]

In the years following Narcisse Pelletier's departure, sailors increasingly enlisted Aboriginal family groups to dive for *bêche-de-mer* and pearl shell. And as in other locations they enticed Aboriginal women aboard their boats for overnight trysts or

semi-permanent company. Some came willingly to escape an
onerous and unhappy life as wife to a much older man; others
from a sense of adventure and release from an oppressive culture.
The outcomes of their encounters were no doubt as disparate as
the vagaries of human nature allowed.

According to Reynolds: 'The predominantly male workforce
of the northern maritime industries sought Aboriginal and Torres
Strait Island women for sexual gratification. The degree to which
blacks assisted them in this pursuit varied widely according to
time and local circumstances.

'On both the northwest coast and around Cape York the
pearling fleets supported a large and lucrative prostitution industry.
Aboriginal clans reorganised their pattern of migration to travel
down to the sea coast when the pearling luggers were paid up for
the monsoon season and remained there till they sailed away again.

'The demand for the young women was such that all other
clan members could live off the proceeds of their copulation for
the duration of the lay-up season.'[5]

Meantime, as the cape's bountiful resources attracted the gold-
seekers, the timber-getters and the cattlemen, the Native Police
Force continued its role as the hard cutting edge of repression.
However, as the Aboriginal people were progressively dispossessed
of their land and their law, the need for a cohort of armed
enforcers became less urgent.

According to historian Timothy Bottoms: 'The Native Police
were financed by the colony itself and the ruling elite therefore
felt that only they had a right to say how the force was run.
British investment in the colony was such that the institutions
concerned did not want to hinder the opportunities for greater
financial returns . . .'[6]

'The tragedy is that in every district and region in Queensland,
indigenous oral history recounts similar tales. Violence was
ubiquitous. And to justify their behaviour, Europeans portrayed

"the blacks" as cannibals and "bad" because they dared to resist the invasion of their homelands and fight a guerrilla war.'[7]

However, in its later years some of its leading lights brought the Native Police Force into public disrepute. Among them was the notorious Frederick Wheeler who, in March 1876 at the aptly named Mistake Creek, was reported to have whipped a young Aboriginal man to death. The location was northwest of Rockhampton where an inquest was ordered and credible European witnesses – including other police – gave evidence against him.

Charged with murder, Wheeler was committed for trial and dismissed from the Native Police the following month. He was consigned to the Rockhampton jail but soon afterwards two prominent graziers offered to provide sureties and bail was granted by one of the colony's senior jurists, Justice Alfred Lutwyche, and approved by Attorney-General Samuel Griffith.

The trial began at Rockhampton in October 1876 but Wheeler failed to appear. He had not only absconded but no warrant was ever issued for his arrest; and two years later the Supreme Court was advised that no further charges would be laid against him. Although he was then technically free to return to Queensland, his whereabouts remained unknown until confirmed reports arrived in 1882 from Java. He had died there of an unidentified disease.

Samuel Griffith claimed that during his first premiership which ended in 1888, he 'had these blood-stained forces disbanded forever', but the reality is that they were never officially disbanded. Their numbers were reduced from the mid-1880s but by then the invaders had largely achieved their aims.

Indeed, by the 1880s, according to Reynolds, the colonial society of Queensland was 'assertive' about its achievements: 'It was taken for granted that the frontier settler would displace the "savage" and that the displacement was inevitable and for the better.'

Griffith would again serve as premier in the 1890s and would take a conspicuous role in the drafting of the Australian Constitution; and as Queensland's chief justice until 1903 he codified Queensland's criminal law.

By then his predecessor as Queensland Premier, John Douglas, had become the long-serving Government Resident and Police Magistrate on Thursday Island. Indeed, the transfer of the official station from Somerset to the island had been taken largely at Douglas's initiative when he was the premier.

Born in London in 1828, Douglas had arrived in Australia with his brother Edward in 1851 and soon after was appointed a sub-commissioner at the southern New South Wales goldfields. Two years later the brothers bought grazing properties and became prominent in political circles. John represented several Queensland districts after separation in 1859 and was appointed to ministerial posts in succeeding governments until becoming premier in 1877.

He was out of office but still in the parliament in 1880 when he led a group of progressive members seeking a royal commission to investigate all aspects of the Native Police Force. According to Reynolds: 'The reformers were modest in demand and cautious in approach. They considered that a war of races was inevitable and that the weaker race would be defeated. John Douglas agreed with opponents that they must look forward to "the eventual extinction of the weaker race".

'Douglas believed that brutalities and murders had been over and over again committed in the north; they had become so common that "the European nature was in danger of demoralization".'

Already Europeans in the north had become 'terribly callous' and had 'almost lost sight of the fact that murder of this kind was unjustifiable'.

But after two long debates, the attempt was rebuffed by a substantial majority in the House of Assembly.

After his political career ended, Douglas travelled to England for a time; and on his return sought re-election but was not successful. He accepted the Thursday Island post in 1888 and held it until his death in 1904.

By then Frank Jardine, who had remained on Somerset, had fathered two sons and two daughters with his Samoan princess bride. They entertained passing visitors royally with dinner served on silver plate made from Spanish dollars he had gleaned from a shipwreck. Frank would contract the biblical disease of leprosy but would survive until the second decade of the new century.

32

Narcisse/Amglo

The exorcism had been a debilitating emotional experience, not least because it quickly became apparent that it was an utter failure. There was no evidence of any intervention by the Virgin, the angels or even the humble martyrs in exorcising the satanic spirits from their grip on Narcisse's soul. The man himself was not only left with the burden of failure but the knowledge that quickly sped through the community that he remained 'possessed'.

It would not have been surprising if he had responded to the despair of his family and the taunts of the townsfolk by seeking the surcease of anger and hopelessness in the red Vendean wine. This would have been doubly understandable when the only employment offered him had been to appear 'on stage' as a curiosity to tell of his life with *les sauvages*.

There is some evidence that he found a congenial companion on the wharves of Saint-Gilles in one Morineau, a sailmaker. Narcisse not only spoke to him at some length but is said to have written notes. They might well have been *aide-mémoire* of his experiences for, on a brief trip to Nantes in late January 1876, he sought employment from the Ministry of Navy and the Colonies and there he met a surgeon-turned-historian, Constant Merland, who wanted to write his story in a book. Narcisse was excited at the prospect. Merland had promised that a portion of the sales would be his; and if the book became popular he would be a rich man.

The notes have never been discovered, but there is very little evidence in Merland's subsequent publication that Narcisse confided any of his adventures and experiences with the Night Islanders to the author. His *Dix-Sept Ans Chez Les Sauvages* is a monologue of faux scientific analysis and European condescension. And according to Marcel Baudouin, the youthful Saint-Gilles *reporteur,* the stories Narcisse told Morineau 'were not those published by Dr Merland'.[1] The book was priced at two francs a copy, sold in modest numbers when published later in the year, and, according to Thompson's *Son of the Vendée*, 'it remains unclear whether the castaway ever received any payment for his collaboration'.[2]

His time with Merland was made the more unsettling by the involvement of a musician, Edouard Garnier. He made an ambitious attempt to have Narcisse perform the chants and songs of the Night Island clan as he transcribed the 'melodies' and 'lyrics' into the Western system of staff notation. It was not successful. He produced four 'songs' but afterwards complained that Narcisse might not have cooperated as candidly as he had hoped. 'I have wondered whether they were not rather Pelletier's unconscious recollection of the tunes of his native land,' Garnier wrote, 'or of the liturgical forms of his parish church which had later become confused with the language, the words and the kinds of more or less fixed sounds of the savages with whom he lived for many years.'[3]

While in Nantes, Narcisse also sat for a series of photographs by the fashionable Peigne. The one chosen by Merland which appears in his book (and on the front cover of Stephanie Anderson's work) is a remarkable portrait of a man who carries on his body the cicatrices of his proud Aboriginal attainments and possesses the dark shadowed eyes of well-guarded secrets. His elongated right earlobe is clearly visible beneath his neatly cut and combed dark hair, but the bamboo plug has been removed. He wears a trimmed moustache and his forearms are those of a particularly strong individual. It is the picture of a man in his prime, comfortable in his body and braced to respond if challenged.

The photographer may well have caught him at the apex of his physical and mental condition, for nothing in the eighteen years left to him suggests that it was other than a steady slide into a solitary and tormented fate.

* * *

Narcisse's visit to Nantes produced a position that could hardly have been more poetically conceived by the French bureaucracy for the lonely, disconsolate castaway. The Ministry of Public Works offered him the post of *gardien* or keeper of the Phare de l'Aiguillon, a cylindrical stone lighthouse on the northern bank of the Loire estuary at Saint-Nazaire on the Atlantic coast of Brittany.

It was more than eighty-five kilometres north of Saint-Gilles and freed the family and himself from their mutual discomfiture. It sheltered him from the stares and the unwanted attention of his compatriots. It provided him with a decent living. And as a shipwreck victim himself, it gave him charge of the means to keep his fellow seamen from a similar fate.

It was a proud posting. The Phare de l'Aiguillon had been erected by marine engineers in 1756 on the orders of the Duke of Aiguillon, the then Governor of Brittany. It would light the way of ships entering the Loire and heading upstream to Nantes. And the town that supported it also had a long maritime history.

Saint-Nazaire began as a fishing village but graduated to seaport in 1838 when Vieux Mole, a pier running along the top of a massive granite wall, formed a breakwater between the ocean and the Loire. It gave protection to river and coastal steamers from the Atlantic's stormy seas. Louis-Napoleon had added two new piers over eight years from 1848, known as the *Griffes de Crabe*, Crab Claws, creating an outer harbour, the Avant Port. And from 1862 the *Compagnie Général Transatlantique* made Saint-Nazaire its home port for a regular service to the Caribbean and South America.

The lighthouse itself was on the Pointe de l'Eve, a craggy headland jutting into the Atlantic some ten kilometres north of the port. It was a remote and isolated spot but of such military importance in the perennial *contestation* with Britain that in 1857 a guardhouse had been built nearby to protect it and was occupied in times of war.

Inside Narcisse's new home, there were comfortable if some-what spartan living quarters. But most of his time was spent in its upper storey where he tended the oil-fired lamp with its Fresnel lens, named for its inventor, the commissioner of lighthouses, Augustin-Jean Fresnel. Its brilliance sent the bright white light great distances out to sea.

We may believe that in his mind and his spirit Narcisse followed the light on a journey that took him all the way across the oceans to that other life that had so thoroughly enveloped him through the years of his maturing. The memories were branded indelibly on his mind and their recall would so easily have become a part of his life, day and night, on the high watchtower. And with the visions would have come the questions: what was the clan doing at this time of the tropical year? Hunting the dugong? Paddling the canoe in wild pursuit, Maademan standing tall on the tiny platform, his mighty harpoon spear raised and poised to plunge as they overtook the great mammal with his tusks that could rip a man's belly . . .

Or were they fishing and swimming in the warm waters of the lagoon, diving among the rainbow corals? Or had the storm-wracked seas forced them inland, where they were tracking the cassowary, silently surrounding it and on sudden signal rising with spears fitted into their *yulis* and flinging them with perfect accuracy into the heart of the great bird.

Maybe they were stalking the young *ayntikanu,* just released to freedom from their nest by the big female who had guarded them from their greedy sire, running one down in the shallows, leaping on its back, one hand gripping its baby jaws together, the other driving the short hand-spear home through its white underbelly.

What of Sassy and his new wife? What of doleful Bruno whose Sabine had never returned . . . or had she? And had he beaten her as was his right, or taken her back and hunted for her until her next departure?

What of his own wives, Mitha and Kanti: who were they given to now? And were they still thinking of him, of Amglo, their provider and *Pama ngathana,* bedman?

But then came the vision so tormenting that it ground away in his mind like the rough rock sharpening a spearpoint: what of his children? Little Markuntha who grew to be Yapu, and tiny Chuchi who hardly seemed to grow at all: what of her? And, the question so infuriating that it made him cry out in despair: what did she really call to him on that last day, the day they took him into the longboat? As she ran down the sandbeach, what did she shout so urgently to him, to Amglo, to *piipi,* to her father?

At first and for a long time afterwards the questions revolved endlessly in his mind. But there came a time when he half-believed that he could set his spirit free to follow the light and take him there, to the sandbeach, the encampment, and he could sit in the branches of a *thanka* tree and watch the comings and goings of his people. He could become one with his totem, the brilliant *tinta,* and he could watch over them; and then − if he tried hard enough − he could warn them when they were in danger, with his sharp cry . . . but then the dream would slowly dissolve and he would be back in the lighthouse, gripping the metal rail as he stared across the endless ocean that separated him from them.

He hated the sea.

* * *

As the weeks turned to months and the months to years, the story of Narcisse/Amglo begins to cloud. And though we have no French Donald Thomson to guide our narrative, there are some beacons of light, occasions dutifully recorded by the French bureaucracy, from which we can make some confident deductions.

We know, for example, from the family tree compiled by genealogist Véronique Guilbaud, that his brother Alphonse relocated to Saint-Nazaire where he worked in his cabinet making-cum-furniture trade. How much time the two brothers spent together we do not know. But as noted, the town was some ten kilometres from the lighthouse and Narcisse's duties were unremitting.

However, it may well be that Alphonse encouraged him to at least venture into the social life of the town since in 1880, aged thirty-six, Narcisse married a seamstress, Louise Désirée Marbileau, aged twenty-two. Both Alphonse and Élie attended the wedding and witnessed the union in Saint-Nazaire. The bride's father, Marc Séraphin Marbileau, had died but her mother, the former Rose Françoise Yver, was recorded on the marriage certificate as 'Widow Marbileau'.

However, by 1890 Alphonse had moved to Nantes where he died of causes unknown. His death was followed the next year by Père Martin. The widow Alphonsine would sell the Saint-Gilles property and take up residence with Élie, who by then had married one Maria Robin and established his *Maison Pelletier – haute fantaisie pour Dames* at Sables d'Olonne. But Élie himself succumbed there in 1892 and was buried in the local cemetery. There is no record of Narcisse's attendance.

Indeed, the fourteen years from Narcisse's marriage may best be understood from the certificate of death that followed the castaway's demise on 28 September 1894. The given cause was 'neurasthenia', a nineteenth century label for the symptoms of fatigue, anxiety, heart palpitations, high blood pressure, severe headaches and depression that today would attract diagnoses ranging from a neurotic disorder, to post-traumatic stress to chronic fatigue syndrome.

Whatever the label, it told of a progressive descent into a mental and physical breakdown; and given the intolerable pressures of his dual existence, the outcome could hardly be wondered at. During the descent, there came a time when he could no longer bear the anguish of a life atop the eyrie that spread before it an ocean of separation from the people he had held so dear. There were no children of the new union and there have been suggestions from later French sources that he and Louise separated, but all available evidence suggests that she remained with him to the end.

By then he had transferred from the lighthouse to a desk-bound position as 'clerk at the harbour' and a modest home at 20 Grande Rue, Saint-Nazaire. And that is where he breathed his last. We can but hope that in his final delirium his spirit carried him back to the home of his people; and that someone, perhaps his daughter, glanced up in the night sky and wondered at the shooting star.

Benjamin Hippolyte had avoided a mother's natural wish for him to join the priesthood and married twice. He would live until 1905 but there is no record of him or their mother at Narcisse's funeral. The only mourners, we believe, were his wife and the mysterious Morineau, the sailmaker to whom he confided the stories he would never tell to another. And Morineau left no record.

At the time of his death, Louise bought a double plot in the cemetery. But she later remarried so the name on the grave is not Pelletier but Tessier, the name of her second husband, Joseph Marie Tessier, with whom Narcisse had to share his space until Louise joined them in 1930.

A rare duality followed him, it seems, even to his grave.

EPILOGUE

Narcisse Pelletier is memorialised in Saint-Gilles by a wide promenade between an avenue of trees along the bank of the Jaunay, a tributary of the River Vie. And at *La Maison des Ecrivains de la Mer,* a maritime museum at the entrance to the Port La Vie, there is a permanent exhibition which chronicles his life. The centrepiece is a striking bronze bust of a naked Narcisse with piercings and bodily markings by the sculptor Jean-Jacques Roussarie.

The fate of his reviled Captain Emmanuel Pinard is contained in the *Archives départmentales de Seine-Maritime* in Rouen. In 1859 after his return from the South Seas, Pinard resumed his career with the French Merchant Marine. However, he was then assigned to mail vessels from Le Havre to other French ports until 1874. In that year, it seems, he went absent without leave and the *Gendarmerie Maritime* searched for him for two years without success.

The immediate cause of his disappearance remains locked in the files of the French maritime police; but it is hard to escape the conclusion that the most traumatic events of his professional life – the shipwreck and the abandonment of both the Chinese passengers and Narcisse – lay at the base of it.

In 1876 Pinard was discovered in St-Germaine-en-Laye, a village twenty kilometres northwest of Paris. He died in Paris on 14 March 1877 not long after Narcisse had returned to France. In the unlikely event that the two made contact, neither the castaway nor the ship's captain made the meeting public.

Narcisse's story is best known in France through the work of the *bande dessinée* (graphic novel) artist, Chanouga, who produced two striking hard-cover graphic novels on the subject. While they take the wildest liberties with the narrative, *bande dessinées* are taken very seriously in France where they are regarded as 'the ninth art'. In 2015 Chanouga travelled to Saint-Gilles for the launch of the second volume, *Narcisse II: Terra Nullius*. However, it was left to the Australian, Stephanie Anderson, to provide the most authoritative academic rendering of the Pelletier story with her 2009 publication, frequently referenced within these pages.

As for the Sandbeach people, it was not until 1924 that the combined forces of the white invaders reached the three 'kingdoms' of the Umpila, the Kuuku Y'au and the Uutaalnganu (Night Island) people. An Anglican mission established itself at Lockhart River in almost the centre of the Night Islanders' territory. It was the most traumatic event in the history of the clans who had lived in harmony with the land and sea, and in competition with each other, for tens of thousands of years.

The missionaries, backed by the Queensland government, followed their standard practice of undermining the cultural foundations of the people. They unleashed their full armoury – tales of a jealous Christian God, a deliberate dependence on Western food and the 'shame' of the naked human body. But the most destructive of their measures was forcing the tribes together, banning their languages and separating the children from their parents. Indeed, by 1935 the superintendent Harry Rowan boasted that he'd increased the mission's population 'by commandeering the children' so that families were forced to live there.[1]

The result was a total dislocation of Aboriginal society, and it is a matter of great good fortune that Donald Thomson – and to a lesser extent Hale and Tindale – should have chosen to visit the area so soon after the missionaries' arrival and been able to record a way of life that was soon to be gone forever.

However, the Sandbeach people are nothing if not resilient. The mission was finally closed in 1967, and historical connections have been irrevocably disrupted; however, some of the mission's practices remain and the Sandbeach people have also adopted the cultural practices of various newcomers.

While there are no known descendants of Narcisse's children living today, the story of his time with 'the old people' is known and they are alive to its tourist (and film-making) potential. Indeed, prior to one of my visits to the cape researching the story, a French television crew had recently filmed elements of a documentary dealing with Narcisse's long sojourn there.

My time at Lockhart was both inspiring and unsettling. In October 2017, I was met at the airport by the Deputy Mayor of the Lockhart Aboriginal Council, Norman Bally. On meeting, Norman falls immediately into that special category of good men: 'the lovely bloke'. He is a bit overweight and with a warm and kindly sense of humour. We were mates the moment we met.

I stayed in one of the well-appointed cabins near the airport. The complex at the time was run by Jasmine Accoom, one of those super-efficient Aboriginal women to whom multi-tasking comes naturally. She was standing in for a friend, the manager of the 'Iron Range' complex, which is eight kilometres from the town. Norman himself was standing in for the mayor, Wayne Butcher, one of a new style of Aboriginal businessmen, with a broad portfolio of investments in the cape. My plane had been delayed and Wayne had been called away to meetings in Canberra.

On this occasion Norman and I were accompanied by two respected elders and over the period we covered an extraordinary range of different landscapes, natural features and significant sites. Beyond the town, apart from the occasional chance meeting with travellers, the Night Island 'kingdom' that had so impressed Narcisse was utterly deserted.

In some places, the traditional burning of the lightly forested grasslands had recently taken place; in others, creeks had turned to waterholes or dry beds that defied any motorised transport except the four-wheeled driving skill of Norman at the controls. We crossed hard, rocky ridges and sweet green gullies; found camping spots secluded by a forest wall where wallabies scooted through the undergrowth as though fleeing the hunter's spear.

We ate Western food purchased by Norman from the Lockhart supermarket and when the time was right, we ventured past the scattered ruins of the mission to the headland just north of Night Island. To our right was the beach where Narcisse had landed with his party of bedraggled French sailors under the command of Captain Pinard; and to our left was the place where the Mabuiags and the Englishmen had taken him into the longboat from the *John Bell*.

It was there on the headland, chatting with Norman and the elders, that I experienced the full force of the 'presence' of Amglo/Narcisse that had been with me through the journey. It was an understandable reaction. There had been reports of 'sightings' of Narcisse in the area from Queensland historian Clem Lack and the distinguished medico Sir Raphael Cilento in the decades following his departure. The bush is full of such tall tales and I took them with the proverbial grain of salt. But I had buried myself for more than a year in the minutiae of his life and times in this place. Combined with the extraordinary work of Donald Thomson, his story had crystallised into vivid life. It was almost as though he was there at that moment, part of the transcendental history of Sandbeach country.

It was time for photographs. I prepared my mobile for the shots just as I always had. I'd been using the phone camera for more than a year and was quite familiar with its workings. I asked my Aboriginal companions to stand together with the sandbeach to the left and the great sweep of ocean beyond.

'All good?'

Norman nodded and murmured assent.

I held the camera at eye level but when I pressed the button to take the shot, a familiar image intervened between us. It arrived in the shape of that other photograph I had looked at so often, the one taken by Peigne, with his dark, brooding eyes and posture braced to meet any challenge.

I put the camera aside. 'Just a minute,' I said. 'I just saw Narcisse.'

I smiled as I said it, but when Norman responded he was serious. 'That's good,' he said. 'That means he approves of you telling his story.'

The elders nodded their agreement.

I then took the other photos without any further interruptions. The first one was never fully resolved. The 'image' of Narcisse was of course some trick of the light combined with the obsessive nature of the long-form writer.

But I couldn't help feeling oddly pleased that it had happened.

ACKNOWLEDGEMENTS

I pay respect and admiration to the Aboriginal elders, past and present, and to all the First Australians who have endured so much for so long.

In addition to the help and guidance of Dr Lindy Allen, Rita Metzenrath and staff at the Australian Institute of Aboriginal and Torres Strait Islander Studies (AIATSIS), I wish to acknowledge the invaluable assistance from the following.

The scholarly work of Stephanie Anderson and her academic associates in their pioneering studies in *Pelletier: The Forgotten Castaway of Cape York*.

My friend and frequent co-author Peter Thompson who travelled from his London base to unearth previously unpublished information on the Pelletier family and Narcisse's time in Saint-Gilles and Saint-Nazaire before and after his long sojourn in Queensland; Peter also read the manuscript and provided advice that corrected and improved it; the late Jimi Bostock for his generous support in connecting me with the Aboriginal people of Lockhart River and Cape York; Norman Bally and Jasmine Accoom for their willing help and friendship during my time in Night Island territory; and Professor Bill Gammage for introductions to a range of academic anthropologists who have produced distinguished work in the area.

The French authorities, from the *Service historique de la Défense* to the *Archives départmentales de Seine-Maritime,* in Toulon and Rouen respectively, were of great assistance. And the French linguist Dr Kerry Mullan very kindly ensured that Narcisse expressed himself appropriately in his mother tongue.

My special thanks to Dr Dawn Casey, the foundation director of the National Museum of Australia, who enjoys the respect and affection not only of her Aboriginal people but the deference and devotion of all who know her, to Professor Henry Reynolds, the doyen of Australian historians of the Frontier Wars, and the rising scholar of Aboriginal anthropology Heather Threadgold, who were kind enough to read the manuscript and provide important advice and generous comments; to my agent Margaret Kennedy, to my regular, steadfast publisher at Hachette, Matthew Kelly, and to the thoughtful editing of the manuscript by Susin Chow. Finally, I am deeply indebted to my wife Wendy and sons Rob and Ben who have contributed more than they know to such an all-embracing project.

ABRIDGED BIBLIOGRAPHY

DONALD THOMSON

Cape York artefacts (collected 1928–33) Donald Thomson Collection, Museums Victoria

'Cape York: Nature's gateway to Australia', *Walkabout*, vol. 35, no. 7, pp. 14–17, 1969

'Ceremonial Presentation of Fire in North Queensland: A preliminary note on the place of fire in primitive ritual', *Man*, vol. 32 no. 198, pp. 162–6, 1932

Children of the Dreamtime: Traditional family life in Aboriginal Australia, Viking O'Neil, Ringwood, Vic., 1989

Children of the Wilderness, Curry O'Neil, South Yarra, Vic., 1983

'Childhood and Play Among the Australian Aborigines', *Melbourne Age Literary Supplement*, September 3, 1955, p. 17

'Exploding the Myths of Smoke Signal and Boomerang', *The Age Literary Supplement*, April 21, 1956, p. 17

Field notes, (Cape York, Arnhem Land, January 1933 – August 1935) Donald Thomson Collection, Museums Victoria

Field notes, (East Cape York Peninsula, 1928) Donald Thomson Collection, Museums Victoria

'In Camp with the Stone Age Men: Life among the nomad tribes of Cape York Peninsula in far north Queensland', *The Queenslander*, January 29, 1931, p. 4, available from: http://nla.gov.au/nla.news-article23134613

Kinship and Behaviour in North Queensland: A preliminary account of kinship and social organization on Cape York Peninsula, ed. H.W. Scheffler, Australian Institute of Aboriginal Studies, Canberra, 1972

'Masked Dancers of I'wai'i: A remarkable hero cult which has invaded Cape York Peninsula', *Walkabout*, vol. 22, no. 12, 1956, p. 17–19

'Papuan Influences in Cape York', *Hemisphere*, vol. 10, no. 4, 1966, pp. 13–18

'The Cassowary in the Jungle of Cape York', *Walkabout*, vol. 16, no. 8, 1950, pp. 34–5

'The Masked Dancers of Cape York: A cult of great pageantry', *The Age (Melbourne)*, June 9, 1956

'The Native People', *Pearl, C.*, 1961, pp. 25–39

'Two Devices for the Avoidance of First-cousin Marriage Amongst the Australian Aborigines', *Man*, vol. 55, 1955, pp. 39–40

'White Man's Life Among Australia's Aborigines', *Melbourne Age Literary Supplement*, September 22, 1956, p. 17

OTHER AUTHORS

Anderson, Stephanie, *Pelletier: The Forgotten Castaway of Cape York*, Melbourne Books, Melbourne, 2009

Austin, C.G., *Early History of Somerset and Thursday Island*, Historical Society of Queensland, Brisbane, 1949

Berndt, R.M. and Tonkinson, R. (editors), *Social Anthropology and Australian Aboriginal Studies: A contemporary overview*, Aboriginal Studies Press, Canberra, 1988

Bloomfield, Noelene, *Almost a French Australia*, Halstead Press, Canberra, 2012

Bottoms, Timothy, *Conspiracy of Silence: Queensland's frontier killing times*, Allen & Unwin, Sydney, 2013

Butcher, Maria, Brown, Irene, Claudie, Winnie, Giblet, Elizabeth, Pascoe, Minnie, Pascoe, Suzie, Moses, Molly and Short, Dorothy, *Ku'unchikamu: Kuuku Ngampulungku – Old Lockhart women yarn stories together*, Aboriginal Studies Press, Canberra, 2004

Carron, William, *Narrative of Kennedy's Cape York Expedition*, Kemp & Fairfax, Sydney, 1849, reprinted by Corkwood Press, 1996

Cole, Noelene, 'Battle Camp to Boralga: A local study of colonial war on Cape York Peninsula 1873–1894', *Aboriginal History*, v. 28, 2004, pp. 156–98

Connors, Libby, *Warrior: A legendary leader's dramatic life and violent death on the colonial frontier*, Allen & Unwin, Sydney, 2015

Davidson, Col, 'The Saga of the St Paul', *Traditional Money Association Journal*, vol. 14, no. 1, 1998, available from: https://www.scribd.com/document/50062696/Saga-of-the-St-Paul

Dixon, Bob, *Searching for Aboriginal Languages: Memoirs of a field worker*, University of Queensland Press, Brisbane, 1984

Gammage, Bill, '*Early Boundaries of New South Wales*', *Historical Studies*, vol. 19, no. 77, October 1981, pp. 524–31

Gregory, Edmund, *James Murrell's Seventeen Years' Exile*, self-published, Brisbane, 1896

Hale, Herbert M. and Tindale, Norman B., *Aborigines of Princess Charlotte Bay North Queensland*, Records of the South Australian Museum, Adelaide, 1934

Jardine, Frank and Alexander, *Narrative of the Overland Expedition of the Messrs. Jardine, from Rockhampton to Cape York, Northern Queensland*, edited by Frederick J. Byerley, first published by J.W. Buxton, 1867, web edition published by University of Adelaide Library, Adelaide, 2014

Kennedy, Edward B., *Four Years in Queensland*, Edward Stanford, London, 1870, p. 4

Lawrie, Margaret, *John Jardine and Somerset*, Royal Queensland Historical Society, Brisbane, 25 October 1990

Loos, Noel, *Invasion and Resistance*, Australian National University Press, Canberra, 1982

McKenna, Mark, *From The Edge: Australia's lost histories*, The Miegunyah Press, Melbourne, 2016

Moore, David R., 'Cape York Aborigines: Fringe participants in the Torres Strait', *Mankind*, vol. 11, no. 3, 1978, pp. 319–25

——'Toward Dispelling a Myth [of the isolation of Aborigines: data from Cape York and Torres Strait]', *Australian Natural History*, vol. 19, no. 6, 1978

——*The Torres Strait Collections of A.C. Haddon: A descriptive catalogue*, Trustees of the British Museum, London, 1980

Peterson, Nicolas and Rigsby, Bruce (editors), *Customary Marine Tenure in Australia*, University of Sydney, Sydney, 1998

Pohlner, Howard J., *Gangurru*, Hope Vale Mission Board, Milton, 1986

Prentis, Malcolm D., 'John Mortimer of Manumbar and the 1861 Native Police Inquiry in Queensland', *Journal of the Royal Historical Society of Queensland*, vol. XIV, no. 11, May 1992, pp. 433–88

——*A Concise Companion to Aboriginal History*, Rosenberg Publishing, Kenthurst, 2008, pp. 466–89

Reynolds, Henry, *The Other Side of the Frontier: Aboriginal resistance to the European invasion of Australia*, University of New South Wales Press, Sydney, 1981

——*This Whispering In Our Hearts*, Allen & Unwin, Sydney, 1998

Richards, Jonathan, *The Secret War: A true history of Queensland's Native Police*, University of Queensland Press, Brisbane, 2008

Rigsby, Bruce and Chase, Athol, *The Sandbeach People and Dugong Hunters of Eastern Cape York Peninsula: Property in land and sea country*, Sydney University Press, Sydney, 2014

Rigsby, Bruce and Peterson, Nicolas (editors), *Donald Thomson: The man and the scholar*, Academy of the Social Sciences in Australia with support from Museum Victoria, Canberra, 2005

Sharp, Nonie, *Footprints Along The Cape York Sandbeaches*, Aboriginal Studies Press, Canberra, 1992

Thompson, Peter, *Son of the Vendée: The prodigal's return*, paper compiled on behalf of the author, May – June 2017

Warby, John, drawings by Ray Crooke, *'You-Me Mates Eh!'*, The Rams Skull Press, Kuranda, 1999

NOTES

CHAPTER 1

1 Municipal archives of Saint-Gilles-Croix-de-Vie.
2 Constant Merland, *Dix-sept ans chez les sauvages*, 1876, E. Dentu, Paris, pp. 2–3.
3 Much of the material for the shipwreck and its aftermath is drawn from 'The Saga of the St Paul' by Col Davidson.
4 Ibid.
5 Anderson, p. 37.
6 Davidson, p. 3
7 Ibid.
8 Ibid.
9 Supplied in correspondence between the author and the *Service historique de la Défense*, Toulon, France.

CHAPTER 2

1 Cook's journal, written in 1770 but not published until 1893.
2 Cook named the island Possession Island.
3 William Dampier, *A New Voyage Around the World*, 2nd edition, James Knapton, London, 1697.
4 Bloomfield, p. 45.
5 Ibid.
6 Ibid.
7 Ibid.
8 Christopher N. Johnson and Barry W. Brook, 'Reconstructing the dynamics of ancient human populations from radiocarbon dates', *Proceedings of the Royal Society B*, vol. 278, issue 1725, May 2011, available from: https://doi.org/10.1098/rspb.2011.0343

9   Reynolds, 1981, p. 71.

10 Robert Macklin, *Dark Paradise*, Hachette Australia, Sydney, 2016.

11 Robert Macklin, *Hamilton Hume*, Hachette Australia, Sydney, 2017,
    p. 219.

CHAPTER 4

1   Connors, p. 2.

2   Ibid., p. 9

3   'Murder of Captain Logan by the Blacks at Moreton Bay', *The Sydney
    Gazette and NSW Advertiser*, 16 November 1830.

4   Bottoms, 2013, p. 14.

5   Ibid., p. 17.

6   Connors, p. 46

7   Ibid.

8   Ibid.

9   Ibid.

10 Ludwig Leichhardt, *Journal of Second Expedition, Moreton Bay to Port
    Essington, a distance of upwards of 3000 miles, during the years 1844–1845*,
    T&W Boone, London, 1847.

11 Ibid.

12 Augustus Charles Gregory, *Journals of Australian Explorations by Augustus
    Charles Gregory and Francis Thomas Gregory*, James C. Beal, Brisbane, 1884,
    p. 188.

CHAPTER 6

1   Turbet, Peter, *The First Frontier: The occupation of the Sydney region
    1788–1816*, Rosenberg Publishing, Kenthurst, 2011, pp. 163, 268.

2   Eric Morisset was said to be a direct descendant of Governor William
    Bligh. Sgt A. Wittingham; Proceedings of the Queensland Historical
    Society, 23 July 1964, p. 510.

3   Report from the Select Committee of the Legislative Assembly on the
    Native Police Force, 1857.

4   Reid, Gordon, *A Nest of Hornets: The massacre of the Fraser family at
    Hornet Bank Station, Central Queensland, 1857, and related events*, Oxford
    University Press, Melbourne, 1982; Bruce Elder, *Blood on the Wattle:
    Massacres and maltreatment of Aboriginal Australians since 1788*, New Holland
    Publishers, Sydney, 1998, p. 94.

5   Hurd, Reginald, 'The Hornet Bank Massacre', *The Queenslander*,
    1 February, 1919, p. 29.

6   Stewart, James, 'The Hornet Bank Tragedy', *The Queenslander*, 15 April,
    1905, p. 8.

7   Bottoms, p. 19.

8 Jonathan Richards, 'Frederick Wheeler and the Sandgate Native Police
   Camp', *The Royal Historical Society of Queensland Journal*, vol. 20, no. 3,
   August 2007.
9 Australian Dictionary of Biography.
10 Noel Loos, *Invasion and Resistance*, ANU Press, Camberra, 1982, pp. 20–1.

CHAPTER 8
1 Loos, 1982.
2 Ibid.
3 Bottoms, p. 44.
4 Ibid., p. 48.
5 Ibid., p 50.

CHAPTER 10
1 Despatch from Governor Bowen to Duke of Newcastle, 9 December 1861.
2 Bottoms, pp. 53–4.
3 Reynolds, 1998, pp. 92–3.
4 Prentis, 2008.
5 Robert Herbert, collected letters, John Oxley Library, State Library of
   Queensland.

CHAPTER 11
1 The initiation ceremony that follows is taken directly from the field notes
   and published reports of the pioneering anthropologist Donald Thomson
   who, in the 1920s and 1930s, spent many months with the Sandbeach
   people and was invited to observe the initiation ceremony of the I'wai
   Tjilbo cult. The duration of the rituals is not entirely clear from his notes
   but might well have extended into months as opposed to the several weeks
   I have employed in my telling. But I have been careful to follow strictly
   the published elements of the ritual.

CHAPTER 12
1 Margaret Lawrie, *John Jardine and Somerset*, Royal Queensland Historical
   Society, Brisbane, 25 October 1990.
2 Kennedy, p. 4.
3 Lawrie, 1990.
4 Loos, 1982, pp. 29–30.
5 Ibid.

CHAPTER 14
1 Lawrie, 1990, p. 9
2 Sharp, 1992.

CHAPTER 16
1 Frank and Alexander Jardine, 1867.
2 Ibid.

CHAPTER 18

1 This quote and all following quotes in this chapter from Frank and
   Alexander Jardine, 1867.

CHAPTER 20

1 Kennedy, 1870, p. 13.
2 Sharp, 1992, p. 46.
3 Ibid.
4 C.G. Austin quotes from the unpublished autobiography of H.M. Chester
   in his *Early History of Somerset and Thursday Island*, read before the
   Historical Society of Queensland, 28 April, 1949, p. 6.

CHAPTER 22

1 Austin, 1949.
2 Sharp, 1992, pp. 27, 28.
3 Ibid.
4 Prentis, 2008.
5 Reynolds, 1998, pp. 97–9.
6 Ibid., p. 98.
7 Ibid., 1998, p. 101.

CHAPTER 24

1 From 'The Pastoral Frontier' in Loos, 1982, pp. 29–62.
2 Ibid.
3 Reynolds, 1995, p. 103.
4 Bottoms, pp. 118–19.
5 Arthur Laurie, *The Black War in Queensland*, read before the Royal
   Queensland Historical Society, 23 October, 1958.
6 Cole, 2004.
7 Ibid.
8 Mark McKenna, *From the Edge: Australia's lost histories*, The Miegunyah
   Press, Melbourne, 2016, p. 170.
9 Ibid.

CHAPTER 26

1 Robert Macklin, *Dragon and Kangaroo*, Hachette Australia, Sydney, 2017,
   p. 61.
2 Dorothy Shineberg, *The Trading Voyages of Andrew Cheyne 1841–1844*,
   Pacific History Series No. 3, ANU Press, Canberra, 1971, pp. 196–9.
3 Loos, 1982, p. 118–23.
4 Reynolds, 1981, p. 176.
5 Commodore John Wilson RN, *Labor Trade in the Western Pacific, 1882–83*,
   government despatch, Melbourne, 1882, available at: https://www.
   parliament.vic.gov.au/papers/govpub/VPARL1882-83No31.pdf

CHAPTER 28

1   Somerset Correspondent, *Brisbane Courier*, 10 November 1875.
2   J.W. Ottley to H.J. Dodd, 30 May 1923, letter reproduced in Anderson, 2009.

CHAPTER 29

1   Letourneau, 'Sur un Français nommé Narcisse Pelletier,' 1880, quoted in Anderson, 2009, p. 327.
2   Extract of the medical report from the *Jura (Rapports Medicaux XIII-9), Service historique de la Défense,* quoted in Anderson, p. 369.
3   Barry McGowan, Marcus Clark and Felix Meyer's cameo roles in the Paris Commune, *The La Trobe Journal,* no. 99, March 2017.
4   Ibid.

CHAPTER 30

1   Thompson, 2017.
2   'Latest Intelligence', *The Times*, 15 April 1880.
3   Thompson, 2017.
4   Philip T. Weller, *The Roman Ritual*, 1964, available from: http://www.ewtn.com/library/prayer/roman2.txt

CHAPTER 31

1   Noel Loos, 'A Conflict of Faiths: Aboriginal Reaction to the First Missionaries in North Queensland 1861–1897', doctoral thesis, James Cook University, Brisbane, 2018.
2   Reynolds, 1981, pp. 189–90.
3   Loos, 1982.
4   Named for an Edinburgh friend, Hugh Lockhart.
5   Reynolds, 1998, pp. 121–3.
6   Bottoms, 2013, pp. 5–6.
7   Ibid., p. 132.

CHAPTER 32

1   Thompson, p. 4.
2   Ibid.
3   Anderson, p. 290.

EPILOGUE

1   Anderson, p. 24.

INDEX

57th Foot Regiment 56

abandonment by *Saint-Paul* crew 23–4,
    47–8
Aboriginal people
    Australia, arrival 27–30
    early European contact 30–2, 39–40
    population in 1788 39
Aborigines Protection Society 224
Accoom, Jasmine 297
Africa 27, 40
Albany Island 148, 152
Albert River 119
Albinia Downs 104
Algernon 122
Alma 102–3
America 40
American Civil War 99, 240–1
American War of Independence 33
'Amglo', naming of Narcisse 51–2
Anderson, Stephanie 288, 296
Arafura Sea 27
Archer, Charles 60
Archer, David 59–60
Archer, Tom 59–60
Ariel 68
Armstrong, Sergeant 225
Arnhem Land 66
arsenic poisoning 60–1
Arthur, George 40, 55
Astrolabe 33
Australia 27, 39, 42, 62–3, 99, 153, 203,
    240, 243, 265, 285

Atlantic Ocean 289–90
Avant Port 290
Awu 208–9
Ayreshire 90

Babin, Alphonsine 48, 182, 257, 259,
    269–70, 274, 276, 292, 263, 292–3
    marriage and children 4–7
    reunion with Narcisse 272
Babin, Grand-père 4–6, 182, 214, 276
Babin, Jean 6
Baki Baki 67
Bally, Norman 297–9
Banjilaka 218–19
Banks, Joseph 39
Banner, Captain William 241
Barkly Tableland 138, 206
'Barney' 161
Baroway 70–1, 74, 77, 92–3, 95, 106,
    131, 154, 183–4
    battle against Umpila 141–4
    death 143–4
    first meeting 49, 51, 52
    funeral ceremonies 145–7
    initiation 127, 131
Barunguan people 199
Bass Strait 35, 41
Bathurst 82
battle against Umpila 142
Battle Camp 226
Battle of One Tree Hill 58
battle of Sedan 264
Battle of the Mitchell 173–4

Battle of the Normanby 226
Baudin, Nicolas 35
Baudouin, Marcel 272, 288
Bay of Biscay 4, 77
Beaujon Hospital 270–1
Bell, John 243
Bendemere Massacre 101
Bendemere station 101
Ben'ewa 55
Billibellary 83
Binney, R.N. 161–2
birth 4–5
Bismarck Sea 4
'Black Line' 40–1
'Blacks' Camps' 224
Blake, station owner 189
Bligh, Lieutenant John 105, 119
Bloomfield, Noelene 32
Bode, Henry 161, 224
Bombay 8–9
Bonaparte, Louis-Napoleon 261, 264, 271, 290
Bonaparte, Napoleon 35, 42, 56, 261
Booby Island 118
'Boralga' 226
Botany Bay 33, 34, 38
Bottoms, Timothy 118, 283
Boussole 33
Bowen 160, 224, 241
Bowen, George 102–3, 117–18, 135, 137–8, 149, 151–2, 153
Bowen–Herbert government 137
Bramston, John 121–2, 135
Brandenburg 62
Bribie Island 57, 59
Briggs, Fanny 102
Brisbane 58, 60, 82, 89, 102, 104, 118, 121–2, 136, 151, 186, 187, 190, 203, 224, 260
Brisbane 254, 259, 261
Brisbane Courier 101, 120
Brisbane River 57, 58
Brisbane, Thomas 54–5, 56, 57, 82
British Army 40, 67
British Crown 42, 60
British Empire 99, 151, 189
British War Office 203
Brittany 289
brothers see Pelletier, Alphonse; Pelletier, Benjamin Hippolyte Jean; Pelletier, Élie Jean-Félix
The Brothers 240

Brown, George 'Black' 58
Brown, Harry 62, 63, 66
'Bruno' 96, 125–6, 156, 181, 184, 193–4, 197, 200, 209, 220, 256
battle against Umpila 140–1, 143–4
canoe 231
crocodile hunt 164–70
expedition to mountains 234–8
tutoring Little Markuntha 229–30
wife 96, 230, 239, 291
Bulletin 204, 205
Bulletin Français 269
Bundaberg 90
Bundjalung country 100
Burke and Wills expedition 100
Burketown 138
Burnett 85
Burnett, Commodore William Farquharson 118
Butcher, Wayne 297
Byerley, Frederick 171–6

Caboolture 101
Cairns 68, 241
Caleb 62–3
Calvert, James 62, 64, 65–6
Campbelltown 82–3
Canada 118
Canberra 297
cannibalism 21, 247–8, 275, 284
Rossel Island 19–20, 37–8
Cannon, Assistant Surgeon Richard 149, 152–3
Cape Cleveland 81 see also Townsville
Cape Regiment 82
Cape River 138
Cape York 27, 90, 117, 135, 137–8, 153, 206, 243, 249, 269, 270, 281, 283
early expeditions 31, 65, 67–9
missionaries 190–1
Somerset station, establishment 117–18, 135, 148–9
Caribbean 290
Carnegie, Captain John 148
Carpentaria Downs 138, 161
Central Queensland 103, 254
Ceylon 82
Channel Country 103
Chanouga 296
Charles II, King 203
Charleville 203
Charterhouse School 103

Chester, Henry Marjoribanks 192, 202–3, 254, 280
Chevin, Dr Arthur 271
children
  Chuchi see Chuchi
  Little Markuntha see Markuntha, Little; Yapu
Chilpu 127–8, 130–1, 142, 154, 198, 212, 218–19, 232, 259
  death 245
China 40, 99, 135, 182, 240
Christianity 55, 243, 280
Chuchi 228–30, 232, 248, 256, 291
Cilento, Sir Raphael 298
Clarence River 84
Colonial Office 137, 205
Colony of Queensland 38 see also Queensland
Colony of Victoria 38 see also Victoria
Comet district 188
Comet River 90
'Commandant' 61
Commune 265
Compagnie Général Transatlantique 290
Connor, Lieutenant Edward 254, 258–9
Connors, Libby 55–6
Cook, Captain James 30–2, 39, 44, 54, 60, 175
Cooktown 226, 254, 259
Cooktown Herald 227
Cooranga 101
Corfu 103
Cork 56
corroboree 29, 94, 101, 198–9, 246
Côte de Lumière 4
Cowderoy, A. 161, 162
Crab Claws 290
Cressbrook station 61
Crimean War 264
Cripplegate 202
crocodile hunt 164–70
  punishment 198–201
Croix de Vie 272
Crown Land 88, 186
Cullin-la-Ringo station 118–19
Cunnamulla 203

d'Adhemar de Cransac, Alphonse 21
Dalla 58–60
Dalrymple, George 137
Dampier, William 32, 39, 241
Darling Downs 58, 62

Darling, Ralph 35
Davidson, Alfred 224
Davidson, Col 19
Dawson River 86
de Bougainville, Louis-Antoine 13, 33
de Galaup La Pérouse, Jean-François see La Pérouse, Jean-François de Galaup
de Gonneville, Binot Paulmier 32–3
de Langle, Fleuriot 33
  death 293–4
d'Entrecasteaux, Bruni 34–5
Deniliquin 85
Denison, William 84
Dent, Corporal David 150–1
Dix-sept ans chez les sauvages 288
Dharawal 82
Douglas, Edward 285
Douglas, John 285–6
Dragoons 135
Dreamtime 28, 39, 76, 91 see also Storytime
Duke of Aiguillon 289
Duke of Newcastle 117–18
Dumfriesshire 135
Dungidau 59
Durundur station 59
Dutch explorers in Australia 31–2
Dutton, Charles 121
Duyfken 31

East Indies 32
'Edmund' 108, 123, 194
Elliott Island 36
Emerald 118
Endeavour River 225
England 39, 62, 68, 122, 186, 190, 261, 286
English explorers in Australia 32–6
Eton 84, 118
Eugénie 7
'Evette' 144, 145, 156
'Evonne' 144–5, 155 see also Kanti
exorcism 276–9, 287

Far North Queensland 224
father see Pelletier, Martin
First Fleet 33, 38
Fisher, Charley 62–4
Fleming, John 42
Flinders Island 41
Flinders River 138
Fly River 203

Four Years in Queensland 186–9
France 6, 33–4, 74, 238, 258–9, 261,
      263, 264–5, 269, 296
Fraser, John 86
Fraser, Sylvester 87
Fraser, William 86, 87–8
Frazer, Joseph 243–4, 249, 253–4
French explorers in Australia 32–6
French government 265
French Merchant Marine 295
Fresnel, Augustin-Jean 290
Frontier Wars 58, 81, 83, 188, 223
funeral ceremonies 145–7, 245

'Gabriel' 127
Gambetta, Leon 264–5
Gandangara 82
Garcin, François 21
Gare Montparnasse 271
Garnier, Edouard 288
Gates of Gibraltar 265
Gayiri people 104
Geographe 35
Germany 62
Gibraltar 118
Gilbert, John 62–6
Gipps, George 43, 62
Gladstone 69, 90, 136, 148, 203
Gladstone, William 103
Goenpul 55
Golden Eagle 148, 149
Gondwana 27
Gold Coast 57
goldrush 36, 38–9, 83, 224–5, 254
Goondiwindi 85
Gordon 260
Government House 149, 192
Grande Rue 293
Great Barrier Reef 33
Great Divide 69, 89
Great Dividing Range 38
Great South Land 27, 28, 30, 33, 38
Green Island 241
Gregory, Augustus Charles 68–9
Gregory, Francis 241
Griffith, Samuel 284–5
Grimes, Charles 54
Gudang people 152, 202
Guilbaud, Véronique 292
Gulf Country 223, 224
Gulf of Carpentaria 65, 67, 137, 206
Gulliver 102–3

Gulmarra 68
Guy Fawkes' Day 163
Gwydir Valley 42

Halpin, J.J. 149, 150
Hamburg 243
Hann, William 282
Hartog, Dirk 31
Haussmann, George-Eugène 271
Hawkesbury Valley 82
Herbert, Robert 103, 121–2, 135, 137,
      149, 151–2, 188
Herston 121–2
Hey, Nicholas 281
Heydon, Charles 225
HMS *Curacoa* 152
HMS *Endeavour* 31, 44, 175
HMS *Orpheus* 118
HMS *Pioneer* 118
HMS *Salamanda* 148, 149
Hodgson, Pemberton 62–3
Hogg, J. 226
Honfleur 32
Hong Kong 4, 9, 36, 135, 254, 259
Hope Valley 282
Hornet Bank 86
Hornet Bank Massacre 86–7
House of Commons 84
Hughenden 100
Hume, Hamilton 42, 83
Humpybong 54
Hundred Years War 32
Hunter, Captain John 34

Ilot du Refuge 16, 18, 36–7
India 8, 82, 99, 148, 254
Indian Navy 203
Indian Ocean 9, 31
Indian Subcontinent 40
Industrial Revolution 39
initiation 125–31
Innisfail 138
Ionian government 103
Ionian University 103
Ipswich 87, 104, 187
Ireland 40
Iserbrook 243
'Ivo' 124–5
I'wai Tjilbo 95, 129, 130, 159, 233

Jack, Logan 282
'Jackey Jackey' 68

Jagg, Francis 190–1
Jagg, Mrs 190
Janszoon, Willem 31
Jardine, Alexander 153
    Battle of the Mitchell 173–4
    cattle drive expedition 160–3, 171–7,
        206
Jardine, Elizabeth 136, 153
Jardine, Francis ('Frank') 153, 190, 202,
    254, 286
    Battle of the Mitchell 173–4
    marriage to Sana Solia 242
    cattle drive expedition 160–3, 171–7,
        206
    Police Magistrate 191, 192
Jardine, John 135–8, 148–53, 160, 173,
    176–7, 189, 190, 191
Jardine, John Robert 150, 153, 176–7
Jardine Matheson 135
Jardine, Sir Alexander 135, 137
Jardine, William 135, 137
Java 31, 35, 284
Jervis Island 243
Jimbour 62
John Bell 243–4, 248–9, 253, 256, 275,
    298
    'rescue' of Narcisse 244
Jones, Harry 226
Julia Percy 241
Jura 263, 265, 269

Kabi people 120
Kanaka labour 241–3
Kanakas 240, 241
Kangaroo Island 41
Kanidji 96, 128
Kanti 155–6, 229–30, 238, 256, 291 see
        also Evonne
    birth of Little Markuntha 207–14
    child, presentation to father 215–20
    marriage to Amglo 214, 215
Keendahn 100
Kennedy, Edmund 67–8
Kennedy, Edward B. 136, 186–9
Kennedy River 226
Kennett, William 190
Kilcoy station 59, 60, 119
King Charles II 203
King Island 35
King of Samoa 242
King, Philip Gidley 35
King's College, London 67

Kio 149
knife attack aboard Reine des Mers 8, 215
Kolan River 90
Kuuku Y'au 94, 155, 157, 158, 164,
        233, 246, 247, 256, 259, 296
    arrival in Night Island country 107–8
    punishment for crocodile hunt
        198–200
    totems 158, 199

La Pérouse, Jean-François de Galaup
        33–4, 38
La Trobe, Lieutenant Governor 83
Lack, Clem 298
Lagnardette, Pierre 21
Lamalama 94
Lamartinière, Alexandre Henri 262
Lamington National Park 57
Landsborough, William 90, 100–1, 117,
        137–8
Lang, Gideon Scott 204–5
Langley, Colonel G.C. 152
Laura River 226
Le Blanc, Madame 195
Le Boulevard Oceanique 276
le Curé, Monsieur 5, 6, 24, 95, 195,
        272–4
    exorcism of Narcisse 276–9
Le Furet 6–7
Le Havre 295
Le Jeune Narcisse 4, 214
Leichhardt 135
Leichhardt, Ludwig 61–7, 161
Lesueur, Charles-Alexandre 35
    letters to family 258–9, 263, 264
Lizard Island 241
Lockhart 297–8
Lockhart Aboriginal Council 297
Lockhart River 282, 296
Lockyer River 58
Logan, Captain Patrick 56–7
Logan River 119
Loire River 265, 289
Loire-Atlantique 271
London 103, 118, 152, 186, 189, 202,
        205, 224
London Missionary Society 280
London Society for the Propagation of
        the Gospel 190
Loos, Noel 100–1, 223–4, 280–1
'Louis' 123, 127 see also Chilpu
Louis XV, King 33

Louisiade Archipelago 13, 14, 33
Lutwyche, Justice Alfred 284

Maademan 95, 97–8, 107, 116, 128,
    146–7, 183–4, 233, 234, 256, 288
  arrival of *John Bell* 245–8
  battle against Umpila 142–4
  canoe 156, 157, 165–6, 181–3
  disputes, settling 123–4, 198–201,
    213–16, 218
  first meeting 24, 49, 51–2, 70–4, 76
  harpooning and hunting 193–8, 228,
    232, 290
  marriages 52
Mabuiag Island 243
Mabuiag people 243–9, 256–7, 298
Macalister, Arthur 254
Macarthur, John 82
Macdonald, J.G. 138, 161
MacFarlane, Reverend Samuel 280
Mackay 203
MacKellar, William 36
Mackenzie, Evan 60
Mackenzie, Robert 206
MacMillan, James 225–6
Maison Pelletier 270
Malay Corps 82
Mantell, Monsieur 50
Manumbah 120
Maori 118
Mapoon 281
Maranoa 85
Marbileau, Louise Désirée 292–4
Marbileau, Marc Séraphin 292
Marchand, Charles 263–4
'Marie' 50, 52, 70, 77, 98, 109, 182, 184
  death 245
Markuntha (later 'Big Markuntha')
    193–7, 209, 228, 231–2, 233, 246
Markuntha, Little 209–17, 218, 228–9,
    234, 235, 291 *see also* Yapu
marriage ceremony 184
marriages
  Kanti 214, 215
  Louise Désirée Marbileau 292
  Maademan's daughter 234, 238
  Mitha 183–5
Marsden family 243
Marseilles 8
Maryborough 89
massacres of Aboriginal people 39–44
Mauritius 35

McConnel, David 61
McConnel, Henry 61
McKenna, Mark 226
McKinley, William 100–1
Meanjin 55
Merland, Constant 287–9
Miller, Captain Henry 54, 55
'Mimi' 96, 108, 139, 194
missionaries 60–2, 190–1, 243, 280–2,
    296–7
missions 281–2
Mistake Creek 284
Mitchell, Sir Thomas 67
Mitha 194, 197–8, 210, 218–20, 238,
    259, *see also* Veronique
  birth of daughter Chuchi 228–30
  marriage to Amglo 183–5, 291
  pregnancies 198, 230
  Umpila 183, 213, 216–17
Monteil, Lauren 21
Moreton Bay 38, 54–6, 62, 81, 89, 186,
    240
Moreton Island 57
Morineau 287, 293
Morinish 205
Morisset, Edric Norfolk Faux 84–5, 89,
    104
Morisset, Major James Thomas 82, 85
Morisset, Rudolph Roxburgh 104
Morrill, James 81
Mortimer, Alexander 120
Mortimer, John 120
Morton, Lord 54
mother *see* Babin, Alphonsine
Mount Warning 100
Muchell 260
Multuggerah 58
Murgon 104
Murphy, John 62, 66
Murray Island 280
Murrumbidgee 83
Muwo 19–20, 37–8
Myall Creek massacre 43

Nahrung, Konrad 101
Nantes 9, 271, 276, 287–9, 292
Napoleonic wars 59
Narcisse II: Terra Nullius 296
Native Mounted Police Force *see* Native
    Police Force
Native Police Force 99–105, 117, 138,
    225

Aboriginal troopers 101–2
Edward B. Kennedy 187–9
Frederick Wheeler 101–2, 104, 119, 203–5, 284
funding 283
government inquiries 85–6, 119, 121, 285
origins 82–90
opposition 119–21
recruitment 82–4, 99–100, 119
Naturaliste 35
Neagle, Henry 87
Nelson, Lord 103
Nerang River 99
'New Albion' 42
New Caledonia 34, 36, 117, 265
New England 90
New Guinea 14, 19, 27, 33, 203, 254
'New Holland' 32, 33 *see also Nouvelle-Hollande*
New South Wales 35, 38, 43, 54, 56, 59, 83, 84, 89, 136, 285
New South Wales Legislative Council 240
New Zealand 118
Newcastle 62, 83
Ngugi 55
'Nicky Nicky' 189
Night Island 96–7, 127–8, 140, 182, 241, 258, 298
landing of *John Bell* 243–4
Night Islanders 52, 75, 92–4, 96, 113, 124–5, 164, 184, 199, 201, 228, 236, 257, 259, 271, 274, 275, 296
see also Uutaalnganu
arrival of *John Bell* 244–7
battle against Umpila 141–2, 144, 145
canoes 156, 157, 231, 247
child, presentation ceremony 207, 208, 210
customs and rituals 124, 145, 155–6, 195–6, 215, 217, 233–4, 245
encampment 107–8, 123, 131
funeral ceremonies 145–7, 245
dugong hunting 195
language 94, 113, 183, 199, 217, 249, 260, 276
laws 155–6, 195, 213–14, 233
seasons 184, 230–1
songs 288
territory 92–4, 107–8, 235, 239, 271, 282, 296, 298

totems 94, 108
Ningy Ningy 60
Nogoa district 188
Norfolk Island 82, 85
Normanby River 225
North Atlantic Ocean 276
North Australian 119
North Queensland 100, 138, 223–4
Jardine expedition 160–3, 171–7, 206
Northern France 32
Northern Territory 63, 68–9, 206
Northumberland 240
Norway 59
Noumea 263, 270
Nouvelle-Hollande 12, 21–2, 33 *see also* 'New Holland'
Nundah 60
Nunukul 55

'Old Eulah' 161–2, 171, 173
Orsted-Jensen, Robert 102–3
The Other Side of the Frontier 39–40, 281
Ottley, Lieutenant John Walter 254–5, 259
Ovitali, Jan-Michel 21
Oxford University 103, 118, 121
Oxley, John 54

'Paddy' 59
Palmer, Arthur 224
Palmer, Edmund 223
Palmer, Edward 138
Palmer, George 191
Palmer River 224–5, 226
Palmerston 103
Palmerston government 103
Palvadeau, Madame 50
Palvadeau, Monsieur 5, 8, 50, 257
Pama Uutaalnganu see Uutaalnganu
Paris 9, 34, 56, 255, 264–5, 270, 296
Paris Zoo 264
Parramatta 55
Pascoe, Lieutenant R.J. 149, 151–2
Passiwodop 190
Patrick, Second-Lieutenant Alfred March 104
pearl-shell industry 241–3, 282–3
Peigne 288, 299
Pelletier, Alphonse 5–6, 212, 257, 272–3, 275
death 292
rescue 5–6, 212

Pelletier, Alphonsine *see* Babin,
    Alphonsine
Pelletier, Benjamin Hippolyte Jean
    272–3, 275–6, 277, 293
Pelletier, Élie Jean-Félix 5–6, 77, 212,
    257, 292–3
  death 293
  reunion with Narcisse 269–73, 275
Pelletier, Martin 4–7, 257, 259, 269–70,
    272–5
  death 292
  marriage 4
Peninsular Wars 56, 82
Per, Adolphe-Charles 21
Peruvian 81
'Peter' 161, 171
Pfalzer 282
Phare de l'Aiguillon 289
Philippines 4, 13
Phillip, Captain Arthur 33–4, 42
Phillips, William 62, 65
Pinard, Captain Emmanuel 47, 97, 243,
    245, 249, 257, 295, 298
  abandonment of Chinese passengers
    17–18
  death 296
  Saint-Paul, voyage and shipwreck 8–9,
    11, 13, 15–18, 21–2, 36–8, 295
Pinya 158–9, 165, 167–8, 181
Pitkethly, Betsey 81
Pitkethly, George 81
Place du Baril 272
Plunkett, Attorney-General John 43
Pointe de l'Eve 290
'Poison Creek' 174
Port Albany 118, 148
Port Denison Times 104, 224
Port Essington 63, 66, 67
Port Jackson 34, 35
Port La Vie 295
Port Macquarie 83
Port Phillip 35, 38, 83
Prince of Denmark 36
Prince of Wales 118
Promenade de la Vie 276
Prussia 62, 264
punishment 198–201, 214–20

Queensland 61, 68, 99, 102–3, 119, 120,
    121, 136, 174, 186–9, 203–4, 206,
    223, 283–5
  colony 39, 44, 54, 102

Frontier War 81, 83–90, 174, 223,
    283–4
government 117, 136, 190, 205, 206,
    225, 284–5, 296
Kanaka trade 240–1
missionaries 296
Native Police Force *see* Native Police
    Force
Queensland Club 187
Queensland Government Parliamentary
    Inquiry 119
Queensland Heritage Register 88
Queensland Native Mounted Police 82,
    83–4 *see also* Native Police Force
Queensland Rifle Brigade 136
The Queenslander 88

'Redcliffe' 54
Refuge Isle *see* Ilot du Refuge
Reine des Mers 7–8, 215
'rescue' of Narcisse 256, 246–9
Reynolds, Henry 39, 205, 242, 281,
    283, 284, 285
Richardson, Archibald 160–1
Rio de Janeiro 263–4
River Vie 5–6, 77, 212, 272, 275, 295
Riverina 83
Roaring Forties 31
Robin, Maria 292
Rockhampton 88–90, 99, 102, 118,
    135–6, 153, 160, 161, 188, 191,
    203–4, 205, 254–5, 259, 284
Rockingham Bay 68
Roebuck Bay 241
Rolleson, Christopher 104
Roma 101, 103
Roma, Diamantina 103
Roper, John 62, 65–6
'Rosine' 50, 52, 77, 98, 182, 184
Rossel Island 17–20, 21, 37
Rouen 21, 295, 302
Roussarie, Jean-Jacques 295
Royal Engineers 84, 254
Royal Marines 148, 151, 152
Royal Mathematical School 203
Royal Military College 84
Royal Navy 54, 118, 148, 149, 152
Royal Society 54
Royal Ulster Constabulary 83
Rue du Calvaire 48, 50, 272

'Sabine' 96, 156–7, 164, 230, 239, 245, 291
Sables d'Olonne 270, 292
Saich, Private John 150–1
Saint-Gilles 4–5, 48, 73, 96, 124, 263, 270, 288, 289
  memorial 295–6
  return 272, 276, 287
Saint-Gilles-Sur-Vie *see* Saint-Gilles
Saint-Nazaire 289–90, 292, 293
Saint-Paul 3–4, 8–9, 11, 18, 19, 20, 182, 261
  Nouvelle-Hollande voyage 12–15
  shipwreck 15–16, 36, 247–8, 258, 295
'Sambo' 161
Samoa 33, 242
Sandbeach country 91, 182, 237, 241, 243, 298
Sandbeach people 75, 141, 183, 196, 206, 229, 230, 236, 238, 243, 262, 282, 296–7
Sandgate 89, 187
Sapphire 148
Sassy 92–4, 96–8, 106–16, 123–4, 139, 146–7, 213–14, 218, 220, 228, 234, 246, 248, 256, 291
  battle against Umpila 142–5
  canoe 155–7, 181–2, 184
  crocodile hunt 165–70, 200–1
  first meeting 51–3, 70–7
  hunting and harpooning 193–7, 216, 228, 231–2
  initiation 125–8
Savage Scenes from Australia 152–3
Schmidt, Reverend 61
Scotland 90, 135
Scott, Andrew 86
Scott, Arthur 137
Scott, Walter 137
Scrutton, C. 161
Seine 270
Service, Sir James 265
Seymour, David Thompson 227
Shark Bay 241
Sharp, Nonie 190–1, 203
shipwreck 15–6, 36, 247–8, 258, 295
Simon, M. George-Eugène 261–3, 265
Simpson R.N., Captain Henry G. 189, 190
Sims 101
Solia, Sana 242
Solomon Islands 34

Somerset 186, 189, 192, 202–3, 249
  arrival of Narcisse 253–4
  establishment 118, 135, 138, 148–9
  Jardines 160, 171, 175–7, 186, 190–2, 202
  missionaries 190–1
  pearl-shell industry 241–2
  Thursday Island, transfer 280, 285
Somerset Bay 148, 149, 258
Son of the Vendée 288
South Africa 82
South America 290
South China Sea 13
South Pacific 4, 32, 33, 263
South Sea Island 243
South Sea Islanders 203, 242
South Seas 240, 295
Southern Confederacy 99
spear attack by Yannick 97–8
spear carving 92–3
Spring Creek Barracks 188
Springsure 103
Squatting Ministry 103
Sri Lanka 82
SS *Brisbane see Brisbane*
St George, Harold 225, 227
St-Germaine-en-Laye 296
St-Malo 21
Storytime 76, 91, 114, 196 *see also* Dreamtime
Stradbroke Island 57
Straits of Malacca 9
Strathdon 224
strychnine poisoning 86–7
Styx 36–8
Sunshine Coast 59
Sweer's Island 138
Sydney 38, 41, 42, 56, 57, 62, 68, 90, 136, 240, 243, 259, 263, 265
Sydney Cove 34
Sydney Harbour 261
Sydney Morning Herald 225, 262, 265

Tangu Chuchi 231
Taroom 87
Tasman, Abel 31–2
Tasman Peninsula 40
Tasmania 32, 34–5, 55
  genocide of Aboriginal people 40–1
Terra Australis Incognita 31, 36
terra nullius 42, 60
Tessier, Joseph Marie 294

Thompson, Chief Constable Andrew 82
Thomson, Donald 292, 297–8
Thursday Island 241, 253, 254, 285
'Tookie' 93, 165, 167, 181, 198
   crocodile attack 157–8
Toongabbie 240
Toowoomba 88
Torres Strait 36, 117, 118, 148, 186,
      241–3, 253, 259
'totem talk' 109
totems 94–5, 108, 109, 158, 199, 218,
      235, 291
Toulon 265, 269
Tours 265
Towns, Robert 240–1
Townsville 81, 188, 206, 224, 241
Tree Island 151
Trieste 7
Tudor reign 40
Tweed River 89

Umpila 52, 106, 146, 157, 183, 194,
      216, 247–8
   battle against 139–44
   country 94, 107, 111, 123, 141, 233,
      296
   raiding party 139
   totems 94
   trespass into country 116, 123–5, 234
Union Bank 203
United States 99, 118, 120
Upper Burdekin 69, 137
Uutaalnganu 52, 131, 233, 296 see also
   Night Islanders

Van Diemen's Land 32, 84
Vanikoro 34
Vendée 4, 8, 74, 97, 261, 271, 272
'Veronique' 50, 52, 77, 106, 143, 145–6,
      183 see also Mitha
Versailles 265
Victoria 38, 42
Victory 103
Vieux Mole 289

Waka Waka people 101–2, 104, 120
Walker, Edward 59
Walker, Frederick 83–5, 100–1, 103–4,
      117
Wanchai 9, 11
wappa 115, 234

Warrego district 203
Warrior Islands 241
Waterloo Creek massacre 42–3
Waterloo Plains massacre 42
Webb, William 225–6
Wellington 136
Wellington, Lord 42, 56
Wentworth, Sophia 240
Wentworth, William Charles 240
Western Districts 42
Western Port 35
Westminster 60
Westminster School 89
Weymouth Bay 68
Wheeler, Frederick 89–90, 99–100,
      101–2, 104, 119, 203–4
   death 284
   trial for murder 284
Whitehall 121
Wickham, John 89
Wide Bay 85, 119, 161
'Widow Marbileau' see Yver, Rose
   Françoise
Wik people 148
Williams, Lieutenant John 138
Wilson, W.B. 149, 151–2
wine, Bordeaux 8, 9, 10, 124, 258
Wiseman, William 135
Wollumbin 100
Wonajo 19
Wondal 199–200
Woodlark 148
Wurudjeri 83

Yaamba 204
Yabba 120
Yangtse Valley 40
'Yann' 123, 144, 213
'Yannick' 106, 123, 155, 156, 234
   battle against Umpila 144
   child, presentation ceremony 207—14
   punishment of Amglo 215–16,
      218–20
   spear attack 97–8, 184
Yapu 235–6, 238, 246, 256, 291
Yardargan people 202
Yeeman 86, 87
Yugambeh 99
Yuggera 58, 60
Yulebah Creek 101
Yver, Rose Françoise 292